The Anatomy of National Fantasy

LAUREN BERLANT

THE ANATOMY OF NATIONAL FANTASY

HAWTHORNE, UTOPIA, AND EVERYDAY LIFE

THE UNIVERSITY OF CHICAGO PRESS
Chicago & London

Lauren Berlant is associate professor of English at the University of Chicago.

The University of Chicago Press, Chicago 60637
The University of Chicago Press, Ltd., London

Printed in the United States of America
00 99 98 97 96 95 94 93 92 91 5 4 3 2 1

Library of Congress Cataloging-in-Publication Data

Berlant, Lauren Gail, 1957–
The anatomy of national fantasy : Hawthorne, Utopia, and everyday life / Lauren Berlant.
p. cm.
Includes bibliographical references and index.
ISBN 0-226-04376-2 (cl.). — ISBN 0-226-04377-0 (pa.)
1. Hawthorne, Nathaniel, 1804–1864. Scarlet letter.
2. Hawthorne, Nathaniel, 1804–1864—Political and social views.
3. National characteristics, American, in literature.
4. Nationalism in literature. 5. Utopias in literature. 6. Fantasy in literature. I. Title.
PS1868.B397 1991
813′.3—dc20 90-26907

♾ The paper used in this publication meets the minimum requirements of the American National Standard for Information Sciences—Permanence of Paper for Printed Library Materials, ANSI Z39.48-1984.

CONTENTS

Acknowledgments vii

Introduction
"I am a citizen of somewhere else." 1

ONE *America, Post-Utopia: Body, Landscape, and National Fantasy in Hawthorne's* Native Land 19

TWO *The Paradise of Law in* The Scarlet Letter 57

THREE *The State of Madness: Conscience, Popular Memory, and Narrative in* The Scarlet Letter 97

FOUR *The Nationalist Preface* 161

FIVE *America in Everyday Life* 191

Notes 219

Index 261

ACKNOWLEDGMENTS

THE NATIONAL ENDOWMENT FOR THE HUMANITIES, the University of Wisconsin Institute for Research in the Humanities, and the University of Chicago provided welcome financial and temporal relief during the emergence of this project. My research assistants, Carrie Klinger, Nguyen Kung, and Megan Shein, performed immensely valuable alienated labor, for which I am truly grateful. A version of chapter 1 appeared in *Arizona Quarterly* 44, no. 4 (Winter 1989); the journal has kindly permitted me to republish it here. This manuscript has been read and improved by many sources and conversations. It is especially indebted to the teaching and the example of Michael Colacurcio. In addition, the commentary of Nina Baym, Laura Brown, and William Veeder came at crucial early moments. Jay Schleusener, Michael Murrin, and Lorelei Sontag said important probing things; Julie Skurski and Jim Chandler offered really wonderful clarifying thinking and debate. Finally, the supreme intelligences of Michael Warner, Claudia Johnson, and most of all Tom Stillinger have been illuminating and inspiring, incalculably.

We must not voodoo the people . . .

Frantz Fanon

INTRODUCTION *"I am a citizen of somewhere else."*

NATIONS PROVOKE FANTASY. WHEN NATHANIEL HAWTHORNE loses his job as the federal Surveyor of the Custom-House (1849)—where his task was to police the national border, regulating what commodities might enter and exit the public space—his imagination runs wild. Now "a politically dead man,"[1] he pictures himself as a victim of the French Revolution, his head "axed" by the federal "guillotine" of patronage (41); he also imagines himself as the Headless Horseman of Irving's "Legend of Sleepy Hollow," a ghostly vestige of the American Revolution who rides a triumphant horse and carries a weapon—his detached head—to throw at any offensive stranger (43). In addition, he writes *The Scarlet Letter*. Even this carries a ghost title and authorship: the "POSTHUMOUS PAPERS OF A DECAPITATED SURVEYOR" (43).

America, which bestows on Hawthorne "the crown of martyrdom—(though with no longer a head to wear it on)" (42), dominates his represented relation to his activity, his knowledge, his affect, his very body. This domination is primarily textual, but Hawthorne does not experience national effects as muted or indirect. The "guillotine," he writes, is "one of the most apt of metaphors," rather than a "literal fact" (41); yet these comic images of revolutionary rupture testify to the intimate violence of political life within the national frame. But the language of violation does not do justice to the tonal ambivalence toward national intimacy that Hawthorne's text also registers. The author expresses pride in federal office, personal embarrassment at being fired, and rage at his own dependency on the symbolic and the actual nation. He mocks his own complicity in the silences that protect national self-privilege, referring to the "causes which I may not have space to hint at" (19) and the "better book than I shall ever write" (37) about what happens to those who seek and obtain too close a proximity to the federal apparatus, "this peculiar mode of life" (19). He also mixes his assorted negations with rhetorical impulses of nationalist pleasure—through intertextual allusion of topical and literary sorts, the modes of satire and sentiment, and a playful fantasy that as author-in-exile from the state he might be a servant, a fount, and a privileged source of a revitalized American memory.

In these nationally based images of citizenship and decapitation, Hawthorne engages in what we might call the fantasy-work of national identity. As an "official" man—a party underling and a federal employee—he says that he overidentifies with many aspects of the national system, and shows that its effects on him are more dramatic and public than they are for the general populace. For the "official," political change is direct and brutal, so dependent is he on a specific configuration of power—for example, on the success of one political party over another, or on the continued identification of political with racial and patriarchal privilege. Moreover, in "The Custom-House," Hawthorne seems always uniquely on the verge of personal transformation: he casts himself as a solitary writer of "native" tales, a radical utopian transcendentalist, a custom-house official, a headless victim of the historical nation, a headless national fiction, a triumphant dead American author, and, at another remove, an "editor" of the American antiquarian material that becomes *The Scarlet Letter*.

Rather than display his transformations simply as exceptional personal crises, Hawthorne suggests that they are also fundamentally a condition of identity: the experience of identity might be personal and private, but its forms are always "collective" and political. The relation of personal experience to public form is not, however, a relation of the "real" to the "inauthentic." In Hawthorne's own represented history, diverse kinds of memory, knowledge, and experience intermingle in his patrilineal and national legacies. The eruption of these pasts into the present does not provide for him a deep and rich sense of self-understanding; the more kinds of knowledge he brings to consciousness, the more defamiliarized he becomes, both with respect to himself and to his geopolitical surroundings. Within the moment of estrangement, he grasps at certain consoling, familiar feelings as well. The figures of consolation also involve permeable boundaries, interfaces between public and private: the federal "Hawthorne" is mentally linked to his later incarnation as a "literary man" (43) by his vernacular intimacy with "Uncle Sam," the American common ancestor (5, 39); and the "literal" Hawthorne turns to the hard fact of his physical body, noting that whatever the fate of his "figurative self," "the real human being" remained, "his head safely on his shoulders" (43). But neither the body, the national ancestor, the New England family romance, nor the vestiges of textual knowledge provide Hawthorne a stable, foundational place from which to live in the modern nation. These are axes of personal identity, in constant and unsettled exchange with a political heritage that is both abstract and affectively invested. Opening with a narrative about Hawthorne's forced discharge from the federal Custom-House, the text begins on a hybrid note of personal/national violence and follows through its myriad aftershocks.

Accordingly, although in "The Custom-House" Hawthorne writes autobiographically, he reveals not "the inmost Me" (4) detached from social inscription but speaks in an exemplary way, as a citizen, taking care to play out the complex regimes of knowledge, power, and desire that transform him into a being intimate somehow with mass political culture.[2] Ending the essay as "a citizen of somewhere else," he acts out how it *feels* to be a citizen by constructing "America" as a domestic, and yet a strange and foreign place. The same structure of personal/national representation obtains in *The Scarlet Letter*. The narrator paradoxically asserts both that state-authored public torture is inhumane and that the purpose of torture—to force a person's private fetishes into the light of public scrutiny—is vital to the reproduction of political legitimacy (55, 260). Locating the possibility of political identity in the linked phenomena of personal depravity and its public exposure, he argues that the citizen should dissolve the state's ethical dilemma by showing "freely to the world" an embodiment, a trace by which her/his "worst" traits might be construed (260). By so construing the subject's "consent" to becoming available to interpellation as a citizen, the narrators of "The Custom-House" and *The Scarlet Letter* secure the linkage between naturalization and nationalization, political estrangement and intimacy.

In humorous and in deeply serious moments, then, Hawthorne depicts national fantasy as fundamental to the political and everyday life of all Americans, whose "Americanness" is as central to their sense of entitlement and desire as any family name and tradition and sensation itself might be.[3] The nation's presence in the generic citizen's daily life is more latent and unconscious than it is in his incidental, occasional relation to national symbols, spaces, narratives, and rituals: still, whether consensually or passively transmitted, national identity requires self-ablation. Citizenship becomes equivalent to life itself and also looms as a kind of death penalty: both activity in and exile from the political public sphere feel like cruel and unusual punishment. It is apparently a quality of nations to claim legal and moral privilege, to inspire identification and sacrifice, as well as to make citizens feel violated in public and private. Thus the complexity of Hawthorne's tone: the pain and pleasure of his citizenship and the sublime jocularity of his exile.

In *The Anatomy of National Fantasy* "America" is an assumed relation, an explication of ongoing collective practices, and also an occasion for exploring what it means that national subjects already share not just a history, or a political allegiance, but a set of forms and the affect that makes these forms meaningful. As his prefaces repeatedly stage it, "we"—that is, the author, Hawthorne, and the readers who consume his fictions—are already inextricably bound together by America, prior to joining in the novel's process. We are bound together because we inhabit the *political* space of the nation, which is not merely juridical, territorial (*jus soli*), genetic (*jus sanguinis*), linguistic, or experiential, but some tangled cluster of these. I call this space the "National Symbolic."

Law dominates the field of citizenship, constructing technical definitions of the citizen's rights, duties, and obligations. But the National Symbolic also aims to link regulation to desire, harnessing affect to political life through the production of "national fantasy." By "fantasy" I mean to designate how national culture becomes local—through the images, narratives, monuments, and sites that circulate through personal/collective consciousness. There is no one logic to a national form but, rather, many simultaneously "literal" and "metaphorical" meanings, stated and unstated. Thus, for example, critics have crossed discursive fields to explain Hawthorne's beheading as a comic embodiment of castration's centrality to citizenship: this composite reading stresses how Hawthorne, figuring the state as a shrewish she-eagle, frets that he will lose his "manly character" by depending on "her" for support (39).[4] Elsewhere he notes that leaving his official position in the political public sphere also transforms him from a "self" into a "man," in an interesting inversion of the Constitutional transformation of embodied white "men" into abstract "persons" (43). These formulations register an intense, complex, and conceptually incoherent experience of Anglo-American manhood. "Hawthorne" here is defined as the subject who interlinks the incommensurate: the individual male body, its patriarchal privilege, the Constitutional "body" of the citizen, with its unstated, embedded racial and gender inflections, and the mental projections of the subject who has been politically socialized within the "*mise-en-scène* of desire" that constitutes the discourse of American national identity.[5]

Hawthorne's work on the body/nation investigates both the technology of collective fantasy and the effects of the nation's semiotic practices on the unstable materials it uses. To comprehend America, he adjudicates these overlapping but differentially articulated positions: the official and popular; the national and the local; the rule of law and the rule of men; the collective and the individual;

the citizen as abstraction and the citizen as embodied, gendered; utopia and history; memory and amnesia; theory and practice. The activity of these various sites of ideological, political, and material stress is central to the "American" novels of the 1850s—*The Scarlet Letter*, *The House of the Seven Gables*, and *The Blithedale Romance*—as well as to much of Hawthorne's early national material. But what kinds of substitutions are we tracing here, in this nexus of shifting systems, terms, minds, and bodies? And *how* has the activity of the National Symbolic worked to make America intelligible, as an objective formation, to citizens en masse and to persons individually?

In this book, the problem of understanding national citizenship in early national America will be read mainly through *The Scarlet Letter*. The tripartite essay on *The Scarlet Letter* that forms the core of my study aims to analyze the different official, popular, and subjective modes and effects of collective/national identity that characterize both the narrator's representation of Puritan culture and his allusive construction of the national-political present tense: this in order to suggest how citizens have been explicitly positioned and explicated within a collective/national domain, through regulation of the body and the coincident conscription of subjectivity. By showing how a subject has been "positioned," I do not mean to represent Hawthorne simply as a champion of the "weak" individual or community struggling to retain authenticity in the face of state power.[6] I use the term "counter-memory," after Michel Foucault, to refer to the residual material that is not identical with the official meanings of the political public sphere—for instance, the material of popular memory in which public or national figures, bodies, monuments, and texts accrue a profusion of meanings. The popular knowledges that constitute counter-memory work in contradistinction to the official material that so often becomes the "truth" of a historical period and political formation. Official memory and popular memory do not, however, necessarily oppose each other. Their relation represents the dispersal of experience and knowledge that constitutes the realm of the "social." Indeed, the popular reframing of national signs is often not politically invested in any explicit way: as I suggest in chapter 1, the personification of the Statue of Liberty in American culture is a prime example of how contradictory interpretations of a sign might *not* call into crisis the meaning or function of that sign, or of the system that authorizes it.

These are the "facts" of modern American citizenship, as Hawthorne represents them and traces their logic. But the complex text of "The Custom-House" and *The Scarlet Letter* also strikes a range of critical positions within these representations. Insofar as the production of "citizens" by "nations" requires symbolic and practical orchestration of a public mentality, Hawthorne critiques and counters the hegemonizing strategies and privileges of "official" national identity. He uses the fact of the popular reframing of official material to humiliate textually the fictive self-presence of the federal system (predicted, in its modes of spectacle, by Puritan juridical practices), thus giving his text a populist tinge.[7] He also imagines, in a set of inchoate theoretical gestures, other routes to the linkage of politics and utopia that the Puritans and the Americans have claimed as foundational to their official political authority. But Hawthorne's critique of the conventional forms these attachments take, his proposals of some counter-forms for the construction of a critical nationalism, run into limits, some of which emerge from his own position as a privileged subject of American citizenship.

The frame around *The Scarlet Letter* in this book establishes its prehistory and projected development as a national fantasy. The first chapter, "Body, Landscape, and National Fantasy in Hawthorne's *Native Land*," describes how a bond between erotic desire and the desire for collective political existence serves the nation, by connecting national identity and more local and personal forms of intimacy. The name for the ideal form of this association, in Hawthorne's version of America, is "utopia." Hawthorne traces the national-utopianism of the body and the body politic to two ideologically (but not territorially) disjunct moments: Puritan and post-Revolutionary War political cultures, both of which used the promise of millennial and secular collective perfectibility to create a sphere of projected political experience and knowledge that competed with and even sublated the pressure of material political realities. The claim to splice the political and the utopian in the nation marks the body, in Hawthorne's reading of American history, via the activity of public patriarchal rule and female symbology in the national and pre-national memory. One key aim of this discussion will be to describe the nationalist *mnemotechnique*—a form or technology of collective identity that harnesses individual and popular fantasy by creating juridically legitimate public memories.

The final chapter, "America in Everyday Life," breaks the "American" frame that dominates both Hawthorne's texts and the bulk of this book. Under the pressure of slavery, economic transformation, rapid territorial and population expansion, and imperialist impulses, American national identity was in a legitimation crisis in the 1850s: but one possible outcome of this crisis, rarely considered by Hawthorne critics, might have been the failure of the federal system to secure the complex emancipatory image America has claimed as its birthright, its natural law. The United States, as we know it, was not inevitable, despite the "American"-utopian claims of its always already constituted status; not all cultural work tended toward the national horizon. In this chapter, I suggest that everyday life, local political identities, and political affect itself are posited in Hawthorne's texts as alternate routes to the revitalization of the political and utopian promises that have distinguished modern national life from other state formations. This chapter reconfigures *The Scarlet Letter* within a discussion of Hawthorne's history book for children, *Grandfather's Chair,* and Lydia Maria Child's story "Home and Politics," both of which provide critical commentary on the project of reproducing the dominant forms of American national identity.

Thus in a sense this is a simple project, tracing out the thought of one man about the complex of factors that citizenship involves. That the man is Nathaniel Hawthorne, canonical forefather of a major strain in the American literary canon, means that his ruminations have an interest for general readers and literary historians, always interested in collecting new ways of understanding the literary logic of an influential author.[8] However, this is not an intentionalist reading of "Hawthorne"; rather, I aim to lay out the complex mechanisms of national identity his texts display, including but not limited to what we can deduce about his interests and positions.[9] Beyond the attempt to reproduce authorial intention, the strongest contemporary critical discussion of how Hawthorne represents America focuses on his symptomatic reproduction of the contradictory logics of liberalism. The work of Myra Jehlen and Sacvan Bercovitch has produced a complex nationalist Hawthorne, critical of American political practices but inscribed in the culture of consensus that absorbs in a pluralist semiotic the fractures of social hierarchy.[10] In contrast, Donald Pease and Jonathan Arac see Hawthorne more powerfully registering and contesting these fractures by, respectively, aligning with populist sentiments and insisting on the productive indeterminacy of national, personal, juridical, and political identity.[11] I am most strongly aligned with the latter, less "symptomatic" readings of Hawthorne and American culture; all of the above, and many others, have influenced positively the way this book aims to explain the relation between official, juridical definitions of the nation and its circulation in the culture at large.[12]

But I also see, in the struggle to explicate the forms and practices of nationhood in Hawthorne's work, an attempt to break the frame of national hegemony itself. Work in colonial discourse and collective identity has demonstrated the political necessity to historicize the rhetorical and practical processes by which nationality has been created, secured, and deployed; likewise, I reconstrue America in its moment of high nationalism by reading its modes of power and practice not as given, but as continuously constructed in difference from and competition with other political and social formations.[13] A specifically feminist component of this argument also motivates my narrative: this book contributes to the ongoing attempt to historicize and theorize female political agency in the democratic social spaces of American culture.[14] Hawthorne's women emerge as uncanny, paradoxical, politically unintelligible: as fantasy projections of patriarchal fear about the imminent end of male hegemony within the political public sphere, as occasions for serious critique of that same patriarchal culture, and as eroticized subjects who speculate that other forms of collective life might be imaginable, even within America.[15] In this sense "citizen" is both an inclusive and an exclusionary noun, naming by negation juridically contested racial, gendered, and class identities. If citizenship is an overdetermined juncture of experience and power in Hawthorne's work, these other always nationally inflected sites of embodied meaning and experience seem often *under*determined—appearing in stereotypes authorized by what Eve Sedgwick has called "the privilege of unknowing," a kind of amnesia available to the legitimate subjects of hierarchical cultures.[16] You will have noted that I have used a "citizen/he" locution throughout this preface: as Hawthorne's experiments in citizenship unfold in this book, this pronoun too will undergo change. The default gender of the American citizen is still, alas, a masculine one.

This description might well raise some questions about the place of historical evidence and narrative in this book, focused as it is on the relays between the practices and materials of life in the United States and the experience of national identity. Having placed the reproduction of authorial intention to one side, and put in its stead a descriptive function, to provide a detailed account of the rhetorical and practical operation of "America" in the social practices of collective life as Hawthorne represents them, I also aim to create another kind of political memory, of how the nation has

worked both practically and affectively. David Van Leer has shown how Hawthorne's philosophical seriousness is communicated, in *The Scarlet Letter*, by his use of conceptual and verbal anachronism.[17] In addition, by crossing over different temporal fields and thus bringing them into sharp conjunction, Hawthornean anachronism also makes present the means by which official political culture configures its own power, and constitutes its "historical moment," while in the present tense. The narrator's continuous flow of allusion in *The Scarlet Letter*—to Catholic symbology, British political and literary history, and to popular or folk knowledge, for example—constantly violates the temporal frame of the narrative in order to adjudicate seventeenth- and nineteenth-century concerns, but also, I argue, to perform in the text a crisis of historical consciousness. Historical horizonality is a necessary fiction, in the Hawthornean revitalization of national life: but the seventeenth- and the nineteenth-century "horizons" of *The Scarlet Letter* and "The Custom-House" are fictions that demonstrate the paradoxically non-synchronic nature of any present tense or horizon of experience. The rough edges of this historical narrative, as it moves among and transcodes temporal and critical registers, produce the affective discomfort of national identity as a reading-effect. In this spirit, I employ anachronism as well. Just as Hawthorne deploys the guillotine and like images of events that happen "elsewhere" to describe crucial nodal points in personal/national history, I mean to defamiliarize national identity, treating Hawthorne as a moment in its vexed operation.

I have tried to stress that there is always an official story about what the nation means, and how it works: not only in the way propaganda enacts a systematic fraud on citizen-readers, but also in the power of law to construct policy and produce commentary that governs the dominant cultural discussion of what constitutes national identity. Chapter 1 addresses the popular logic of national fantasy, both in nineteenth-century America and in Hawthorne's early work, and the chapters on *The Scarlet Letter* read the logic of Puritan juridical discourse in the novel. But alongside public iconography and popular narrative is an official story of "citizenship": the juridical discussion of what membership in the nation implies and requires. To construct the anatomy of national fantasy as Hawthorne writes it, it is necessary to track the history of American citizenship to the moment of his articulation of it: What does it mean, in 1850, to be a "citizen" of here or elsewhere? How does it happen that national identity has become, in America, fundamental to the person, akin to gender, race, and family? Like any consolidating term of national identity, "citizen" was an elastic trope: and in the epoch of *The Scarlet Letter* its meaning was suspended in a struggle of national proportion.[18]

During the time in which Hawthorne was negotiating his own national identity, the question of where the generic "person" derives his national identity was a vexed one: although many of the famous cases that addressed this issue, like the *Dred Scott* decision, took place after *The Scarlet Letter* was written, the cultural movement toward the crisis was already, during and after the 1830s, a matter of great concern in the courts and in public political discourse.[19] Being an American citizen wasn't "natural" for white men, but it involved the possession of a gendered and racialized body; it wasn't simply "familial" or "local," but still involved a historical inheritance in the form of *jus sanguinis* and *jus soli*; citizenship depended on how one adjudicated state and federal identities; it depended on adult consent to participate in national culture—such that Hawthorne's self-willed "citizenship" of "somewhere else" was, indeed, a right uniquely conferred upon him by America; and finally, it depended on the existence of an intelligible national culture in which to participate. In addition, the crisis of relation among these affiliations threatened the national frame of reference itself: within the political public sphere, it became a matter of fierce contention whether the nation truly fulfilled its juridico-utopian promise to protect the local while abstracting the person from his body and everyday life experience to another, more stable, symbolic order.

Modern citizenship operates according to rules and conventions barely alive in the juridical imaginary of Hawthorne's time. In contending that citizenship involves the state's obligation to care for the psychic security of the citizen (along with the political protections promised by the Bill of Rights), Hawthorne anticipates a virtually current juridico-ethical turn in citizenship jurisprudence. In this section, I wish to stage the difference between what we currently understand by citizenship, in the modern juridical present tense, and the problems posed by and for national identity that faced the nation most acutely in the period of Hawthorne's nationalist work, prior to the Civil War.

In a landmark case of 1958, the U.S. Supreme Court ruled that it would be cruel and unusual punishment to strip a citizen of his national identity. *Trop v. Dulles* is an undramatic case of a soldier who deserts an army unit and who is then stripped of his citizenship by virtue of congressional statute.[20] Mr. Trop did not mean to expatriate himself, or to choose another national affiliation. Thus, wrote Earl Warren for the majority, denuding Trop of citizenship would be taking away his right to be protected a priori by the nation:

> We believe . . . that use of denationalization as a punishment is barred by the Eighth Amendment. There may be involved no physical mistreatment, no primitive torture. There is instead the

> total destruction of the individual's status in organized society. It is a form of punishment more primitive than torture, for it destroys for the individual the political existence that was centuries in development. The punishment strips the citizen of his status in the national and international political community.[21]

In the Court's opinion, forced, involuntary expatriation violates the citizen through a virtually ontological torture: *Trop v. Dulles* is a landmark case because it situates citizenship in the citizen's "body," the abstract body that can, nonetheless, feel pain as well as the humiliation of being vulnerable, feminized, "fair game for the despoiler at home and the oppressor abroad."[22] Everyday life might continue—the man without a country "may perhaps live, work, marry, raise a family, and generally experience a satisfactorily happy life"[23]—but the modern state's assurance of national identity as more fundamental to the person than any of his other historical affiliations provides the citizen his fundamental sense of power, protecting the citizen as he negotiates everyday life, as he lives his own privileges.[24]

In making such an argument for national citizenship's essential status for an actual person, Warren departed from the conventional logic of official discourse about the citizen's rights and obligations.[25] His understanding of citizenship is anticipated by Hawthorne, who likewise understands the crucial interface between the state and the person as affectively invested and experienced. Usually, citizenship is adjudicated by interpretations of the Fourteenth amendment: in fact, as I will discuss below, modern American citizenship is derived primarily not from Enlightenment Constitutional dicta but rather from the enfranchisement of African-Americans. Indeed, it is possible to see the history of the Constitution as a record of the nation's gradual recognition that it needs officially to theorize an ideal relation between its abstract "citizen" and the person who lives, embodied, an everyday life. This crisis of definition took place because "[o]ne of the most important terms in the Constitution which the Framers did not define or explain is the term 'citizen.'"[26] Benjamin Ringer, among many other historians of race in America, suggests that the Constitution's vagueness about this crucial matter was strategic on the part of the framers: "the Convention sanctified not one but two models of society. On the 'visible' level of the Constitution is the society built on the concept of the sovereignty of the people and on the rights of the governed. And on the 'invisible' level of the Constitution is the society built on the concept of 'unequal rights' and on the enslavement of subjugated 'other persons.'"[27]

Prior to passage of the Fourteenth Amendment (1868)—which guarantees to all citizens the protections of the Bill of Rights and which intended to confer the franchise on all African-American (male) persons—American discourse on citizenship did, indeed, traverse an overt and a covert semiotic, although racial difference was not the only determining site of distinction and exclusion.[28] Two competing ways of conferring citizenship have dominated the modern state's political strategies. These are generally called birthright citizenship, which incorporates both *jus soli* (place of birth) and *jus sanguinis* (nationality of fathers) lines of political entailment, and consensual citizenship, which derives the polity from the aggregate consent of individual subjects. The birthright model is a monarchical trace, involving communities of natural allegiance to the king and assumptions about national identity's organic situation within the person. Peter Schuck and Rogers Smith have recently renamed this category "ascriptive citizenship," so that it might include all suprapersonal, objective conditions determining the person's rights and obligations.[29] In their view, racist cultures situate race as an ascriptive quality, an inherited, "natural" delimitation of the subject's power. The consensual model, in contrast, assumes no natural state of political participation but rather a historical one, involving the abstract "person" who lives outside of objective or natural political systems and who has chosen to enter a political frame. For instance, although the Constitution implicitly defined a "natural" legitimate subject (white, male), who was privileged to be "disembodied" by national identity, not all white males inherited the national covenant (their franchise status was determined by states); therefore the abstract realm of nationality relied on some archaic conventions of political participation, but only as a route to constructing political alliances based on the subject's *intention*. The framers of the Constitution felt it important to reject "the doctrine of perpetual allegiance" that operated in England; they tried to construct a national form which would assure that America was not only "chosen" in a millennial sense but to-be-chosen in historical time by "the people."

Still, while the model of consent motivated the overt dominant political discourse of America, even up to the Civil War "the nature of United States citizenship was still vague and undefined," for two major reasons.[30] First, even freed African-Americans were excluded from access to consensual membership via an argument from birthright; second, alongside the racial fracture soon to rend the nation, there developed a widening fracture over the relative political priority of the federal state to the local state. Insofar as *jus soli* arguments still obtained, conferring citizenship according to place of birth (with the ongoing assumption that adults "consent" to citizenship by not expatriating themselves), the struggle for sovereignty between the state and the federal nation was, some say, the real issue that motivated the Civil War. Did property, even property in a "person," have a national character?[31] By 1789, it was clear that state membership was primary, and the only route to federal citizenship. But the purchase of the Northwest Territory (1787) also made it possible to think national identity without a state affiliation (this possibility was codified by statute in 1795).[32] This ambiguity, in which racial and territorial hegemony were twined, was brought to a crisis in the *Dred Scott* decision (1857). A major axiom in Justice Taney's argument against conferring the franchise on African-Americans was that persons of African descent were not persons in the Constitutional sense: "Can a negro whose ancestors were imported into this country, and sold and held as slaves, become a member of the political community formed and brought into existence by the Constitution of the United States, and, as such, become entitled to all the rights, and privileges, and immunities, guaranteed by that instrument to the citizen?"[33] His answer was negative, because slaves did not inherit citizenship by birthright: Dred Scott had no right to petition the Supreme Court because he wasn't a federal citizen; nor was he a state citizen, according to the Constitution.

This decision foregrounds a number of crises in national self-definition contemporary with Hawthorne's own moment: What is the relation of one's parentage to one's local affiliation, and the relation of these to the federal state? The Fourteenth Amendment consolidated the priority of federal citizenship over state—although, as anyone who has seen D. W. Griffith's *Birth of a Nation* will attest, this amendment hardly put to rest suspicion of the federal "nation," a suspicion that currently survives in civil rights litigation.

No wonder exile seemed to Hawthorne like a solution to the difficulties of feeling intensely both local and federal "native" identification. Hawthorne's response to this crisis is to return to the body, to subjectivity, to material experience, and to everyday life to reconfigure what it means to be an American citizen. He does this in part by critiquing the claims of official nationalist discourse, but mainly by writing a new kind of history, a "genealogy" of national identity, from 1640 to 1850. The word "native" that peppers Hawthorne's "national" work ambiguates and also retheorizes the relation between the local and the national. In addition, we will see that two affective strains of representation and systems of power—the patriarchal and the utopian—characterize America throughout its history, viewed both regionally and federally, through Puritan and post-Revolutionary War lenses. But we will also see that even within the limitations of this inquiry—one man's mind working on an assortment of historical and literary material—there is no inevitable "America," no ur-American "citizen," no simple emergent, archaic, and dominant ideological or political formation that "means" America. *Seven Tales of My Native Land* and *The Scarlet Letter* (as well as the later American novels) show Hawthorne experimenting with citizenship, with the abstract political affiliations nations require, and with the different forms of fantasy that circulate through the local experience of the national context.

This is not to assume an unbroken continuity between local self-expression and the national condition: it is to assume, rather, that no such national totality exists, and that the struggle to control the dominant meanings of America and the variety of emergent means of exercising counter-hegemonic power are key in Hawthorne's reformulations of national history and ideology, as they create "citizens" and "the people." In Hawthorne's national work we see the suspended meanings of the national "map" through characters whose experiences vary because of their own gender, class, ethnic, racial, religious, and political identifications. Hawthorne's "American project" questions the filiopietistic self-representations of the "nation" and the "people"; it suggests different ways of articulating a "people" out of historical materials, refusing to see history or culture as a fixed and lasting pool into which the literary pen can dip, finding the material for the literary reproduction of an exemplary microcosm; it questions the prospects for utopian social theory in a context in which the "utopian" has already been politically appropriated by an official apparatus of national identity. The usual opposition in this sort of discussion is between utopia and ideology, the latter being the discourse of "interest" that blocks the realization of the former. But in America utopia has not simply been a condition occluded by the imperfect techniques of political practice. Instead, as Bercovitch has argued, utopian discourse has been a crucial component of American political practice, such that in the national frame (as in the New England experiment) utopia is both "utopia" and "ideology." The preeminence of law in Hawthorne's representation of pre- and postnational American culture reveals that the ethos of "government by law" has long absorbed national-utopian fantasy; Hawthorne's emphasis on patriarchalism reveals the coterminous operation of "government by men," in both a utopian and a vulgar practical sense. For our purposes, then, the utopia-ideology distinction is neither a code for "theory" and "practice" nor for "pure" and "corrupt," nor an opposition of any kind in its own right. In each of the following chapters, the utopia-ideology *relation* establishes, instead, a field of social activity within which individual and collective fantasy become, nationally, embodied.

ONE

America, Post-Utopia: Body, Landscape, and National Fantasy in Hawthorne's Native Land

> A nation and a woman are not forgiven the unguarded hour in which the first adventurer that came along could violate them. The riddle is not solved by such turns of speech, but merely formulated differently.
>
> Karl Marx
> *The Eighteenth Brumaire of Louis Bonaparte*[1]

IN THE *EIGHTEENTH BRUMAIRE*, MARX DEVELOPS AN aesthetic of revolution that explains the political content of mass movements by their relation to symbolic forms. He does not simply read the content-logic of the forms themselves—so that the "meaning" of a metaphor like "the nation is a woman" would not reside primarily in the way "woman" expresses national qualities. Rather, Marx evaluates the *techniques* through which a movement formulates or articulates itself. "Bourgeois revolutions," he writes, ". . . storm quickly from success to success; their dramatic effects outdo each other; men and things seem set in sparkling brilliants; ecstasy is the everyday spirit. . . . There, the phrase [goes] beyond the content."[2] In the case of bourgeois revolutions, the overpresence of spectacle indicates the poverty of the movement's political self-conception: the public is asked to "believe" that these ecstatic images "express" the political subjectivity of the movement, and the political content of the revolutionary moment is in turn displaced to an atemporal and globalized activity of spirit and affect. To Marx, here, what is significant is the delirium that accompanies the production and deployment of bourgeois images, and less whatever political fantasy is contained in the images themselves.

So, too, when Marx addresses the "riddle" of national vulnerability by conjoining the image of the nation with a new image, that of woman, he does not aim to express the problem of national unconsciousness through an evaluation of the conditions of female vulnerability. He does not claim to "solve" the national riddle by looking to woman; crossing over and joining the national to the feminine code, he reformulates the question in order to refine the question itself. This "refinement" does not produce clarity but opens up new fields of inquiry: for one, Marx's use of gender to formulate the national question emphasizes the need to evaluate the riddled relations between political forms and the subjective conditions of historical experience.

My aim in this chapter is to reformulate Marx's concern with the mutual implication of language and subjectivity by considering specifically the conditions under which national identity takes shape: within dominant or "official" culture, and for persons who come to know themselves as national "citizens." To provide this analysis of national consciousness I will refer to the formation and operation of what I call the "National Symbolic"—the order of discursive practices whose reign within a national space produces, and also refers to, the "law" in which the accident of birth within a geographic/political boundary transforms individuals into subjects of a collectively-held history.[3] Its traditional icons, its metaphors, its heroes, its rituals, and its narratives provide an alphabet for a collective consciousness or national subjectivity; through the National Symbolic the historical nation aspires to achieve the inevitability of the status of natural law, a birthright. This pseudo-genetic condition not only affects profoundly the citizen's subjective experience of her/his political rights, but also of civil life, private life, the life of the body itself.

Modern citizens are born in nations and are taught to perceive the nation as an intimate quality of identity, as intimate and inevitable as biologically-rooted affiliations through gender or the family.[4] National subjects are taught to value certain abstract signs and stories as a part of their intrinsic relation to themselves, to all "citizens," and to the national terrain: there is said to be tional "character."[5] Nathaniel Hawthorne wrote at a ica when literary culture was doing much of the worl such a constellation of national signs, both to provide for the people a National Symbolic, the common language of a common space, and to shore up the shaky state apparatus, which as yet had no cultural referent whose expression it could authentically say it was.[6] "Alice Doane's Appeal," the tale I will address in this chapter, stages the problem of constructing an effective National Symbolic as a riddle that can be posed in two ways: How does the experience of space and time influence the formation of national identity? And, how can the woman, perhaps "taken" unawares, serve the nation? Hawthorne sees as central to this enigma the need for writing to harness the libidinal energies of the American "people" for the purposes of national fantasy.

But how do we locate this thing called "national fantasy," in order to excavate its general techniques of operation? Frantz Fanon's classic investigation of national identity in *The Wretched of the Earth* argues that it is the purpose of national culture "to make the totality of the nation a reality to each citizen. It is to make the history of the nation part of the personal experience of each of its citizens."[7] Ideally, the national culture feeds the "passionate"[8] fantasy of the citizen to be empowered by a collective activity and identification that is also realized and preserved by a politically legitimate nation-state: "A national culture is the whole body of efforts made by a people in the sphere of thought to describe, justify, and praise the action through which that people has created itself and keeps itself in existence."[9]

Yet, as Fanon himself realized, national cultures rarely work only in this positive, expressive fashion—just as definitions of "the people" are constantly in flux within the nation's political sphere.[10] The cultural expression of national fantasy is crucial for the political legitimacy of the nation: it is evidence of the nation's utopian promise to oversee a full and just integration of persons, "the people," and the state. However, a national culture simultaneously records the discontinuous, contradictory, ambiguous, antagonistic, and simply confusing elements of civil life[11]—sometimes to provide for "the people" protocols that at once make intelligible and "manage" the complexities of the public sphere, sometimes to provide politically invested "materials" on behalf of one or another version of national identity.[12]

The National Symbolic thus seeks to produce a fantasy of national integration, although the content of this fantasy is a matter of cultural debate and historical transformation. One prominent event in the history of American national-popular imagining was the construction of the first national icon built by "the people": the Statue of Liberty. Now fully saturated by a century of collective fantasy, the "Lady" provides an exemplary study in how the fantasy-work of the National Symbolic has worked to produce and to mobilize American citizens.

The Statue of Liberty (1886) was the first American monument financed completely by public contributions. The significance of this fact must be underlined: it is the first national monument "owned" or generated by "the people" themselves—or this is how the citizens who sent their pennies to Joseph Pulitzer's newspaper, the *World*, saw it. "*The World* is the people's paper, and now it appeals to the people to come forward and raise the money. The $250,000 that the making of the statue cost was paid in by the masses of the French people—by the workingmen, the tradesmen, the shop girls, the artisans—by all, irrespective of class or condition. Let us respond in like manner. Let us not wait for the millionaires to give this money. It is not a gift from the millionaires of *France* to the millionaires of America but a gift of the whole people of *France* to the whole people of America."[13] The letters from contributors Pulitzer published repeated this message: "We, as workmen poor in pockets, but rich in patriotism, contribute our mite in hope that the example will be followed by workingmen generally, and shame the close-fisted millionaires if that be possible."[14]

Articulating the national symbol as an expression by "the people" and of "the people," the *World*'s popular capitalization of the statue provided an opportunity for the self-styled "masses" to take ownership of the symbolic material of national fantasy—a populism of the symbol long reinforced by the Statue's crucial placement in the American experience of immigrants who saw it as the national boundary. A century later, in 1986, a spate of coffee-table books and national magazines heralded a crisis of national proportion: the Statue of Liberty was in dire need of what was quaintly called a "face-lift." The president, Ronald Reagan, seeing the opportunity for a patriotic event, turned the responsibility for the statue from the National Park Service over to the American "people": and, many proclaimed, it was a "wise decision," because it gave the nation for the second time the opportunity collectively to acknowledge and to demonstrate "our" spiritual obligations, "debts" we owe both to "the Lady" and to the nation.[15]

The public relations campaign that accompanied this spectacle aimed to create tremendous national anxiety at the thought of the dissolution of a national symbol. Why would the statue's dismemberment create such anxiety? Critics of the Statue universally comment on how its appearance of timeless monumentality is central to the populist fantasy that animates the fantasy of American nationhood. Indeed, the sculptor, Frédéric Bartholdi, is said to have subscribed to a current theory of the symbolic politics of public statuary that stressed its unifying, totalizing function:

> When a figure rears itself above the sea at the entryway to a harbor, and will be seen from a distance by navigators on one side and those who live on the seashore on the other, it is important that its mass be compact, indivisible—in a manner of speaking without a single noticeable jutting salient, without any detached accessory, without any gap. And more, so that the statue can be 'read easily' at the distance at which it will be seen, it is essential that its movement be simple and that it display in silhouette almost unbroken lines . . . and in the actual model, major planes in which individual planes are dissolved and lost.[16]

In other words, the statue's stability as a point of national identity depends on her body being indivisible, like America. The iconic body provokes the translation of subjects in time and history into an unmarked plane or space of consciousness, unperforated by "gaps" or "protrusions": a whole body, indivisible although clearly divided, that represents the promise of the nation, which is a utopian promise, to provide a passage for the individual subject to the abstract identity of "citizen," which includes but is autonomous from the historical person. Thus the icon's body is liminal: it marks the limit of historical time, promising the immortality of identification, suspended outside any historical moment although fundamental to the subject's local historical experience. By passing into citizenhood through inscription in the National Symbolic of the body politic that expresses her/him, the citizen reaches another plane of existence, a whole, unassailable body, whose translation into totality mimics the nation's permeable yet impervious spaces. According to this logic, disruptions in the realm of the National Symbolic create a collective sensation of almost physical vulnerability: the subject without a nation experiences her/his own mortality and vulnerability because s/he has lost control over physical space and the historical time that marks that space as a part of her/his inheritance. Fanon's representations of "native" subjectivity within a colonized nation repeat this structure of anxiety and sensation of dismemberment. Fanon describes how the colonized subject becomes a part-object, or "amputation," to himself,[17] without a nation to be "sheltered behind."[18] National identity provides, then, a translation of the historical subject into an "Imaginary" realm of ideality and wholeness, where the subject becomes whole by being reconstituted as a *collective* subject, or citizen.

The "collective" nature of this individual citizen loses its paradoxical quality when seen through the national icon's ambiguation of the relation between its multiple planes and its aura of totality. One recent critic of the statue suggests that although its "unwieldy iconographic machinery rusted, leaving the observer with a kind of polymorphic iconographic blank that might be invested with a variety of changing, up-dated symbols . . . the *total* configuration of the statue became itself the symbol of liberty,"[19] unchanging and unchangeable. The Statue, exemplary among national icons, is what Walter Benjamin identifies as a "dialectical image," an image that functions like a montage in which objects are made part-objects by their relation to a larger simulacrum of wholeness.[20] The national dialectical image works in a utopian way to create multiple spaces that coexist in time despite contradiction, without threat of annihilation.

Such a promise of a totality that overwrites the object status of individuals and property through a transformation of micro-spaces into larger, neutral, impermeable sites defines the utopian promise of the nation as such—all modern nations, not just America. The nation enacts this promise by positing collective identification as the way in which atomized sites become sutured by a synchronous participation in the perpetuation of a political and cultural collective life. So, for example, the Statue of Liberty carries a tablet, Mosaically inspired, which constitutes the "law" of American liberty: the "content" of this text is simply *JULY IV MDCCLXXVI*, the space of time that sutures "the people" and the territory to the "nation." I use the term "suture" deliberately here, to signify the way in which the national totality does not demand the dissolution of the micro-boundaries of individuals or property within its borders; rather, as is the case with the statue's iconic construction, internal boundaries are conferred on citizens of a geographical and political territory and are legitimated as traces of the nation's promise of sovereignty, however vaguely defined in the conjunction of the state, the civil society, and "the people."

The political operation of these sutured spaces adds a crucial dimension of time—both of history and of modernity—to our spatial consideration of the construction of national identity. Benedict Anderson writes that the modern nation developed a notion of territorial simultaneity to explain the experience by atomized citizens of collective life and consciousness:

> In the course of the sixteenth century, Europe's 'discovery' of grandiose civilizations hitherto only dimly rumoured—in China, Japan, Southeast Asia, and the Indian subcontinent—or completely unknown—Aztec Mexico and Incan Peru—suggested an irremediable human pluralism. . . . The impact of the 'discoveries' can be gauged by the peculiar geographies of the imaginary polities of the age. More's *Utopia*, which appeared in 1516, purported to be the account of a sailor,

> encountered by the author in Antwerp, who had participated in Amerigo Vespucci's 1497–1498 expedition to the Americas. . . . (The meaning of these settings may be clearer if one considers how unimaginable it would be to place Plato's Republic on any map, sham or real.) All these tongue-in-cheek utopias, 'modelled' on real discoveries, are depicted, not as lost Edens, but as *contemporary* societies. One could argue that they had to be, since they were composed as criticisms *of* contemporary societies, and the discoveries had ended the necessity for seeking models in a vanished antiquity.[21]

Thus as a result of the discovery of new spaces, new frontiers, a notion of contemporaneity became integral both to the modern utopian formulation and to the modern nation. The modern nation always represents itself as immanent in the movement of historical forces and always operating within the scope of a "limitless future"; at the same time, however, the nation operates according to an idea of " 'homogeneous, empty time,' in which simultaneity is, as it were, transverse, cross time, marked not by pre-figuring and fulfillment, [as in prenational America], but by temporal coincidence, and measured by clock and calendar."[22] The iconic operation of monuments like the Statue of Liberty implies such a liberation from what Julia Kristeva calls "cursive," or linear time, the time of traditional national narratives.[23] As Emma Lazarus's "The New Colossus" suggests, the very *sight* of the statue erases the exiled subject's historical temporality by performing the individual's rebirth as a citizen.[24] Passing through the gaze of the "Mother of Exiles," the subject—who is at this point nationless, having left behind a prior national identity—is translated into a new Symbolic order, as well as into a new territory and a transformed experience of time, mapped out according to a specifically national agenda.[25]

The power of this "Mother" to make citizens out of exiled subjects derives largely from her placement—both within an already potent National Symbolic and at the fixed and permeable outer boundary of the nation. But one other intimate quality must be addressed in this construction of the means of national fantasy: this is the Lady's gender. The allegorical figuration of political desire in the body is conventional to all points along any political spectrum and is limited neither to the woman nor to national discourse.[26] However, the political deployment of the female icon often thematizes her "power" as a quality of her gender.

In particular, the female icon tends to derive her centrality to the scene of power through her implicit association with what Teresa de Lauretis calls her "consent to femininity"—"the (impossible) place of a purely *passive* desire."[27] Even "The New Colossus" has the statue acting without moving, speaking: the "Give me your tired, your poor" speech is cried with "silent lips," the eyes glow, the flame is imprisoned lightening—her power in short, is her immobility.[28] Just as the statue's body is powerful because it refuses and erases the dismemberment of the immigrating bodies once emigrating, and then in exile from national affiliation, so her immobility and silence are fundamental to her activity as a positive site of national power and fantasy.[29]

More than one centennial text tells how immigrants and workingmen still express desire for "the Lady": "A blacksmith working on molds of the ribs said: 'I guess, whether we admit it or not, we are all in love with her.' Bob Conmy, a member of the scaffolding crew, did not have to say anything. He was one of the first to reach the level of the statue's face and look her in her enormous eye. He leaned forward and gave her a kiss."[30] Another more scholarly text closes off its analysis of the Statue by taking her off her "pedestal," fantasizing that "not as we see her, but as we know her, this decent woman takes on an altogether different character—for a fee she is open to all for entry and exploration from below." [31]

The construction of the national genitalia of our national prostitute reminds us that the National Symbolic is there for *use*, for exploitation, to construct a subjective dependency on what look like the a priori structures of power. It would not be too strong to say that the political deployment of the feminine icon has a pornographic structure.[32] A popular site of collective fantasy that "solves" the problem of staging collective life by providing for itself a legible sex/text, the female body of the American National Symbolic eternally desires to be relieved of desire, to be passive and available for service, to contribute to the polis by being and needing where it needs her to be.[33]

The regularity with which Miss Liberty becomes an object of sexual speculation and erotic fantasy evokes the way citizens formulate the nation as an object of idealized love—this is one of Benedict Anderson's main aims, to reestablish the genuineness of the utopian promise that characterizes the experience of the national. Still, when the body of the woman is employed symbolically to regulate or represent the field of national fantasy, her positive "agency" lies solely in her availability to be narrativized—controlled, as de Lauretis suggests, by her circulation within a story.[34] To Kristeva, addressing the placement of the woman in specifically national terms, the woman becomes the nation's common *symbolic denominator*, "designed as the cultural and religious memory forged by the interweaving of history and geography."[35]

In short, the transcoding of the national scene along gender lines, in addition to creating spatial and temporal intelligibility for the nation, has provided a powerful relay between the utopian and the political prospects of national identity. Indeed, historians of the American early national period point out that the iconic body of the American woman provided a major mystic writing pad for national identity as it emerged: "her" availability as an object of collective fantasy gave very formal expression to the utopian promise of the United States. But clearly the symbolic logic of figures invested with national meaning from circulation through public spaces does not tell the full story of how modern American national identity emerged in practice. Two other coextensive fields of relation come into contact, in this intense moment of national articulation. First, I will address the complex relations between cultural nationalism and political nationalism as they developed in America through the nineteenth century; next some practical implications of the America-utopian coupling that helped to structure the particular elasticity of the federal political public sphere.

The Statue of Liberty came late in the movement toward cultural nationalism, and served mainly as a figure of the need to integrate into the nation the immigrant groups entering America in and after the 1880s. Eric Hobsbawm writes that "Americans had to be made. . . . The immigrants were encouraged to accept rituals commemorating the history of the nation—the Revolution and its founding fathers (the 4th of July) and the Protestant Anglo-Saxon tradition (Thanksgiving Day)—as indeed they did, since these now became holidays and occasions for public and private festivity."[36] Hobsbawm here describes national culture as citizens ordinarily experience it—through periodic "patriotic" returns to the National Symbolic. The centrality of these official moments to national identity demonstrates how the citizen's primal territorial affiliation produces the ritual, liminal time of national "simultaneity": participation in national celebration connects the citizen to a collective subjectivity constituted by synchronous participation in the same national rituals, the same discursive system.

But prior to the production of symbols for the "nationalization" of immigrants, the nation produced a body of material that staged its own "nation-ness" to itself, internally.[37] The American National Symbolic burgeoned during the early and mid1800s. But this cultural self-articulation did not take place "naturally": the "American Renaissance" emerged under widespread pressure to develop a set of symbolic national references whose possession would signify and realize the new political and social order.

Historians of American nationalism consistently comment that the pressure to develop a distinctively American discursive space was not identical to the pressure to create an indigenous culture experienced by many other national movements: in the American case, political facticity as a nation preceded the development of a shared culture among the citizens themselves. Kenneth Silverman writes of the late 1780s, when the call to develop a national culture began: "In calling for an American literature, most political nationalists required little more than that writers style themselves 'American.' Others dimly hoped that claiming a national identity might help to create one."[38] Without an ancestral religion or a coherent ethnic tradition, nationalists argued, a loyalty to the nation-state had to be formed that would have the strength of customary loyalty to a sovereign king. Silverman notes that theorists and prophets of the nation's future thought they recognized the absence of a mutually confirming political and cultural system; they saw dire possibilities for the state should it remain represented as new, or as outside of history, rather than as an inevitable product of historical action both revolutionary and legitimate, according to established, traditional standards. Thus the movement toward creating an "indigenous" American culture aimed to rectify a weakness in the relation between the state and the nation, for without the operation of an indigenous cultural system of self-expression the state itself would not be perceived to be integrated with the nation as a whole, for there was no stable set of customary references that constituted the expression of an "American people."

In addition to managing and/or symbolically resolving contradictions that threaten the political future and cultural intelligibility of the state, national-cultural productions were called on essentially to recast the state as an expression of a collectivity that had yet to be created. The need to form, formulate, and represent this collectivity for "the people," as if by "the people," resulted in the production of a set of discursive conventions whose internal logics provided the means for the symbolic—but not necessarily the coherent or the political—embodiment of "the people" in a simulacrum of the American state that images an integrated popular will. Anne Norton has argued that the National Symbolic has tended to achieve this populist aim through the elaboration of opposing terms. These oppositions, which come to signify metaphorical schemas of power, are entirely unsurprising: masculine and feminine, sovereign individual and system, North and South, white and any number of racially contested groups.[39]

The power of these oppositional locutions in antebellum American culture resided in their elasticity: they were powerful because they could be used to "clarify" and therefore to "manage" any number of contested situations. Lawrence Friedman suggests, for example, that the deployment of gender conflict in national rhetoric expressed patriarchal ambivalence about the nation's utopian claims; in particular, woman's "seeming ability to embrace both rooted security" and perfectibility made her a figure of great investment and ambivalence in early national discourse.[40] Maternal or monstrous, Friedman argues, the image of the woman became the "safety valve" for American culture, which exploited patriarchal ambivalence toward woman by making her knowledge, her body, and her reliability the focus of the reproduction (symbolic and actual) of the nation.

In contrast, Norton argues that the main deployment of gender in early national culture is as a metaphor for regional conflict between the North and the South. The very conventionality of the opposition (even the "war") between the sexes provided the deep structural struggles between these regions with an aura of natural inevitability. Here—as in the case of Marx's reading of bourgeois revolutionary aesthetics—the specific meaning of gender deployment for the purpose of national self-representation is less important to this analysis of the National Symbolic than is the way analysis reveals gender's political centrality as a source and structure of collective identity.

Such an ability to develop mechanisms for staging unity as a virtual *effect* of difference is not unique to the image of woman, the National Symbolic, or America. What is specific to America is the way it has politically exploited its privileged relation to utopian discourse: the contradiction between the "nowhere" of utopia and the "everywhere" of the nation dissolved by the American recasting of the "political" into the terms of providential ideality, "one nation under God." In addition, I have previously suggested that post-Enlightenment national cultures always claim to express the spirit of "the people" in one way or another. Yet even when "the people" is a political "body," the claim to represent its spirit is a fictive one, deployed on behalf of or in opposition to a particular national Real. In the words of David Forgacs, "'National-popular' designates not a cultural content but . . . the possibility of an alliance of interests and feelings between different social agents which varies according to the structure of each national society."[41] Whereas other modern nations are constituted in part by an implicit and often contested national covenant—that the nation (as political formation) will unify to express and protect "the people" in a state of ideal relations—in America the possibility of a sutured national-popular consciousness has been a central distinguishing mark of state mythic utopianism. America has from the beginning appropriated the aura of the neutral territory, the world beyond political dissensus, for its own political legitimation.

It would be impossible to map out all of the political and cultural implications of the "nationalization" of utopia that takes place in the American context. My main interest is to chart how utopian discourse specifically refracted the theory and experience of "America" for the citizen who is theorized/brought into being in this abstract and collective context.

Since the experience of "the nation" as nation is primarily a "symbolic" one—communicated through the subject's understanding that certain spatial and temporal experiences reflect, perform, and/or affirm her/his citizenship—the spatial and temporal ambiguity of "utopia" has the effect of obscuring the implications of political activity and power relations in American civil life. If the "meaning" of the nation is its utopian "promise," then: is America utopia incarnate, the already-realized fulfillment of the assurance of universal sovereignty postulated by Enlightenment political thought?

Or is the "utopian" nation an imperfect formation constituted by a promise for future fulfillment, a "promissory note," imminently in the state of perfection but to be achieved within history? These contrary possibilities are not mutually exclusive: as Sacvan Bercovitch has shown, the logic of national-utopian discourse has produced antithetical models of national temporality that are fundamental to what has been the dominant mode of American self-description.[42]

This suspension of national-historical time has political implications that do not pertain when utopian theory remains a fully fictive discourse. One result, in America, of the temporal transformation of history that traditionally accompanies utopian thought, is the *denigration* of "the political" or, in its more traditional formulation, "the ideological." Louis Marin—making an argument also made by Karl Mannheim and Paul Ricoeur—has argued that utopian thought traditionally introduces "into narrative history and geography the sudden distance that breaks apart closely held spatial and temporal surfaces. Lightninglike, before coming to a hard and fixed image in the utopic figure and 'ideal' representation, the *other* appears: limitless contradiction."[43] In other words, utopian theory reveals the fabricated identity of time and space with their textual description. The unifying utopian figure, which in theory brings time and space into the realm of (discursive, systemic) perfection, shows, in relief, the impermanence and instability of the historical frames within which persons gain (self-)knowledge and experience. In addition, the American deployment of the simulacrum of utopian neutrality, embodied in the Statue of Liberty's aura of transcendent symbolic and physical indivisibility, figures the national Other as the cause of internal division: a site of monstrous political discourse that embodies the presence of hierarchy, inequality, separate interests, and unjust oppression within the political space of America. It has been suggested, indeed, that early American utopian nationalism developed a fundamental antagonism between the National Symbolic, with its emphasis on the dream of collectivity and unity, and pragmatic political discourse, which seems fractious and debased in comparison.[44]

Nathaniel Hawthorne's intervention in cultural nationalism takes on the contest between the political and the utopian in often contradictory ways. Hawthorne sees the nation's utopian heritage as a fundamental fact of America's meaning and participates like a loyal subject in the movement to map out national culture. As any reading of his prefaces reveals, his repeated desire to find the "immunities" of the "atmospherical medium"[45] that constitutes a "neutral territory"[46] "so like the real world, that, in a suitable remoteness, one cannot well tell the difference,"[47] may be read as his attempt to provide, for the nation, the very semiotic that will allow citizens to experience America in a new form of utopian ideality: one in which these officially contested forms of discourse and reference no longer seem antithetical, mutual negations. In so articulating a sutured political-utopian realm, he aims to recast his readers as national subjects within the workaday world of civil and historical life newly seen through the lens and the interests of the National Symbolic.

In addition, however, central to Hawthorne's expression of the Nation is a search to create a space of cultural critique that is not appropriable by the will-to-absorb-difference or contradiction that characterizes a dominant strain of liberal-idealist "utopian" ideology.[48] American pluralism, as I have said, is distinguished by an insistence that the legitimacy of micro-formations (states, individuals) is conferred by the nation-state itself: the nation in theory sees dissent as a sign of the paradoxical permeability and permanence of its political/territorial authority and thus welcomes the opportunity to contain political opposition.[49] Hawthorne remains attracted to the national utopian promise of universal legitimation, but wants to transform the way it works to contain, to neutralize, and to disavow internal antagonism. Since he sees the context of national identity as fundamental to his subjectivity, he is forced to identify and to devise spaces *within* the system, national "heterotopias," within which he might maintain a critical edge.[50]

To do this Hawthorne offers a counter-National Symbolic marked by a hermeneutic of negativity and defamiliarization. In response to the ideal intelligibility of the national-utopia, he constantly makes illegible the American landscape; in response to the national elevation of the woman as the privileged source and future of culture, he substitutes her denigration and her negation, erasure, or absence; in response to the call to make citizens at home in their culture he posits the ideal citizen as tourist. In conflating the citizen and the tourist, and in making strange the domestic political space, Hawthorne also opens up other political vistas, based not on mass consent to be politically collective but on a politics of experiment, experience, subjective identification that might or might not refer to or reauthorize the national horizon. As to the question of how these tactical moves revise the operation of the National Symbolic—let this remain for the moment a critical question.

In theory, the National Symbolic sutures the body and subjectivity to the public sphere of discourse, time, and space that constitutes the "objective" official political reality of the nation. To install such a field of reference requires the production of what Friedrich Nietzsche calls a "mnemotechnics,"[51] an official technology of memory whose purpose is to burn into the minds of subjects their intrinsically social existence and responsibility. In Hawthorne's career we can see a transition within his representation of the function of the

American mnemotechnic. While his earliest tales posit the past as a ratification of a certain version of collective identity, he comes to see the past as a problem for modernity, and to understand that the National Symbolic must also inscribe in the subject/citizen an authentic relation to the present in order for national identity to be both effective and legitimate.[52]

Hawthorne's 1835 tale, "Alice Doane's Appeal," is a revision of a now lost tale of 1829, probably titled "Alice Doane." Hawthorne intended to publish this tale in his postulated first volume, *Seven Tales of My Native Land*. This volume remains postulated because Hawthorne, in a fit of desperation about his inability to find an audience for his version of his native land, burned the manuscript. To this day, only two stories remain, apart from the traces of "Alice Doane," and these are "The Hollow of the Three Hills" and "An Old Woman's Tale."[53]

The very conjunction of "My" with "Native Land" in the title of this volume demonstrates Hawthorne's determination to participate in the creation of the National Symbolic through the double articulation of subjectivity and landscape. Hawthornians nonetheless tend to be embarrassed by these texts, because their hermetic gothicism reveals none of the literary, historical, political, or moral self-consciousness so vital to the later, canonized work.[54] But these early tales can illuminate the later national tales and novels: first, because they all center on a scene of oral transmission that demonstrates the tangled relations between discursive power and "native"-historical knowledge; second, because they transcode national consciousness through the construction of narrative linkages between landscape, historical time, and sexuality; and third, because they each employ the gothic and the uncanny to represent the surplus affect attaching to the social forms of power.

Central to both "The Hollow of the Three Hills" and "An Old Woman's Tale" is a pedagogical tableau: the reader is educated in how to identify and attain a proper relation to the knowledge s/he receives through the narrative s/he hears. In this sense the tales construe the nation through its inscription in subjectivity—but in each case the text sets up an allegory of reading in which knowledge is transmitted from an individual subject to a scene of intersubjectivity. Such knowledge—which in these tales is always knowledge of "pastness," more than textbook history—gives the knower power over nature, over life and death. Accordingly, each tale splices, in the mode of the dialectical image, the scene of historical knowledge and discursive power with images of grotesque, ancient women. The representation of woman as the caretaker of national history is not unusual during this period, as I have mentioned; but Hawthorne's introjection of national history into the always already decaying body of woman here sets the stage for his future suggestions that the conjunction of woman and special historical knowledge reveals a serious problem in the historical scene and a rupture of patriarchal authority that needs immediate repair.[55]

"The Hollow of the Three Hills" opens in "those strange old times," with a meeting between a previously beautiful woman "smitten with an untimely blight" and "an ancient and meanly dressed woman, of ill-favored aspect, and so withered, shrunken and decrepit, that even the space since she began to decay must have exceeded the ordinary term of human existence" (199). The memo-

ry of the old woman in "An Old Woman's Tale," who told her stories "in a mumbling, toothless voice," not only "included the better part of a hundred years" but "strangely jumbled [the woman's] own experience and observation with those of many old people who died in her young days; so that she might have been taken for a contemporary of Queen Elizabeth, or of John Rogers in the Primer" (240).

"The gradual accretions of a long course of years" (241) during which the personal and historical material of her culture are absorbed makes the female narrator of history powerful, but not legitimate: in both tales, the decrepit woman is explicitly an unacceptable and improper source of national culture, although she is also the only available source of what is valuable about "our" collective past. These tales register anxiety about the discrepancy between the value of "private" historical knowledge and its grotesque origins. They manage this anxiety by casting historical narrative in the form of an artifact whose possession enhances the "owner's" prestige. Therefore, in the tales' structural logic, the place of privilege shifts with the narrative transmission. Elevated in the teller's place is the audience, poised as a critical listener: skeptical about the truth-content of women's tales but desiring the narratives that connect him to the popular or repressed details and habits of the past, the male auditor is himself empowered. In contrast, the simply credulous female listener in "The Hollow of the Three Hills" dies from hearing the conjured tale of her own life.

Clearly the modern critical response to the remains of *Seven Tales of My Native Land* repeats Hawthorne's contemporary problem. On the face of it, these tales build no bridges to the readers already lacking in the interest and knowledge that give one privileged access to the empowered, intersubjective, critical mind of the collectivity on whose behalf Hawthorne was clearly writing allegory. In addition, the allegory itself did not simply reproduce the sunny version of national history and national identity: the gothic semiotics of historical transmission in these tales locates the power over the American historical materials in strange and deformed old crones, implying that the past is not our *heimlich* origin, but a place of potential exile from understanding, control, and identification. With no concessions made to American idealist self-revisionism, the reader might have been forced to come consciously to terms with the complex American past—but this was not to be.

One might surmise, from the revision to "Alice Doane," that Hawthorne took from this experience two lessons: that for a tale to be powerful as a vehicle for proper historical consciousness, the text must somehow realize the contemporary scene that "receives" cultural transmissions; and that the personal authority of the storyteller is crucial to literary nationalist pedagogy. Accordingly, in "Alice Doane's Appeal" Hawthorne recasts the nativist project by suturing a contemporary autobiography onto the historical-gothic tale.

The revised "Alice Doane's Appeal" provides a genealogy of Hawthorne's national mnemotechniques and presents them in the synchronicity of narrative space. It is thrice-told according to its historical placement: simply, there is the original gothic tale that aims to exemplify the Salem witchcraft crisis of 1692 by a gothic story of Indian massacre, incest, witchcraft, and law; second, a contemporary scene in the realist mode of autobiography, in which a desperate narrator who could find no public for his gothic love story takes two women on a tour of Gallows Hill in Salem, where the witches were hung, thereby situating historical "facts" within the context of personal narrative; finally, a frame with no proper boundaries that performs for the reader the liminal translation of one form of time, space, and the body to the other, as I have just described—this is the frame in which the appealing sexuality of the icon, Alice Doane, becomes the indirect appeal of the author, Hawthorne, to his largest, national audience. Alice Doane, in the central tale, pleads for affirmation of her unspoiled virginity in front of a court of ghostly and horrible specters; she "appeals" to the court to provide for her the authorized version of her own autobiography. At stake in the success of her appeal is the future legitimacy of her genetic line. The narrator, in turn, asks his readers to endorse the political authority of his fictions, in order to harness our rambling passions to his love of national history. At stake in his appeal is the emergence of a new technology of national identity that legitimates both a certain version of the American past and the place of literature as the means of cultural/national self-transmission. Her successful "appeal" to the audience to confer legitimacy on her body will thus result in his successful "appeal" to be installed as the author of a new form of American historical consciousness: it is in this aim that the "narrator" and the author, Hawthorne, are united in purpose.[56]

The narrator of "Alice Doane's Appeal" establishes immediately that this is a text in and about a crisis in historical representation, whose operation redounds not only on the practice of historical methodology but on the shape of American culture and self-consciousness as well. We, he writes,

> are a people of the present and have no heartfelt interest in the olden time. Every fifth of November, in commemoration of they know not what, or rather without an idea beyond the momentary blaze, the young men scare the town with bonfires on this haunted height, but never dream of paying funeral honors to those who died so wrongfully, and without a coffin or a prayer, were buried here. (267)

Like the "ahistorical and formalizing reader" Fredric Jameson describes, who resists "that dry and intolerable chitinous murmur of footnotes reminding us of the implied references to long-dead contemporary events and political situations in [authors like] Hawthorne," we, the people, are characterized here by a mass identity organized around exhausted political ritual.[57] To the narrator the scandal of "every fifth of November" is hardly that the scary and libidinous young men do not know that they mark Guy Fawkes Day, an official English nationalist holiday that celebrates the state's spectacular suppression of, and juridical violence against, revolutionary conflagrators.[58] His point is that the young men have no consciousness of acting politically, in spite of the formally political semiotics of their behavior.

That they nonetheless act as if they possessed a political memory is evidence of the power of national fantasy and the juridical mnemotechniques of the National Symbolic; however, the citizens' occupation of the present tense is not a critical one but one organized around the public spectacle of the will-to-*not*-know. "The people" are of the present but are also estranged from it. The narrator differs from these empty citizens because he is motivated both by "stronger external motives, and a more passionate impulse within" (269); his aim is to harness their "passionate impulses" to an external "motive" to live historically in the present tense. In response to the American citizen's profound amnesia about his/her own or any national-political context, the narrator wrote the gothic tale I have identified as Hawthorne's "Alice Doane"—but which now carries no proper title of its own. The historical locus of this tale is the witchcraft crisis of 1692, which here stands as the negated version of American history, a historical space unmarked even by empty ritual.

"Alice Doane" meant to install in the reader-citizen a symbolic memory of the political psychogenesis of the American people: when it was first written, says the narrator, there were no histories of that period through which the now nationally constituted people might understand themselves as having a nonnational or prenational historical genealogy. But the histories of the witchcraft trials written five years later incited the narrator to try disseminating his story again: for these histories, especially Charles Wentworth Upham's *Salem Witchcraft*, treat "the subject in a manner that will keep [the historian's] name alive, in the only desirable connection with the errors of our ancestry, by converting the hill of their disgrace into an honorable monument of his own antiquarian lore, and of that better wisdom, which draws the moral while it tells the tale" (267). In other words, according to the narrator, the nationalist historian of 1835 makes a name for himself by arguing, in the utopian mode, what "the people" want to hear, the "moral" always implicit in the American "tale": that the American people as now symbolically constituted transcend their own history, having embarked on a mission of moral and political perfection in which the problems of the past appear, when they appear, as an abyss from which the national project has liberated us.

The scandal of juridical and communal excess that marked the witchcraft prosecutions becomes, in this positive (and therefore "negative") nationalism, a "monument" to our superior honor. In both "Alice Doane" and "Alice Doane's Appeal," Hawthorne takes us to Gallows Hill in order to question whether "Paradise . . . were rightly named" (266) to plant us collectively within

the history of scandal that is equally and perhaps primally a part of American history. Such an origin in a political reign of law, death, and self-generated unconsciousness calls for the use of the gothic apparatus; but Hawthorne's initial translation of the historical material into the gothic tale does not involve simply the masquerade ball of popular historical romance. The historical method of this fiction is romantic in the sense identified by Hayden White and David Levin: the field of narrative implies a larger ideological and sensational context for the properly historical scene.[59] The internal tale represents witchcraft not as a scandal, but as an agent in a gothic love plot in which private desires have exploded into the jurisdiction of public law through the murder of Walter Brome.

Thus we might say that love is the mnemotechnic of the internal tale, "Alice Doane." But to say this is to say nothing about the kinds of knowledge love generates or about the way it operates as a narrative drive. A veritable piece of what Michael Taussig has called the "virginal historiography" of cultures in transition, "Alice Doane" articulates the historical moment as a crisis over a hymen.[60] The narrative of the love story as we receive it focuses on the catastrophic results of Walter Brome's boast that he has carnally "known" Alice Doane. The major effect of this speech act is that Leonard, Alice's brother, murders Brome, for "here was a man, whom Alice might love with all the strength of sisterly affection, added to that impure passion which alone engrosses all the heart . . . [and] more than the love which had been gathered to me from the many graves of our household—and I be desolate!" (272).

But this incestuous-style act of brotherly love reveals other buried relations. Looking at Brome's dead face, Leonard Doane recalls:

> I know not what space of time I had thus stood, nor how the vision came. But it seemed to me that the irrevocable years, since childhood had rolled back, and a scene, that had long been confused and broken in my memory, arrayed itself with all its first distinctness. Methought I stood a weeping infant by my father's hearth; by the cold and blood-stained hearth where he lay dead. I heard the childish wail of Alice, and my own cry arose with hers, as we beheld the features of our parent, fierce with the strife and distorted with the pain, in which his spirit had passed away. As I gazed, a cold wind whistled by, and waved my father's hair. Immediately, I stood again in the lonesome road, no more a sinless child, but a man of blood, whose tears were falling fast over the face of his dead enemy. But the delusion was not wholly gone; that face still wore a likeness of my father . . . (273).

Prior to this *après coup*, Doane had thought he recognized himself entirely in Walter Brome: it was "as if my own features had come and stared upon me . . . [and] the very same thoughts would often express themselves in the same words from our lips" (271). After the murder, however, Brome turns into the *father's* spitting image, while Doane, the "man of blood," assumes the position of the wild Indian, or the young man who lights bonfires for fun, violating a sacred communal space.

Critics generally think this paternal image is conclusive evidence that Brome is a long-lost and still-repressed brother of the Doanes. This emergent fact would mean that in addition to murder and possible seduction, fratricide and incest are also circulating as unmentionable horrors for Leonard and Alice. But the literal fact is that in this tale all young men look alike, and all are vulnerable to two things: a love of law and a love of resemblance. It is when things *don't* look alike that violence enters the scene—as in the case with the Natives, and as in the possibility that Alice Doane became physically and emotionally different from her "gentle and holy" self by distributing her love differentially (271).

The obsession with effacing difference drives the rest of the tale, during which the lovers of the law get their fill of repetition. After Leonard Doane commits the fratricidal/patricidal murderous act it is all he can do to keep from murdering Alice, "tortured" as he is "by the idea of his sister's guilt" (273); so he goes to a wizard and tells the wizard the tale—which the wizard already knows because *he* turns out to be its vile author, although it is unclear what that means. What is the wizard a wizard of? Transforming difference into similitude: "But when the young man told, how Walter Brome had taunted him with indubitable proofs of the shame of Alice . . . the wizard laughed aloud. . . . but just then a gust of wind came down the chimney, forming itself into a close resemblance of the slow, unvaried laughter . . . " (272).

But like the shaman Taussig describes, who "is said to be the one who truly *sees*, and by virtue of this capacity provides the healing images . . . for the patient, the one who cannot see,"[61] the wizard is forced under what the narrator vaguely calls "certain conditions" to give "his aid in unravelling the mystery" for Leonard (274). He takes the pair to the community graveyard to raise the spectral image of Walter Brome so that Alice might speak, be named "virgin," and be spared her shame or her death.

Significantly, when the wizard does this, and when Brome absolves Alice "from every stain" wrought by the imputation that she has secret sexual knowledge (277), the wizard raises the ghostly images not only of Brome but of the entire historical Puritan community. "All, in short, were there; the dead of other generations, whose moss-grown names could scarce be read upon their tomb stones, and their successors, whose graves were not yet green . . . and whenever a breeze went by, it swept the old men's hoary heads, the women's fearful beauty, and all the unreal throng, into one indistinguishable cloud together" (276–77). Here the wizard conjures the community as a negative totality: "Yet none but souls accursed were there, and fiends counterfeiting the likeness of departed saints" (276), "too shadowy for language to portray" (277). Yet Leonard Doane's desire to contain difference, to keep Alice intelligible to the law of his desire, does not evidently provoke skepticism about the wizard's representations. Although the truth or falsehood of the wizard's specters cannot be determined one way or another, and even after he discovers his own and the community's political unconscious, Doane believes the discourse of the image because he needs to believe in the clarity of evidence and the sovereignty of the law of his desire.

Thus it turns out that love, in the central tale of "Alice Doane's Appeal," is not romantic, or even sexual, but a love of law, which is aligned with a love of resemblance and a suppression of difference. Read as Leonard Doane's story, this internal tale maps out how the Puritan anxiety to insure the colony's juridico-theological authority over even unauthorized signs led it to self-destruct on Gallows Hill. Hawthorne constructs an allegory of love from this political scene by making an oxymoron of the phrase "spectral evidence": loving the law, and desiring that passions be recontained within the patrilineal family that makes the law intelligible and intimate to the Puritans, Leonard Doane reads apparitions as objective monuments to the "truth" that serves him. In this sense he is a most typical Puritan: although fiery battles ensued over what the precise meaning of heavenly signs and embodied spirits might be, the very objectivity of spectral evidence was fundamental to the American Puritan hermeneutic.[62]

The graveyard scene is also a devastating parody of the way civil procedures privileged the discretion, and therefore the desire, of the judges of the court of Oyer and Terminer who presided over the witchcraft scandal. Alice's appeal to Brome for truth and mercy is made by a victim to her victimizer; Brome is not only the possible agent of sexual trespass and the only other authoritative witness to the act of crossing the hymen—he is the accuser and the jury as well. And Alice's brother, because of whose desire this case is brought to trial, will not believe her testimony, because the very fact of her subjectivity makes her a discredited witness to her body. She is the only living witness who knows, but her capacity for knowing discredits her in the eye of the law. In addition, Hawthorne's sexualization of witchcraft not only reflects the scandalous passion that brought the community together against the possibility of trespass but also paradoxically trivializes the will to power of the judges, who claimed to act on behalf of history and society while located in the seat of passionate motive.

And yet despite the tale's narration of the fateful ideology of resemblance and congruence that marks the political structure of seventeenth-century Puritan New England (and implicitly that of nineteenth-century positivist America), it still relies on the spectral image of the woman to represent the collectivity to itself. The admission of the spectral hymen to the court of Leonard Doane deconstructs the law and the society's claim for their own foundations in reason: for though the center of the tale, she is yet an entirely discredited witness, as well as a mirror of her brother's excess. Moreover, her availability as an index of social value both to her brother and in the tale itself reveals how intertwined is Hawthorne's revision of American history with his examination of patriarchal practice. In literature and the law she is always unrepresented, like the transparent membrane that represents her value to her brother: indeed, her appealing value lies in her ability to make her appeal without claiming the authority of representation. Neither she nor her appeal is represented directly in either version of Hawthorne's narration, although the story is named after her and although her brother's confession takes up much narrative space; her body is never described, although the male body materializes frequently. She, the "problem" that generates the historical narrative, is the fold around which the story takes form, its lovingly represented representative of "a happier culture" (272): her autobiography, like her virginity, can be articulated only by a ghost. As with the Statue of Liberty, discourse about history, society, and knowledge is organized around the nonrepresentability of Alice, her discourse, her impassive hymen; it passes through her, she embodies it as she is disembodied by it through her nonrepresentation in the configuration of the "native" narrative.

However powerful this representational apparatus might be for the tale's critique and revision of patriarchal-nationalist practice, it was not powerful enough to forge the links between private desire, collective identification, and historical self-consciousness Hawthorne wanted to effect. Still, in seeming affirmation of his practice in *Seven Tales of My Native Land*, Hawthorne recycles his gothic narrative in "Alice Doane's Appeal." He predicts the representational conventions of his later national novels as well by maintaining the link between the symbolic logic of gothic and the construction of national identity: narrating in particular the interpenetration of surplus sexual and political desire, especially as each encounters patriarchal juridical apparatuses in the public and private realm. Gothic narrative here apparently provides security for what he calls the "vestiges" of history (268), investing these fragile, spectral national signifiers with a power usually limited to questions of sexual desire.

Yet the failure of the first tale, "Alice Doane," to demystify its readers suggests some limits of gothic narrative as well, for the project of reconstructing the individual reader into a communal/national subject. The revised narrative installs a new mnemotechnique to augment the force of Alice's appeal: the narrator addresses his audience directly, bringing together the scene of narrative transmission and the sensual experience of the body, not simply in narrative time but also in the space of landscape. In this revision, he constructs history as an authentic experience of the sensual memory of the body that sees and redefines itself in the heteronymous contexts of mute landscapes, monuments, and other bodies. It is in these sites that "Alice Doane's Appeal" plays to the formalism of the modern audience by conjuring the landscape as the vehicle of national historical identity, as if standing on a historical spot makes the subject experience all of national history simultaneously, as a totality, in the same "space of time" (273).

"For my own part, I have often courted the historic influence of the spot," he notes (267). The narrator's relation to the locus historicus is neither instinctive nor motivated by a desire to civilize it through knowledge, as it has been for the liberal historians who have walked through the same material. Rather, the language of the relationship is curious, simultaneously denoting love and the law. He "courts" the historic influence of the spot; the spot "beckons" to him, requesting that he "obey the summons of the shadowy past" (267). Being a lover of the law, he comes to Gallows Hill. He comes to know it like a lover, a "curious wanderer" (267), and not like a "distant spectator" (266). He derives special, privileged knowledge by so responding: whereas distant spectators see a hill of golden flowers, he knows that "all the grass, and every thing that should nourish man or beast, has been destroyed by [wood-wax], this vile and ineradicable weed" (267). Such fantasies of immersion in the demystifying influence of history inspire the narrator to make an experiment as to whether physical, sensual immersion in a landscape invested with history and fantasy will provide an effective context for the narrative transformation of all desiring persons into historically thinking national subjects.

But the two women never know that they are subjects of an experiment. For all they know, they are taking a walk "on a pleasant afternoon" around Salem, where "all was prosperity and riches, healthfully distributed" (268). The narrator turns this walk into a guided tour in which the women become tourists in their hometown—just as they are, in his view, tourists with respect to their history. He shows them the hometown they didn't know they lived in, in which the weedlike, uncanny historical truth overwhelms the specter of wealth and glory. No longer relying on what would normally be considered proper contexts, proper names, or established landmarks, he grounds the telling of the gothic tale not in a place that the women will recognize but in a place they've never seen, because it hasn't been named, in "the bay and its islands, almost the only objects, in a country unmarked by strong natural features, on which time and human toil had produced no change" (268). The women's defamiliarization from the familiar landscape takes place gradually, as the narrator builds on play fantasy about witches to provide a sense-saturated context for his tale.

Along with establishing for history's and his own sake the utopian perfection of a new landscape, the narrator conjures another historical event: the oral transmission of the written text from an author to a captive audience. No longer mediated by the text, and by the time and space and human toil that conventionally mark the text's transmission, the author here self-consciously coerces the women to hear him out, by secretly bringing the manuscript in his pocket: "The ladies, in consideration that I had never before intruded my performances on them, by any but the legitimate medium, through the press, consented to hear me read" (269). The narrator sees his love letter all the way through to its addressees, reading it to them and manipulating their responses to it. He does this in part so that his text—his *kind* of text—will hit the affective and intellectual mark for which he aims—the revised articulation of national identity in a moment of libidinally charged collective fantasy.

The "audience" of identical female listeners is monitored intensely: every facial expression is viewed by the narrator as an index, a chronicle, evidence of the success or failure of his project—the seduction of the female reader, a.k.a. the libidinally and politically charged subject of history.[63] Here he can see through to the end the experiential transformation of their subjectivity into something collective and fully historical: along with using the gothic and *unheimlich* sensations of the audience to make a space for the comforting totality of national-historical consciousness, the narrator also gives them a visceral, sensational, physical experience of it. "Though with feminine susceptibility," he writes, "my companions caught all the melancholy associations of the scene, yet these could but imperfectly overcome the gayety of girlish spirits. Their emotions came and went with quick vicissitude. . . . With now a merry word and next a sad one, we trod among the tangled weeds, and almost hoped that our feet would sink into the hollow of a witch's grave" (268). Here he enacts a theory of history: history is what we *choose* to believe is here, right next to us, or buried under the deceptively beautiful weeds.

The importance of will and imagination to the future of history goes deeper than the true observation that neither history nor memory has preserved the exact places where the witches died (268). It also foregrounds how profoundly transitional "historical landscapes" are: to choose to create a national landscape out of a plot of land is to participate in a history-*making* process that involves the continual re-creation of invested "spaces" for different generations of subjects who live in the same territory. In its negative version, one might see this revisionary process as involving the exile of persons from their feeling of home, but this exiling has a dynamic relation with the sensual textuality of historical knowledge that is also, in this tale, history's great attraction.

Having so chosen to believe, both the narrator and the audience willingly locate themselves liminally, on the hymen of history, both mediating the present and the past in the scene of textual transmission and also occupying them fully. This is why the seduction discourse of historical narrative tries simultaneously to transform the body and the mind from their shallow inscription in girlish gaity to a deep understanding of the necessity that they develop into individual and corporate subjects steeped in history: at its climax these narrations, these bodies, and these minds are indistinguishable.

> By this fantastic piece of description, and more in the same style, I intended to throw a ghostly glimmer round the reader, so that his imagination might view the town through a medium that should take off its every day aspect, and make it a proper theatre for so wild a scene as the final one. Amid this unearthly show, the wretched brother and sister were represented as setting forth, at midnight, through the gleaming streets, and directing their steps to a grave yard, where all the dead had been laid, from the first corpse in that ancient town, to the murdered man who was buried three days before. As they went, they seemed to see the wizard gliding by their sides, or walking dimly on the path before them. But here I paused, and gazed into the faces of my two fair auditors, to judge whether, even on the hill where so many had been brought to death by wilder tales than this, I might venture to proceed. Their bright eyes were fixed on me; their lips apart. I took courage, and led the fated pair to a new made grave, where for a few moments, in the bright and silent midnight, they stood alone. But suddenly, there was a multitude of people among the graves. (274–75)

Here we see that through the medium of narration, the hill becomes the site and the index of a material transformation: characters in the story led to a "new made grave" become syntactically indistinguishable from the fated pair of readers being brought to death by wild tales; the narrator merges with the wizard, who still needs the proper reception from his audience—that is, a successful seduction—for the vitalization of his power. Thus revealing his method to us, the narrator shows that history is made vital not by a narrative gloss on a temporal event, but rather by an experience of transformation that unhinges temporal, material, and sexual knowledge and re-forms these dislocations into the unity of the simulacrum or spectacle. This is the American utopian promise: by disrupting the subject's local affiliations and self-centeredness, national identity confers on the collective subject an indivisible and immortal body, and vice versa.

If the story ended here, I might conclude that in "Alice Doane's Appeal" we witness the victory of the sensuous spectacle of history over its narration. But the narrator is not always victorious in his containment and transformation of the girls within his historical scene: the story turns, in fact, on what he perceives as their repudiation of his project. Reading his page of wonders to the ladies, narrating the final view of Alice and her brother left alone among the graves, his voice mingles with the wind, "which passed over the hill top with a broad and hollow sound, as of the flight of unseen spirits." This wind transforms, translates, interpenetrates the scene of 1692 with the present tense, and, the narrator embellishes the moment: "Not a word was spoken, till I added, that the wizard's grave was close beside us" (277). The ladies' response to the wizardlike narrator's lurid representation is to burst out laughing; and the narrator, furious that his scene has been violated by the women's suspension of the suspension of disbelief, decides to make "a trial whether truth were more powerful than fiction" (278).

He makes this trial by violating the narrative terms he has so carefully set up in the transmission of his gothic tale. No longer attempting to reconstruct historical identity through a sensuous, symbolic logic, he stages a spectacle of a procession of falsely accused witches walking up Gallows Hill toward their executions. He executes this scene with an eye toward creating personal, humanist identifications with the represented victims. No longer committed to transforming the mode of identification that had so limited the girls as national subjects in the first place, the narrator now uses all the tools at his disposal to effect what he considers the proper response to this historical moment. He plunges into his "imagination for a blacker horror, and a deeper woe" with which to frighten the women (279); he brandishes horrific representations for their gaze until he possesses "the seldom trodden places of their hearts" and finds "the well-spring of their tears" (280). Only when he achieves what he calls his "sweeter victory" over the ladies' resistance to his historical project does the narrator relent. He thinks, by making this trial, that he has done history justice, for he is history: "And now the past had done all it could" (280).

He may have done what he could—but what he could was to decenter, discompose, and coerce the young girls into affirming his superior literary technique. Their agreement, at the end, that "here in dark, funereal stone, should rise another monument, sadly commemorative of the errors of an earlier race, and not to be cast down, while the human heart has one infirmity that may result in crime" (280) cannot be read as an endorsement of the women's self-conscious assessment of the need for a certain kind of national subjectivity. For they respond to his "truth" as they have responded to contemporary historical truths—sensationally, not in a sensuous conjunction of the body and the mind. Similarly, the narrator's reversal of position, to argue for "truth" instead of "fiction" and to be on the side of Doane's law rather than against it, reveals that he is as much a formalist as the historians against whom he has posited his own writing.[64] The narrator displays his own capitulation to amnesia here, as he forgets about the critical national memory he meant to create, in his desire to replace Cotton Mather as the author, the interpreter, the judge, and the jury of American history, viewed from the conjunction of ethics and politics.

Thus what has appeared to be a land reclamation project—the revitalization of American history in a new national-historical subject who reads her place in history through its displacement onto a family romance set in the year of a particular historical scandal—turns instead into the collapse of all these mediations into a narrative landscape made virtually incomprehensible in the narrator's desire to create an effective historical space, or what he calls "a proper theatre" (274).

But this is where the analysis of the narrator and that of the tale must split: while this narrator forgets the lesson he has learned, the text formally "remembers" it. For a third narrative frame, which is incomplete and indeterminate, provides the form for the implantation of a critical national identity that does not rely on identification with totalized images and seamless narratives—the traditional technique of the American National Symbolic. This frame, which opens the tale and surfaces periodically throughout, transforms semiotically what Hawthorne has developed in this search to construct a non-totalizing, historical mnemotechnique of national subjectivity: to summarize, it requires the defamiliarization of the subject who has an active sensuality but no sense of history; a demystifying tour through her own civic backyard that includes a constant shifting of representational modes, of placenaming, of talespinning, in order to reveal that there is no natural anything that is not also fully textualized according to some prior author; finally, it requires that the subject's body and sensuality be central to the construction of a self-conscious collective subjectivity.

This frame opens with the narrator's ruminations on geography and on the proper space for narrative. "The direction of our course being left to me, I led [the young girls] neither to Legge's Hill, nor to the Cold Spring, nor to the rude shores and old batteries of the Neck, nor yet to Paradise; though if the latter place were rightly named, my fair friends would have been at home there" (266). In light of the tale's subsequent move to immerse the represented reader in the sensual landscape in order to provide proper immersion in the national narrative, this opening can be seen as an attempt to do to the readers through text what he will do to the auditors through travel. From his experience with the tale of Alice Doane he learned that if one aims to install a subject properly within a discursive field, it is not enough to represent an allegorical context that makes no explicit bridge to the reader reading the narrative. The reader needs to pass through the landscape itself. Only, rather than the kind of passing through represented by the Statue of Liberty, where one imagines or is an exile in order to experience his/her enfolding within the national bosom, Hawthorne's readers here are enveloped in a textual landscape in which exile from totalizing affiliation is explicitly the a priori condition of being.

The landscape is abstracted here into the language of maps. But this is a falsely clarifying language, since the narrator's nominalization of points on this map does not make Salem more legible to the readers abstracted from the town: he provides us with no situation within the civil context as he demonstrates his familiarity with it. The reader's association with the geography is therefore limited to the textual context. Here, geography is seen as the interspace between seduction and war or political violence. The landscape looks like a dismembered female body: legs, necks, skirts, and even the promise of a vaginal paradise, a locus amoenus which "if rightly named" would be the perfect context for the American ladies. Failing that, he takes the women to his paradise, Gallows Hill. And what we, the readers, see on Gallows Hill while the young girls look at the wood-wax, is something much worse: the primal scene of history.

> [The] tufted roots [of the wood-wax] make the soil their own, and permit nothing else to vegetate among them; so that a physical curse may be said to have blasted the spot, where guilt and phrenzy consummated the most execrable scene, that our history blushes to record. For this was the field where superstition won her darkest triumph; the high place where our fathers set up their shame, to the mournful gaze of generations far remote. The dust of martyrs was beneath our feet. We stood on Gallows Hill. (267)

The reader here develops a consciousness of the sexuality of social relations, the politics of the landscape, and the symbolic logic of their interaction long before the young girls have a clue about their purpose—if they ever do. By the top of the second page, we have seen the landscape turned into a collection of dismembered female body parts and then further transformed into the scene of primal national/sexual horror. History's point of view, which we textual tourists are then taught to take, is one in which blushing and shame and writing are all essentially related acts. We also witness an entirely abstracted double transfer of control over history from one gender to the other, in much the same way as the stories from *Seven Tales of My Native Land* figured the problem of history as a problem of which gender knows, tells, and writes. Superstition used to be the author: she won her darkest triumph by the public, pornographic staging of monstrous intercourse—guilt and phrenzy's execrable scene. History, whom we later learn, is indistinguishable from the man with the pen, receives the transmitted event and revises it, banishing superstition from its midst. At the same time the shame of "our fathers" is handed over to the collective contemporary audience, here figured as two young girls, who must learn how to copulate with or otherwise suture themselves to it.

The writing interpellates the reader into this initial instance of the National Symbolic in a few important ways: the narrator speaks in the plural, and slips back and forth between a "we" that refers to the three characters there and one that refers to "we, the people." At the same time, he estranges us from unconscious absorption into this collectivity by shifting constantly and unexpectedly between direct and indirect discourse, between historical moments within each of the tales themselves, and in the very styles of writing he uses. By foregrounding the formal mechanics of national discourse formation, and by restlessly revising, spinning different narrative and spatial models of how national identity operates within the boundaries of the given text, he keeps the reader a tourist in the textual landscape, one who never knows what hole she will fall into—and only this tourist, who knows that she is a tourist, can fully answer the appeal of national history.

Karl Mannheim writes that "the danger of 'false consciousness' . . . is not that it cannot grasp an absolute unchanging reality, but rather that it obstructs comprehension of a reality which is the outcome of constant reorganization of the mental processes which make up our worlds."[65] In other words, false consciousness is specifically located in the obstacles to comprehension, their forms. In "Alice Doane's Appeal" and throughout his corpus, Hawthorne relies on such a formalist model of false consciousness to explain how the federal state has politically deployed American utopianism, by transcoding the complexities and ambiguities of collective experience into a symbolic logic of national fantasy. The critical hermeneutic of defamiliarization Hawthorne develops in response counters the formal obstacles to comprehending the terms of national identity not by dissolving the rhetoric of collective form as such, but rather by producing counter-forms, in the guise of monuments that will never allow the citizen to forget—that is, to become the typically amnesiac American.

But Hawthorne's monumental mnemotechnic move, Mosaic in its inspiration, appeals to the formalism of collective identity. In this sense the solution in which we construct negative monuments rather than attempt to transform the operation of the National Symbolic itself can be read as a "fantasy bribe" to the subjects whose formalism is already fundamental to collective consciousness.[66] Furthermore, even in the Paradise of monuments and counter-monuments, one can always choose not to read the traces critically—even if "one" is their author. For example, "Alice Doane's Appeal" itself contains explicit references to Native Americans, in Leonard Doane's representation of his father's death. Yet the narrator provides no historical explanation for their participation in the tale. Readers of "Alice Doane's Appeal" who notice the "Natives" see them as simply the stock figures of American historical paranoia.[67] But the very landscape of Gallows Hill is marked by this unwritten history, which runs a kind of interference on the tale even as the tale heroically inserts noncongruence back into American consciousness. The rampart that we see on the first page was built on Gallows Hill in 1674, to protect Salem against the bloody uprising known as King Philip's War.[68] This war had nothing to do with the Salem witchcraft crisis, which happened about twenty years later. But it very likely could have been the event that triggers the foundation of the story's action—by which I mean the Doane patricide.[69]

In addition, this critical tour guide might also reveal to us traces of another kind of military history that intersects symbolically with this scene of scandal and shame: *A Visitor's Guide to Salem* reveals Gallows Hill's Revolutionary War connections as well.[70] Donald Pease suggests that Hawthorne's ambivalence toward representing the Revolutionary War stems from his disgust with the way it was used, in American culture, to insist on the nation's world historical transcendence of politics.[71] In any case, the narrator's lack of metacommentary on the inscription of these histories on this landscape is a sign of the care with which he chooses the witchcraft scandal as the metonymic moment of national identity. While the central gothic tale names no "historical event" in the way that heirs of a national history might receive it—"the Salem Witchcraft Scandal," the "Revolutionary War"—the frame narrative explicitly reveals the tale's aim to represent the "time" of the witchcraft episode to the current inhabitants of Salem's actual and America's symbolic landscape.

It is in places like these that we see limits to Hawthorne's antagonism toward the hegemonic mode of production of American "national" identity. While refusing, in this tale, to be "seduced" by identification with the attractive and self-deceptive utopian-idealist version of the National Symbolic, he quite comfortably reproduces some of the hierarchies and prejudices fundamental to national culture, both in its official and popular forms. Even accepting the range of critique behind Hawthorne's critical reformation of national identity and collective consciousness, details like the elision of Native American history join the tale's use of the female body as a pedagogical tool for the purposes of creating collective memory to suggest whole other bodies for whom this liberatory theory of the defamiliarizing National Symbolic may not be at all germane. The traditional blindness of nationalism to the symbolic disempowerment of certain citizens—in this tale women and Native Americans; elsewhere, African-Americans, the poor—acquires in his work an oppositional voice even within the critical nationalist literary project in which Hawthorne is engaged.

Perhaps the utopian content of "Alice Doane's Appeal," and of the project of cultural nationalism as Hawthorne practices it, lies on the other side of defamiliarization: by which I mean "theorization." If one direction of Hawthorne's refusal of the sunny Symbolic order is to construct an ever shifting set of terms within the context of the promised symbolic resolution that characterizes utopian thought, the other is that new models of political and everyday life are always being produced, even within the utopia of textuality. And so the still-colonized viewer of American history must do the same, seeing out of the corner of her eye the hymen, like an asterisk, pointing her in another direction.

TWO *The Paradise of Law in* The Scarlet Letter

THE TOURIST SEEKS TO EMBRACE THE UNFAMILIARITY of the place she investigates: its unique history, its "foreign" customs and fashions, the material expressions of its local culture. She brings to her investigations a sense of her own social context; indeed, contact with an alien place intensifies her identification with the traditions and qualities of her "home" culture. As Hawthorne proposes it in "Alice Doane's Appeal," the tourist's healthy self-immersion in alien contexts becomes, paradoxically, an alternative model for American national identity. On the one hand, a communally held collection of images and narratives—which, viewed as a field of force, I have called the National Symbolic—makes the national subject or citizen at home in "America." But this domestic political comfort leads to a kind of amnesia, as events and signs that potentially disrupt the nation's official-historical meaning are excluded from its public version of itself. Thus in addition to command of the National Symbolic, Hawthorne's ideal citizen must maintain a critical and skeptical attitude toward the officially sanctioned clarity of the "nation." She should seize, like a tourist, opportunities to add "unofficial" and/or "local color" knowledge to that offered by the dominant culture. The result of such a critical practice will be to transfigure that culture's meaning, largely by transforming its *way* of meaning. Critical nationalism will historicize dominant ideology by showing how it circulates among the many kinds of knowledge that distinguish the national space. Nationalist discourse, as Hawthorne's tale practices it, thus requires discomfort: it ratifies the utopian desire for an inclusive national identity while exposing the kinds of censorship that have marked America's promise of collective self-legitimation. It also aims to fuse new knowledge about social life to the set of things citizens recognize as "national."

Like "Alice Doane's Appeal," *The Scarlet Letter* begins by articulating a crisis in the power of official meanings to effect credible linkages within civil society. We can see this crisis in the narrative instability that marks the opening of the novel: indeed, we can say that the novel opens twice. The first two chapters, "The Prison-Door" and "The Market-Place," each begin by mapping out the "same" topography differently, according to divergent points of reference that emanate from a central scene—the "public sphere" of Puritan culture, figured as a space where the permanent and transient inhabitants of the Massachusetts Bay Colony convene for performances of collective political sentiment. This space is made legible—to "the people" and to the reader—by the co-presence of many different public monuments and signs.

In "The Prison-Door," a prison door and a graveyard mark the dark, hidden spaces of social life. The "antique," dusty quality of the door and the graves makes the modern moment itself seem archaic, the present a metonym for an exhausted past. These forms designate juridical and natural constraints: social life is figured as an aggregation of negations, witnessed by a "gloomy" public. In contrast, the scaffold so central to "The Market-Place" is not a sign of negation, although it is a machine of social discipline. Rather, the scaffold here functions as a fulcrum for the production of collective identity. The scaffold is necessary to the creation of the community in the present, for the future. In short, two ways of staging the operation of public monuments and signs characterize the first two chapters: first, sin and legal transgression are equated in the proximity of the prison and the space of death, and these are "the facts of life" of Puritan culture. But in the succeeding chapter, the penal machine is a sign of social positivity, as collective identity is generated by the scaffold's operation.

This shift in the way the technology of public constraint works reveals an anomaly in the terms of the novel's representation of Puritan culture. In "The Prison-Door," the narrator relates the dismal negativity of the gathered "throng" that occupies the Puritan public sphere to the failure of a "Utopia of human virtue and happiness" to impregnate the "virgin soil" with its theoretical "projections" (47). Death, sin, and legal transgression are the evidence the narrator wields to prove the failure of utopian theory. In "The Market-Place," the negative post-utopian language vanishes, as the scene now casts the technology of Puritan discipline—like that of "religion and law" (50)—as the fundamental fact of the Puritan public sphere. Here the law does not conceal sin, death, or Hester Prynne, but brings these into the light of day, much as this second chapter reveals the "fact" of Pearl: the law makes things possible.

But does this succession of images and discourses mean that *The Scarlet Letter* replaces the phantasm of utopian discourse at the core of the Puritan machine with the productive, political reality of law? Does this logic of substitution reveal either the historical or the ethical preeminence of law over utopian speculation? Is it possible, in contrast, that the law functions as the false front of utopian desire? Or might we read the shifty relation of these two formulations of the Puritan public sphere differently: as positing the proximity of utopia and the law as the *problem* of Puritan/American culture? "The Prison-Door" might be the *méconnaissance* replaced by the reality of "The Market-Place." But the appearance of Hester Prynne on the scaffold convenes "the people" in a simulacrum of the utopian collectivity imagined by the Puritan fathers. The confluence of people in the public sphere is sponsored by utopian speculation: it is the productive face of the negativity marked by the graveyard and the prison door. This suggests that utopia and the law are not antitheses in *The Scarlet Letter*. Each involves social theory and social practices within the Puritan community; each discourse requires the other to be installed as a dominant "ligament" in the body politic.

Utopia and the law, then, are brought into an estranged proximity. While they occupy the same public space, the temporal shift between these formations in the narrative of *The Scarlet Letter* stages their complex relation within Puritan culture. The terms of the novel's inquiry into utopia and the law are both political and ethical: but this is to say that, at a certain conceptual point, they come into contradiction. In utopia, the ahistorical values of ethics, of "our common nature" (55), and the political necessities of civil life will, in theory, occupy the same "space." But the particular form of their divergence is the enigma and the interest of the crisis of collective identity that marks the Puritan/American project in *The Scarlet Letter*. Neither of these discourses (rhetorics that also perform as theories, practices) gains ultimate ascendancy in the novel's moral universe, nor does one erase the other as a force in the social life that the novel represents, whether circa 1642 or 1850.[1]

One aim of *The Scarlet Letter*—and the primary aim of this and the following two chapters—is to investigate the mutual operations of utopian speculation, legal theory, and material legal practices within Puritan/ American culture. These chapters represent the Puritan/American scene by providing two shifting, contending, but not fully antagonistic views of the novel's engagement with the affiliation between utopian and juridical formations.[2] These readings of how Puritan collective/individual identity is organized around utopia and the law might be briefly summarized as marked by either "official" conscience or "counter-memory."

In chapter 2, "The Paradise of Law," I will address the official juridical theory and practice of Puritan identity as it operates in *The Scarlet Letter*. The years the novel spans, approximately 1642 to 1649, were a time of legal turmoil in the Massachusetts Bay Colony—a time when the interests of the law and of utopian social theory appeared to diverge. But the period the novel occupies excludes the originary moment of the new utopian experiment, as the narrator quietly points out on the novel's opening page. The Bay Colony was established in 1630: the crisis in law of 1642 was a response to the prior historical moment, when the political hierarchies of the colony were first established and first challenged. The narrator points to this buried history in a few ways, to be elaborated on below: his allusions to the Antinomian crisis and the Pequod War (both 1637) designate a prior time when the colony's legitimacy and ability to police itself was tested sorely.

Here, I will argue that the novel goes farther than to allegorize the historical predicament of how to install "utopian discipline"[3] in a "people" through the deployment of "ciuill" and "ecclesiasticall" law[4]: it also represents the limits of the law in its patriarchal mode of legitimation, of social address, and of imagination. As many have noted, crucial to both the law's effectivity and the novel's critique of dominant culture is Hester Prynne, in her "transfiguration" of sexual difference into a vehicle for revealing the intricacies of patriarchal power in the utopian state. "The Paradise of Law" will examine the mechanisms by which Puritan law *intended* to deploy the utopian promises of collective identity. It will address the law as a discourse represented by official theories and practices, enacted by the Puritan fathers en masse.

But *The Scarlet Letter* also articulates the crisis of the law in the way these official theories, intentions, and practices intersect the persons of the "fathers." In this essay, Governors Winthrop and Bellingham will be addressed as figures of the law: its agents and its subjects. The patriarchal privilege that links these individual bodies to the law's legitimating machine will provide a point of reference for our understanding of the novel's adjudication of the relations of power that saturate the bodies and practices of its more "literary" figures, Hester Prynne, Arthur Dimmesdale, and Roger Chillingworth.

Hawthorne's representation of the sites on which collective political identity is inscribed expresses an interpretation of the problematics of Puritan culture—in its hegemonic, official form. In conjunction, the novel also projects a nationalist genealogy, by calling into question the modes of intelligibility that have characterized national consciousness over the course of America's first two centuries.[5] But *The Scarlet Letter* does more than to frame the birth of a nation. Nor is it simply an analysis and a representation of the ways dominant cultures control the machinery of power and the construction of individual and mass consciousness. It also aims to lay out the mechanisms by which individual subjectivities get caught up in progressively more abstract collective identifications, like colonies and nations, by providing readings of the ways people live according to standards and sensations that do not reflect the state's desires: specifically, the novel reformulates consciousness through people's historical memories and everyday life relations as well. This mode of public consciousness, which I call, after Foucault, "counter-memory," is not necessarily a liberatory oppositional force in the novel, or even a more benign safety valve for dissent—although counter-memory does provide important material for the narrator's critique of the "official men." The novel's representation of individual and corporate memory, of conscience, and of the public character of social life—which overlaps with, but does not mirror official points of view—is the material of chapter 3, "The State of Madness: Conscience, Popular Memory, and Narrative in *The Scarlet Letter.*" There I will argue that counter-memory has multiple effects in the novel: one, the novel's use of popular individual and collective experience shows the moral and political limits of the state's ability to theorize "from above" the activity of individual and collective subjects, however saturated they might be by mere consciousness of the state, or even by faith in it; two, counter-memory is the material from which individual and collective subjects produce their own kinds of theoretical speculations, which run the gamut from superstition to social theory, problematizing the notion that there is one official "public" sphere dominating the Colony; three, counter-memory produces, mainly in the novel's psychologized characters, a new "body," new sensations, which carry their own political force and represent another way "collectivity" is constructed. The second essay on *The Scarlet Letter* will lay out how these different logics of counter-memory work mutually in the novel, ultimately to allay, if not resolve, the crisis of utopia and the law. The present chapter will stage this crisis in the official bodies of state patriarchs; in the next essay the crisis of the body, and of the agency of the person, is located radically "elsewhere," in the popular public sphere, in private homes, in transitional landscapes. The novel's overdetermination of popular life is further complicated by the narrator's investment in linking the two historical horizons the text occupies, in the 1640s and the 1850s.

In chapter 4, "The Nationalist Preface," utopia and law, official memory and counter-memory, the local and the national, and their circulation through the body are rearticulated within a new genealogy of America's juridico-utopian problematic. In the national context that "prefaces" this and all of Hawthorne's American novels, Puritans become the archaic horizon of historical consciousness, while Hawthorne focuses on laying out the contemporary mnemotechniques of national identity. "The Custom-House" bears witness to a taxonomy of "national characters," federally-underfunded bodies and minds debilitated by two centuries of state patriarchalism, which has made the male body preternaturally vital while short-circuiting the memory, intellect, and will of those who have overidentified with public political forms for personal legitimacy. In the shift between the local collective and the national identity we can trace how a relation to time, space, and a body becomes saturated with different, but crucially linked, *historicity*: the implications of this shift in the templates' meaning designate memory, consciousness, sexuality, and official state interests as crucially political concerns, even in the narrowest sense of "political."

The semiotic anomalousness of "The Market-Place" and "The Prison-Door," then, emblematically suggests that the formal problem of mapping out collective/national culture, even in its most "primitive," local form, results from the difficulty of adjudicating personal subjectivity, subcultural alliances, and dominant cultural formations, like the state or the church. This synthetic difficulty exists in any present moment and also in the cultural history of a political territory, over time. But, contra the critical tradition, it is not that *The Scarlet Letter* (or this chapter) plays off the "individual's" interests against those of the "society." In this drama of juridical discretion, a discourse of citizenship and of responsibility to the public sphere dominates all affective and material signs: but the "people" clearly have their own minds as well, both in their individual and collective constellations, during official events, during the activities of everyday life, in the ephemera of public opinion. A member of the "mob" is also a member of the "people"; a citizen is also a woman; a woman is also a mother; a mother is also a criminal. The very landscape is transfigured by historical and topographical point of view; point of view is itself always negotiated, within the individual subject as well as within the nation. So too the narrative of *The Scarlet Letter* shifts the terms and the values of its analysis as it describes shifts in the position of its subjects, in order to incorporate the range of positions included in the collective/national project. This incorporation is crucial to the utopian context of this novel's semiotics: the variety of represented interpretations of the "same" event and its signifier—the A—signify the "problem" to which national identity is the "answer." Law—both natural and juridical—emerges as the vehicle for the proto-nation's cohesion: conscience and sexuality emerge as both the vehicles and the obstacles to the nation's successful realization.

Thus when *The Scarlet Letter* plays out the Puritan logic of law, which includes a theory of the place of Scripture and natural law in the patriarchal state apparatus and the church, it engages with law's historical and political *effects*: juridical authority is in general constituted by its ability to transfigure its participants. The topos of "transfiguration" (53; 164)—which is what the A does to Hester—stands, in the novel, as the model for the generation of elastic linkages between disparate subjects, discourses, and historical moments. "Transfiguration" implies a model of meaning in which a sign retains its original shape, even as it accrues new meanings, new shapes, by being articulated in different contexts: as such, these signs (for example, the materials of the National Symbolic) provide the material for contemporary identity and historical memory. But the *way* this semiotic material takes on meaning is a matter of interpretation.

In the spirit of such interpretation, *The Scarlet Letter* incorporates a philologically learned appraisal of Puritan discourse into its analysis of the Bay Colony's political and libidinous practices, in order to show how the culture's official semiotic habits influence collective and individual subjectivity, conscience, and memory. Hester Prynne, constantly embodied and transfigured by the A, is the point of exchange between all of these areas of relative social disarticulation, even of conflicting interests. By providing a space and time for the production of a collective experience, her marked body traverses the fractures that otherwise characterize Puritan civil life. The state "intends" to use her this way, as a juridical signifier who calls people to assume their civil identity. But Prynne's "needlework" (81) is "deemed necessary to the official state of men" (82) in more ways than one. The following discussion of the state's legal "intentions" toward Prynne will address the institutional activity that produces the A: the conflation in Prynne of her "necessity" as a legal instrument and as the Bay Colony's foremost fancy-worker transfigures her into a professional, if "convex," mirror of the law, its disciplinary designs.

Stating the Case: The Sumptuary Laws

> Should I not keepe promise in speaking a little to Womens fashions, they would take it unkindly: I was loath to pester better matter with such stuffe; I rather thought it meet to let them stand by themselves, like the *Quoe Genus* in the Grammer, being Deficients, or Redundants, not to be brought under any Rule: I shall therefore make bold for this once, to borrow a little of their loose tongued Liberty, and misspend a word or two upon their long-wasted, but short-skirted patience: a little use of my stirrup will doe no harme.[6]

Nathaniel Ward's *The Simple Cobler of Aggawamm in America* (1647) treats female fashion in a context otherwise saturated with concern for a spiritual and political crisis wracking the English nation. Ward speaks literally of female fashion—to dress down, with the "stirrup" of his language, the ornamental excesses of worldly English women. But more important, the degraded fashion in female fashion is made equivalent to the political "opinions" of Englishmen. In Ward's work, which is contemporaneous with the period represented in the novel, the very relevance of "female" metaphors is a sign of the culture's spiritual and political crisis. As in the Puritan discourse of *The Scarlet Letter*, women and their "common or worthless" handiwork (82) here provide multiple ways to address the culture at large: female fashion reflects directly on women and symptomatically on men, in terms of a complex set of self-defeating patriarchal-nationalist practices. For not only do women "derive a pleasure, incomprehensible to the other sex, from the delicate toil of the needle" (83), but "our stern progenitors . . . cast behind them so many fashions which it might seem harder to dispense with" (82).

Hester Prynne embroiders the letter of the law in gold and places it on her garment. The A is of the law because it signifies law—it is illegible outside the legal code that makes it an abbreviation. A kind of legal jargon, a portable "penal machine" (55), the A transforms the "sphere" in which it operates into an "ugly engine" (55) for the reproduction of juridical authority. The letter is the formal embodiment of the Puritan mnemotechnique: collective identity takes shape in the condensed and isolated time and space of a state sponsored juridical display. The actual method of textualizing prisoners to represent their legal transgressions was not unique to the New England Puritans. Hester Prynne's historical namesake, the English dissenter William Prynne, was branded on each cheek with the letters SL—not meaning "Scarlet Letter," but "Seditious Libeller."[7] But the Puritan hegemonic project required its own complex and elaborate apparatus of legal conscription: for the text of the letter not only addresses Hester Prynne's sexual/legal transgression but also participates in establishing the political authority of the young Puritan community, whose legitimacy derived no authenticity from established tradition.

How does the operation of the letter reflect the state's intentions to install its legal authority within the colony? The A's effectivity as a public monument is overdetermined by literary and more properly "historical" protocols. In its initial moments, the A turns Hester into a mystic writing-pad, a palimpsest: "But the point which drew all eyes, and, as it were, transfigured the wearer,—so that both men and women, who had been familiarly acquainted with Hester Prynne, were now impressed as if they beheld her for the first time,—was that SCARLET LETTER . . . " (53). Just as the text moves into capital letters to demonstrate the A's impact, so the moment of Hester's public conscription by the legal apparatus results in her own "physical" transformation, which touches a variety of signifying contexts. Her body, reborn in a half-parody of Christ's transfiguration, most directly evokes the ultimate juridical authority of Scripture, in turn alluding to the providential-utopian promise that the history of fallen humanity still carries the assurance of future individual and collective saintly transformations.

In addition, the iconography of the A reveals the law's dependence on sexual difference to naturalize its claim to represent God's law for the community's best covenantal interests. The A's inscription of patriarchal privilege is represented manifestly: the letter is crucially "authored" by the collection of patriarchs who gather to gloss the significance of its inscription on Hester. But, just as the historical Puritan "fathers" appropriated the language of the church's "bosom" to describe the spiritual "milk" of their own "breasts," so this paternally authored A appropriates the female bosom to figure, for citizens, their pseudo-biological "need" to be handled by the state juridical apparatus.[8] Hester is, so to speak, the "A" the state wears on its "bosom." She is the "mother" of the A, as the narrator loves to remind us, via Pearl; but she is structurally also its wayward wife and inarticulate child.

There is no rhyme, but there is reason to this collection of interventions into gender. Michael Colacurcio's essays on *The Scarlet Letter* remind us that the Puritan fathers saw sex itself as a serious threat to the state's authority;[9] countless readers of *The Scarlet Letter* see Hester's sexual will as her mark of superiority to her culture.[10] But in these opening chapters, gender—and sexuality, gender's "problem"—is deployed to humanize and universalize the law, to situate law, from every point of view, within the sphere of individual human passion and affect. Naturalized law, then, operates like affect: the expression of juridical sentiments seems like intuition; conscience seems to work like an organ. We see the manifestation of the state's intention and desire to use the law to merge with its subjects' bodies and minds when "the ugliest as well as the most pitiless of these self-constituted [female] judges" in the crowd queries, "Is there not law for it? Truly there is, both in the Scripture and the statute-book. Then let the magistrates, who have made it of no effect, thank themselves if their own wives and daughters go astray!" (51–52). Here, legal laxity leads in a direct line to sexual license, at least in theory. These lay judges are delegitimated in the text for being over-legalistic: they are, rather, "literalistic," and the letter they have "read" is one that was "written" for them by the Puritan fathers. We will return to this habit of reading below, in discussing how the letter of Puritan legal theory legislates this "coarse" hermeneutic practice.

Just as the juridical symbol is empowered to transform the individual body and conscience, it also aims to create a public, collective "body" from among the dispersed spectators. The "mob" contains a multiplicity of opinions, but its stony collective gaze, organized around the A, effaces dissension. Thus when the state sponsors an act of "public discipline," the referent "A" extends both to the prisoner and to the "people amongst whom religion and law were almost identical" (50). As readers of the A, they become the eyes of the law, enacting its penal aspirations. They become "impressed" by the law as well, convening in a new identity, a new affective time and space, as if a fully new regime of law has been installed through the A's transfigurations. To stress the "New Law's" effect on political subjectivity, the narrator calls this site of collective memory "their *imagination*" (68–69; emphasis mine).

What emerges from this set of descriptions is the form of Hester's necessity to the state semiotic apparatus. She is forced to become a legal exemplum, the "text of the discourse" continuously preached in the Puritan churches and streets (85). She circulates among the townsfolk according to the law's intention: her efficacy is measured by the "burning" feeling that comes from having any kind of physical or ocular contact with the A. She also performs and represents the link between the everyday life of the polis, the achronic authority of the patriarchal state, and the utopian promise of collective justice. But Hester's case is both unique to her position and a magnification of a generalized social process. The letter transforms the body of its wearer for any wearer, which forces her subjectivity to change as well—a problem for the law, to which we shall return. The letter's public operation also, in theory, merges individuals into a public collectivity, a "body" with an "imagination." In addition, the scene of the letter initiates individual consciousness of the law. Consciousness develops into collective and individual conscience: to see the A and to feel the burning (in part a sympathetic memory of Hester's own display and humiliation) ought to produce proleptic self-reflection, self-policing.

Finally, the role of conscience in turning the individual into a "citizen," complete with an affective and psychological dependence on her identification with the state, also predicts the form collective memory will take, at least in theory. The historical mnemotechnique of the Puritan state, as Hawthorne represents its strategies of authority, is to turn to the juridical theater for its political legitimation. Each juridical event appears to make the old law a New Law, as the terms of public discourse and private knowledge change to accommodate the local content of the law's text. But what would appear to be new—a new letter, say, reconfiguring the private and public body—would also affirm the monumentality of law itself, for the collective self-intelligibility of the Colony. Hester's body registers the shift between these political "moments." *The Scarlet Letter*, too, reproduces the formal centrality of the law by situating the narrative/historical moment not in great military or political victories but in prosaic, popular, even banal scenes of juridical scandal and its reception.

By so defining Hester as outside of the law, the state brings her into the law. It supports her with "his iron arm" (78) and she supports it with her golden A. In this view, she is not simply Other to the law, the private place inaccessible to its coercion. Instead, she is the law's fantasy of an Other, because she seems to resist the state's desire while absolutely fulfilling its need for effective symbolic loci, effective "texts." That is, from the position of the state she is perfectly comprehensible as a figure of the law's effects. This is why the conservatism of the populace with respect to Hester's A is most extreme on days when the rituals of state such as Election Day are being played out. The narrator notes occasionally that the people's "larger and warmer heart" (64) erodes the negative significance of Hester's A, over time; but on Election Day, seven years after the A's emergence into the public sphere, the townspeople reexperience the "repugnance which the mystic symbol inspired" (246). In the presence of the formal scene of legal display, the letter's force as a legal document is, throughout the novel, at its height.

The state's intent to construct a law-abiding people through the juridical reframing of Hester Prynne runs into internal obstacles. The law's power to mark its prisoner as a negative example is immense, yet inconsistently effective. John Winthrop wrote that "The Lawe is allwayes the same":[11] but in "the incomplete morality of the age" (233), "practice" reveals the limits and the insidiousness of "theory," even utopian theory. We can see this in our very first exposure to Hester, the A, and her fancy-work:

> On the breast of her gown, in fine red cloth, surrounded with an elaborate embroidery and fantastic flourishes of gold thread, appeared the letter A. It was so artistically done, and with so much fertility and gorgeous luxuriance of fancy, that it had all the effect of a last and fitting decoration to the apparel which she wore; and which was of a splendor in accordance with the taste of the age, but greatly beyond what was allowed by the sumptuary regulations of the colony (53).

In wearing the A, Hester, "[k]nowing well her part," (55) fulfills legal requirements. Yet the A constitutes still another legal transgression: it violates the colony's sumptuary laws. In contrast to the law against adultery that Hester breaks,[12] her violation of the sumptuary laws seems trivial—indeed, her transgression goes unnoticed by the Magistrates. But sumptuary laws exist in Massachusetts Bay for an important reason—to maintain and to police the appearance and the appearances of class hierarchies.

This colony is what Winthrop calls a "mixt Aristocratie";[13] thus, as Edwin Powers writes, much of the gentry was "exempted from the restrictions on the wearing of 'Gold or Silver lace, or Gold or Silver buttons or any bone lace . . . silk hoods . . . or scarfs . . . allowable to persons of greater Estates, or more liberal education yet . . . intollerable in persons of such like conditions'."[14] When Hester appropriates the semiotics of gold ornamentation, she evokes the excesses endemic to the privileged "taste of the age" as well,[15] and figuratively aligns herself with the same magistrate class that populates the juridical apparatus. It is no accident that she is frequently taken or mistaken for "a personage of high dignity among her people" (246). Her ornamental alignment with that class is deadly ironic: the magistrate class is distinguished here by being *exempt* from legal restrictions.

Thus if Hester breaks the sumptuary laws by wearing her own luxuriant handiwork, she also reinforces them by providing the signs of class distinction on which the political and social structure of the town relies. She reinforces these in other ways: the narrator notes that Hester sews for all classes, making clothes that mark the ritual and class situation of each of her clients. Since Hester is seamstress to the collectivity, in her work she reweaves and reinforces the world as it already is, even as she is isolated from it and judged by it. Indeed, she becomes necessary to the legibility of the community at large—and not only as its resident outlaw. As a result of her punishment, the narrator notes, Hester's "handiwork became . . . the fashion" (82). Through her ornamental interpretations of class relations, Hester contributes to and reinforces the proto-National Symbolic, the collectively held semiotic system essential to the production and maintenance of the Puritan law that binds her.

But her embroidery does more than stage the hegemony of the upper classes. She in fact helps this new state to establish itself. One could posit that along with all the meanings of the A we know—Adultery, Angel, Angel of Mercy, Art, Affection—the A might stand for Advertising. Hester not only embellishes the sign of its legal power so prominently on her breast—a sort of sandwich board for the state—but provides for it a much larger "alphabet":

> Public ceremonies, such as ordinations, the installation of magistrates, and all that could give majesty to the forms in which a new government manifested itself to the people, were, as a matter of policy, marked by a stately and well-conducted ceremonial, and a sombre, but yet a studied magnificence. Deep ruffs, painfully wrought bands, and gorgeously embroidered gloves, were all deemed necessary to the official state of men assuming the reins of power; and were readily allowed to individuals dignified by rank or wealth, even while sumptuary

> laws forbade these and similar extravagances to the plebian order (82).

The official doctrine of Puritan political legitimation, in which magistrates represent God's will in the City on a Hill, also includes a theory of the fashion system: by virtue of Hester's necessity for the law's symbolic elaboration, the "female problem" of appropriate fashion (commented on by Ward, represented by Hawthorne) here emerges as a *political* problem within the Puritan "state of men." As Reverend Wilson himself comments (in reference to Dimmesdale), "A pure hand needs no glove to cover it!" (158).

The problem of sumptuary excess is associated explicitly with Governor Bellingham—a good customer of Hester's. On her judgment day he wears "a dark feather in his hat, a border of embroidery on his cloak, and a black velvet tunic beneath" (64). Later Hester brings him a pair of those "gorgeously embroidered gloves" to wear at an affair of state (82). The narrative returns, again and again, to descriptions of his extravagant personal style. Matching his lavishness in dress, his home is compared to Aladdin's palace (103). When we first see him there, "expatiating on his projected improvements" to his property, "the wide circumference of an elaborate ruff . . . caused his head to look not a little like that of John the Baptist in a charger" (108). Later, he is disclosed in "a white night-cap . . . and a long white gown" (149). When not acting *in loco parentis* to both Pearl and Hester, he collects "appliances of worldly enjoyment" (108). The narrator's tone toward Bellingham ranges from solemnity to ridicule: he dignifies the public Bellingham while demeaning the luxuriant private man.

Why this kind of attention to Bellingham's vanity? One commentator suggests that the governor's courtly tastes align him with Old World values inappropriate to the new Puritan Utopia.[16] But this explanation is inadequate. For if Bellingham, here a vain fop, is merely irrelevant to the Puritan ideal, he is so as the representative of his class—which has already been characterized, with respect to sumptuary laws, as distinguished by their exemption from the law of the land.

But this exemption has divergent implications in the ethical and political logic of the novel. On one hand, in their private lives, the rulers did not make "it a matter of conscience to reject such means of comfort, or even luxury, as lay fairly within their grasp" (108). Here, the narrator evaluates their exemption from sumptuary laws as a luxuriant love of luxuriance. In contrast, the public symbolic apparatus of the new colony seems to have required the magistrates to assume a formal dignity of appearance that conveyed their technical superiority to the people at large. The magistrates "were distinguished by a dignity of mien, belonging to a period when the forms of authority were felt to possess the sacredness of divine institutions" (64). "Mien" is not only an expression of class affiliation and juridical status: it is a "*form* of authority," a signifier as visible as the gold ornamentation on Hester's embroidery. Thus while the narrator disparages the magistrates' private cultivation of material excess, he sees excess as the necessary rule of political survival in the public sphere.

Embroidery, which here evokes a politics of social position that crosses over the borders between public and private actions, brings to the surface a crisis in the semiotics of juridical expression that emerges in the novel under the pressure of the hyperclarity of Hester's golden A. The "problem of Bellingham" in *The Scarlet Letter* thus occupies the same *visual* space as "the problem of Hester Prynne." But this space, like all spaces in the novel, is transfigured in accordance with the subject's structural position within the political public sphere. Hester experiences these fractures between the public and private implications of juridical semiotics as a citizen interpellated within the law; Bellingham is both a citizen and lawmaker, positions which do not wholly overlap, as we have seen in the case of sumptuary laws.

The Scarlet Letter refers to the historical problem of Puritan juridical representation in its interest in Bellingham's exemplary materiality and, through a far different strategy of representation, in its staging of the death of John Winthrop. Through the story of Bellingham, whose "official life" (40) merges "public" and "private" biography—as all men's lives do, in this novel—and the (dis)appearance of Winthrop, the novel refers to struggles over legal representation that fractured the state apparatus of the Massachusetts

Bay Colony in the 1630s and 1640s. This was a determining moment in the formation of the Massachusetts legal code: at stake was the internal distribution of power within the Puritan state and the forms of the law's written codification.[17] After explicating the complex legal implications of Bellingham's self-fashioning, I will follow the novel's return to the politics of the Puritan collective alphabet in its staging of the death of Winthrop. Winthrop, the Bay Colony's central political theorist and, in these years, its customary governor, is himself woven into the novel by Hester's embroidery (the first reference to him comes when she has just measured his death-robe), and apparently produces an A of his own at the moment of his death.

What is the governors' historical relation, and how are they connected in the novel? Their personal relations were vexed. Bellingham, a magistrate, constantly worked against Winthrop to diminish the concentration of power held by the magistrates, actions deeply resented by Winthrop.[18] But in the political logic of *The Scarlet Letter* these men occupy the same space: the crossroads of politics and utopia (at which, in order to preserve the "utopian" aspirations of the civil society, acts of political suppression take place).

The presence of "the sainted Ann Hutchinson" (48) in *The Scarlet Letter* has been explicated by reference to the respectively passional and spiritual self-"consecration" (195) of Hester and Dimmesdale:[19] but the Antinomian drama has more political meanings as well. During 1637, the same year that John Winthrop prosecuted and exiled Hutchinson, Richard Bellingham led the colonial forces in the massacre of the Pequod Indians. The narrator comments specifically that Bellingham's armor had "glittered . . . at the head of a regiment in the Pequod war" (105–6). The confluence of these two events, in the period just before *The Scarlet Letter* opens, puts deadly quotation marks around the word "utopia" on the novel's first page: in the proximity of these two Puritan fathers Hawthorne signifies the heritage of exile and annihilation in the name of civil purity that "produces" the legal problematic of *The Scarlet Letter*.

In sum, antinomian threats have been exterminated by the fathers: the novel represents Puritan culture as thus being saturated with the law and with civil propriety. The Massachusetts Bay Colony was not invented in 1642: but its prior history has been banished to the narrator's allusions. The people of the colony are, from the novel's first page, constantly being reinstated in the "new" "present tense" of the law. This moment of historical amnesia is, then, simultaneously a "new" origin of historical consciousness: the effects of history's burial and juridical containment are signified by the two institutions, the graveyard and the prison, which mark, on the text's first page, the postutopian condition of the colony. In the double articulation of these two patriarchal Puritan narratives, I will map out how *The Scarlet Letter* imagines the utopian intentions of the Puritan state judiciary: as we have seen in this discussion of the A's formal function in the Colony, not only is the rhetoric and practice of law at issue, but the *persons* and the *bodies* of the legal subject produce problems in their own right. Bellingham and Winthrop provide the traces for seeing the personal and collective problem of law—in its *own* terms—in *The Scarlet Letter*. The following chapter will then restate the question of how legal discourse works in the novel, this time from the point of view of the subjective, not official or public, "spaces" the letter of the law creates.

Governor Bellingham and the "Demeanour of Natural Authority"

Historically speaking Richard Bellingham was many things in the Massachusetts Bay Colony[20]: magistrate, governor, deputy governor, major general of the colonial forces. But he was not actually governor of the colony in the year of Hester Prynne's punishment, 1642.[21] Chapters 7 and 8, "The Governor's Hall" and "The Elf-Child and the Minister," which "accurately" describe his relatively less powerful condition, suggest that Bellingham's presence has another kind of utility in the text. The narrative of Hester's visit to the governor's hall is the scene of three anecdotes about political flux, the conjunction of which raises questions about the legitimacy of state jurisprudence.

The first political tale we read is about hierarchical descent:

> Hester Prynne went, one day, to the mansion of Governor Bellingham, with a pair of gloves, which she had fringed and embroidered to his order, and which were to be worn on some great occasion of state; for, though the chances of a popular election had caused this former ruler to descend a step or two from the highest rank, he still held an honorable and influential place among the colonial magistracy (100).

Bellingham's departure from the governor's office is attributed to the vicissitudes of political life, which—as I will consider shortly—is not quite the case. As we suspend the question of his personal history, we read the second installment of the story, this time about the rulers' desire to police the family. Hester actually visits Bellingham for a "far more important reason than the delivery of a pair of embroidered gloves." For it "had reached her ears, that there was a design on the part of some of the leading inhabitants, cherishing the more rigid order of principles in religion and government, to deprive her of her child. . . . Among those who promoted the design,

Governor Bellingham was said to be one of the most busy" (100–101). Hester feels that natural law is on her side: she approaches Bellingham "conscious of her own right . . . backed by the sympathies of nature"(101).[22]

When Hester imagines that her "right" to retain custody of Pearl is supported or authorized by the "sympathies of nature," she might mean simply that she has a mystical bond with the child because of their "natural" relation. But Hester's reasoning is more specific than this. Her "indefeasible rights" (113) are "natural" because the "world," in making her an "outlaw," has left her only the fundamental space of existence on which to live—the space "God" makes, on which only a "mother's rights" have dominion, especially "when that mother has but her child and the scarlet letter!" (113). To Hester, natural law, derived from God's justice, is that which opposes the claims of the civil order. The Puritan civil order, in turn, also claims the sacred sanction of natural law. This version legitimates neither individual sovereignty nor the bio-social authority of the mother, but rather the juridical privilege the patriarchal state assumes, which derives from God's covenant with the community.[23] The implicit struggle over the "sympathy of Nature"—here a synonym for the "derivation of law"—evident in the relations between Prynne and the state enters into a complex seventeenth-century debate between "the people" and "the sovereign" over where natural authority resides.[24] In sum, Hester, who is said to have "imbibed" the spirit of the revolutionary theory of the age (164), constructs a radical logic of political alliance: on one side, the sovereignty of the mother over her child, the sympathy of nature, and a refusal to acknowledge the rights of mere "men" to determine her franchise; on the other side, the patriarchal Puritan state, which is unnatural precisely because it claims the covenantal right to violate her natural sovereignty—which, again, is not simply individual but social in its own construction of "birth" right.

So far in these two political anecdotes, the "rigid order of principles in religion and government" is posited in opposition to the equally rigid concept of the individual's natural rights: the latter is certainly where the narrator's sympathies lie, at this early point in the novel. Yet the final addition to this triad calls into question the worth of juridical thinking as such. "It may appear singular," the narrator comments,

> and, indeed, not a little ludicrous, that an affair of this kind, which, in later days, would have been referred to no higher jurisdiction than that of the selectmen of the town, should then have been a question publicly discussed, and on which statesmen of eminence took sides. At that epoch of pristine simplicity, however, matters of even slighter public interest, and of far less intrinsic weight than the welfare of Hester and her child, were strangely mixed up with the deliberations of legislators and acts of state. The period was hardly, if at all, earlier than that of our story, when a dispute concerning the right of property in a pig, not only caused a fierce and bitter contest in the legislative body of the colony, but resulted in an important modification of the framework itself of the legislature. (101)[25]

Quite explicitly, the narrator deflates the juridical prerogatives Bellingham claims—again as representative of the colony's "leading inhabitants"(100)—in his intent to intervene in Hester's child-rearing. "[S]tatesmen of eminence" act in a "strange" and "ludicrous" way: Bellingham wants to do the right thing by Pearl, but he shows a symptomatic Puritan inability to adjudicate properly, due to his oversaturation with juridical consciousness and prerogative.

Hester's legalism is not explicitly parodied by the narrator: yet isn't the implicit analogy between Hester's Pearl and a pig an implicit satire on Hester's assertion of natural rights? Is it possible that the high drama of the scene to come, in which the Mother throws her body in front of the State's masculinist meddling in Nature's Law, denigrates the struggle over nature, sympathy, and legal prerogative that occupies the rest of the narrative? The story of the sow to which the narrator alludes involves a conflict between different views of where legal discretionary powers "naturally" lie. This crisis in Puritan polity, commonly called the crisis of the "negative voice," is further relevant to a discussion of *The Scarlet Letter* because of its crucial historical placement in the history of juridical scandal that marks the novel's own construction of a proto-national mnemotechnique.

The term "negative voice" itself derives from a constitutional debate over who in a given government would have final veto power over any proposed legislation; Timothy Breen calls this a struggle between the forces of delegation and the forces of discretion.[26] In particular, the crisis centered on the question of whether the magistrates of the Massachusetts General Court ought to have the final say in all matters of law. The General Court was, as of 1634, composed of two kinds of legislators: the deputies and the magistrates. Deputies were elected by the freemen; magistrates were "elected" by God, and were also the original, more aristocratic holders of the colony's charter. The constitutional crisis erupted because, as the number of deputies increased (which happened naturally, as the colony grew), the power of the magistrates was potentially diminished. Since the magistrates represented themselves as God's vicegerents, ruling by divine covenant, they attempted to retain veto power over any law passed by the General Court as a whole. Giving the deputies equal franchise would be, in Winthrop's view, an affirmation of "the democratical spirit,"[27] a "Monster"[28] in its denial of Godly hierarchies.

The issue of the negative voice is about class as well as legal prerogative: not the unpropertied against the gentry, but essentially the bourgeoisie against the aristocracy. The deputies argued that the dominion of the magistrates might lead to the practice of arbitrary government in the self-interest of the aristocrats; the magistrates asserted that democracy transgressed all historical wisdom, scriptural precedent, and natural (sacred) hierarchy. In 1634 John Cotton proposed a compromise to the crisis of the negative voice by asserting that a society consisted of three elements, the magistracy, the ministry, and "the people," and that the concurrence of all three was essential to the maintenance of the state: thus all parties must approve every law.[29] This proposal was not accepted into law.

Again in 1642, a divergence between the votes of the deputies and the magistrates renewed the crisis of discretionary power. "[T]here fell out a great business," wrote Winthrop, "upon a very small occasion."[30] Goody Sherman's pig strayed into Captain Robert Keayne's pen; later he slaughtered one of his sows and Sherman claimed it was hers. A lower court supported the captain's right to slay his sow; but on appeal the deputies in the General Court collectively overturned the lower-court decision, voting for the woman's claim. Finally, the magistrates voted among themselves to sustain the lower court move, simultaneously nulling the woman's claim to her property and the deputies' claim to their political voice. And so the negative voice question exploded once more. At stake in this decision was the power of the aristocratic class to control the franchise of the freemen.[31] This time, after much speechmaking, Cotton's compromise was more or less ratified, and a bicameral legislature, in the modern mode, was formed, in which the magistrates' veto power was nonetheless preserved.

Legal and moral issues raised by the Puritan difficulty with adjudicating discretionary power underlie all of the juridical activity in *The Scarlet Letter*: it is "strangely mixed-up," (101) extravagant, like the fashions of eminent men. Bellingham's own person, as constructed by the narrator, gives local form to the kinds of historical contradictions that circulate around discretionary power.[32] Bellingham's legal fame is established in the novel by the narrator's disclosure that Bellingham was "accustomed to speak of Bacon, Coke, Noye, and Finch, as his professional associates" (106). What does it mean to be the colleague of these famous men? To unravel this chain of associations would, not accidentally, be to reiterate the discourse on discretionary legal power that the story of Goody Sherman has already provided.

These are among the most prominent lawyers in seventeenth-century England, and all were deeply involved in the political struggle between the king and Parliament over state control. Christopher Hill describes the legal chaos that prevailed during the reigns of James I and Charles I as a conflict between the common-law courts, which operate according to legal precedent in the tradition and spirit of the Magna Carta, and the prerogative courts, which judged in the interests of and according to the Crown's self-interest. "The common-law courts—King's Bench and the Court of Common Pleas—increasingly defended absolute property rights, the right of every man to do what he would with his own. The prerogative courts became more and more organs of the government."[33] One thrust of the Puritan revolution, in fact, was to enforce the values of the common law, and, finally (when the common law itself was charged with relying too rigidly and conservatively on precedent), to make the law linguistically and conceptually accessible to the people. The "Puritan hero" Sir Edward Coke—whose work *On Littleton* was edited by Hester's namesake, William Prynne[34]—is heralded as the codifier and the defender of the common law—although early in his career, as counsel to Queen Elizabeth, he defended the royal prerogative zealously.[35] Sir Francis Bacon, Coke's arch-enemy, was equally the great defender of the royal prerogative; he too occupied the opposing position early in his career, and was in his own way an important theorist of the common law.[36] William Noye, attorney general from 1631 to 1634, also occupied both positions with respect to the locus of legal power in the state during his career, but is most notorious for his prosecution of William Prynne; and Sir John Finch was charged with "conspiracy to produce arbitrary and tyrannical government" during his tenure as lord keeper and in his advice to the king against Parliament.[37] To be the "colleague" of these men, as Bellingham is, is to contain the contradictions of seventeenth-century legal history. He embodies, in this light, not the relations between the government and the governed, but those within the state: in him we see the almost arbitrary struggle over position and prerogative that motivates much nationalist rhetoric and political activity, even when at the same time great moral and political issues concerning personal and collective justice are also being worked out.

It is not surprising, then, that Bellingham's term as governor in 1641 was marked by two crises in legal discretion: one a conflict which arose from the selection of a legal code, and the other a scandal which exposed Bellingham's extravagant, even antinomian, association with the law. From the moment in 1634 when the deputies, led by William Hathorne, joined the General Court, they pushed the magistrates to codify—to write down and to publish—the laws of the new colony.[38] The magistrates, led as always by John Winthrop, were reluctant to do so: first, because of fear that England would become aware of the way the new colony had deviated from English law; second, because insofar as the colony's tendency was toward establishing common law rule, Winthrop wanted time to create a set of precedents specific to the colony itself; and third, because he did not want to limit his own and the magistrates' discretionary power. As in the case of the issue of the negative voice, Winthrop felt strongly that his and the magistrates' election by God was assurance enough that the law would be just. The deputies, typically, felt that Winthrop's reasons were self-serving and unfair, tending toward arbitrary government; and all of the eloquent speech-making in the world would not convince them otherwise. This conflict, then, as with the other legal controversies I have examined, reflects problems not only with the disposition of state power but with class conflict as well.

In 1636 John Cotton was commissioned to draft the laws of the colony. Cotton's "An Abstract of the Laws of New England," which Winthrop renamed "Moses his judicialls," assumes that the law has a negative, coercive force; its function is both to punish transgression (according to biblical precedent) and to ensure the subjection of the citizenry to the magistrates, who are absolutely the Lord's representatives on earth.[39] Thus Cotton, even while maintaining the magistrates' assertion of their ultimate legal authority, actually limits their power by denying them any legal discretion. Everything, literally, goes by the Book.

In contrast, Nathaniel Ward's *Body of Liberties*, commissioned in 1639, is like a Bill of Rights;[40] while Ward's version too cites chapter and verse in its delineation of capital crime, it lists twelve of these in contrast to Cotton's twenty, and spends the rest of its time setting out what it calls man's "freedoms" and privileges. Ward knew the common law; and the force of this document is to establish general areas of precedence on which future particular laws (also called "rules," or the local applications of general laws) might be based, at the lawmaker's discretion. Neither Winthrop nor any contemporary writer comments on why Ward's laws were chosen over Cotton's in 1641, but the General Court's defense of the *Body of Liberties* in 1646, in response to Child's remonstrance,[41] suggests that while Scripture might always set the tone or the intent of juridical law, the English common law and Magna Carta were more directly the models and the justifications for the colony's laws.

The Scarlet Letter displays the contrast between these two modes of discretionary power: as a legal tool used by the ruling classes to establish and maintain hegemony on one hand, and as a relatively humane, nonauthoritarian mode of government on the other. From the perspective of the common law (especially in the seventeenth century), discretionary jurisprudence is "always of the manner rather than the matter, and always external to the law";[42] from the perspective of discretionary law, common law tends to be too democratic and too rigid to deal adequately with the complex legal and spiritual needs of the state with respect to the individual.[43] Bellingham, novelistically rendered, is caught right inside the contradiction of legal discretion; he is a well-meaning, benevolent man who truly wants to use his discretion to render legal, moral, and spiritual justice for Hester and Pearl; and he is entirely inadequate as a judge.

A tension between rigid legalism and the desire to step outside the law (to use "discretion") is evident even on Hester's first judgment day, when the state is eager to negotiate with her by reducing or eliminating her punishment in order to seduce her to reveal the name of Pearl's father. This is to say that Hester's spiritual welfare is not really the concern of legal judgment as such, despite the state's assertions to the contrary. The A itself is imposed by the discretion of the court because Hester is young, beautiful, possibly a widow, and easily tempted because without moral, i.e. male, guardianship. And when the judges cannot loosen Hester's tongue, they make her another offer: should she repent and reveal the father's name, she might not even have to wear the A. What investment does the state have in bargaining this way, especially if the public spectacle of Hester's humiliation is indeed supposed to advertise the power of the law and the seriousness of the transgression?

Here, as elsewhere, the answers to this question come from an overdetermination of textual logic and historical precedent. All uses of discretionary power were potentially problematic in the 1630s and 1640s because of the potential charge of arbitrary government that arose repeatedly in the Bay Colony during the previous decade.
Indeed, adultery was an important example in the struggles over judicial prerogative during the 1630s and 1640s. Winthrop's speech "Arbitrary Government" (1644), for instance, lists the biblical precedent for "discretionary" judicial punishments for "Adulterye" in his defense of the judges' license to adjust punishments for crimes according to the merits of individual cases: "David his life was not taken awaye for his Adulterye and murder . . . in respect of publ[ic] interest and advantage. . . . Bathsheba was not putt to deathe for her Adulterye, because the Kinges desire, had with her, the force of a Lawe."[44] The negotiations with Hester can be read as symptomatic of larger internal tensions in how the law takes shape—through the precedent of the "letter" or through the discretionary wisdom of its representative judges and statesmen.

Another way of explaining the magistrates' leniency toward Hester is that the "fathers," who were made fathers of the collectivity by virtue of their power over the law, misread the alliance between patriarchy and the juridical apparatus, in seeing themselves licensed to act as official "men" toward this vulnerable, victimized, isolated, and beautiful young woman. Certainly they feel this toward Pearl, as they speculate about the father's identity. Reverend Wilson waxes eloquent, theorizing infinite paternal substitutability: "and still better, it may be, to leave the mystery as we find it, unless Providence reveal it of its own accord. Thereby, every good Christian man hath a title to show a father's kindness towards the poor, deserted babe" (116).[45]

Another answer, also a symptomatic effect of the alignment between Puritan political power and male privilege, is specific to Bellingham's own tenure as governor. His was a brief and shaky reign, controversial from its very inception[46]; Winthrop's journals record case after case in which Bellingham is accused of being temperamental and of delaying justice; even the deputies, who were usually his allies (to the disgust of Winthrop), officially protested his misuse of power. In addition, as Colacurcio has shown, Bellingham was sexually scandalous in a way that reflected directly on his discretion (and his discreetness). He married a woman who had been promised to someone else—the first infraction. Indeed, he actually "married" himself, playing judge at his own wedding. He also broke the law by doing this secretly, refusing to publish the banns. Finally, on being called to answer for his actions, Bellingham refused to "answer the prosecution" by stepping off the bench as a judge. Rather than allowing the charges to be aired, he told Winthrop that he would not go off the bench unless he were commanded to do so. And Winthrop did not want to humiliate Bellingham by so commanding him, even while "not thinking it fit he should sit as a judge when he was by law to answer as an offender."[47]

The parallels between Bellingham's story and the love plot of *The Scarlet Letter* are clear: in a sexual triangle involving two men and a woman, the man in the socially prominent position steals the woman from the man to whom she is legally promised and bound. Each man abuses his covenant in a different way, however; as Hester's pastor, Dimmesdale has charge of her soul, and so breaks scriptural, ecclesiastical, and civil law by extending his guidance to her body. Therefore, as Chillingworth loves to point out, Dimmesdale would have had no protection from the law's penalties had Hester revealed his name to the world. Bellingham, on the other hand, can use his legal position paradoxically to break the law and to protect himself from its recriminations. He refused to publish his banns, not unlike Hester and Dimmesdale; moreover, by virtue of his official position he was able to "consecrate" his own private wedding ceremony.

Finally, Bellingham's refusal to descend from the judge's chair to be tried for malfeasance uncannily echoes Dimmesdale's; indeed, the two seem to have a great affinity for each other. We always see Bellingham in proximity to Dimmesdale: in the marketplace, the governor's hall, on the scaffold (when Dimmesdale screams, Bellingham—along with his sister, the witch, Mistress Hibbens—wakes up and searches the night, even though he can see no further than into a "mill-stone"), and in the final episode of Dimmesdale's life, the governor, "although a man not readily obeying the vague intimations that pass from one spirit to another" (252), intuitively understands Dimmesdale's desire to separate himself from the external support of the church (Dimmesdale actively rejects the Reverend Wilson's help) and the state in order to make his final confession.

As represented, Bellingham's understanding with Dimmesdale is essentially unspoken: we assume that they are always together because the young minister advises the governor on affairs of state. Yet this explanation does not illuminate the sympathy between the governor and the minister: never unraveled is the relation of the story of sexual transgression in *The Scarlet Letter*—told mainly in the text's undertones, as in one of Dimmesdale's sermons—to the story of legal excess. Are these stories analogical? Some evidence would support this conclusion: Winthrop turns Bellingham into an exemplum of bad (self-)government through the tale of his sexual imperiousness, and so sex might in this light be the place where the efficacy of the law collapses.[48] Sex would then mark the place called the "outside" of the law, the place where "outlaws" dwell. The insistence of the analogy between God the father, the ruler as father, and the paterfamilias would "naturally" place Hester, the mother, on the "outside" of the phallic lineage, in opposition to the governors with their "demeanour of natural authority" (238). And Dimmesdale, constantly forced to mediate between the claims of law's "natural authority" and the claims of female privacy, which includes here the woman's maternal relations, would provide the linkage between these two sites. Such a mapping out of the social relations of power in the colony tells the story of love's clash with the law from the "law's" privileged point of view.

Yet we must distinguish Hester's position in respect to the state from Dimmesdale's and Bellingham's. Their position is analogous to hers (because each, separately, breaks the law through sexual transgression), but hers is not analogous to theirs, because they enjoy an access to the law quite different from Hester's. The men, Dimmesdale and Bellingham, are also frequently referred to as "the minister" and "the Governor": their titular "names" reveal their structural relation to the law, and as individuals they are explicable only in terms of this relation. In contrast, Hester's position with respect to the law is signified, and mystified, by the "name" A: her position is always unclear, and must be tediously explained and explicated by official state discourse, by the church, by gossip, and by the narrator himself. From these sources we learn that when Hester bears Pearl she bears the law, and yet her intelligibility within it is always mediated, never reciprocal, albeit requiring her consent to passivity in the face of the law's needs for her. The sexual act that generated this configuration of kinds of signs—the maternal A, the patriarchal title—is the place where civil, ecclesiastical, and natural law intersect for public consumption and threaten to collapse. Hester enacts the possibility of this collapse in her various and contradictory relations to these legal systems, just as Bellingham displays it in his own ludicrous behavior and personal style.

But it is only Hester who forges the "new" "New Law": by giving her body and her labor over to the state, and by "forging," as in "lying," out of loyalty to the *appearances* of the "high place." In so dedicating herself, through sumptuary production and the self-imprisoning "lock and key" of her own silence, she figures the law, as metaphorical father/husband, and she transfigures the law by representing it on the maternal body as well. In divesting her public body of personal agency she substitutes her representations of legal authority for the ones that had marked the immediate past—the Pequod War—when suits of mail, not embroidery, were worn.

Through the suturing of bodily and mental transfiguration via the agency of the juridical letter, Hester enacts the intention of Governor John Winthrop, the "founding father *par excellence*"[49] of the Puritan colony, to theorize and to install a new form of collective identity among its citizens. If Bellingham is the historical sign of the haywire effects of Puritan juridical activity, Winthrop provides the evidence of its utopian value. Each legislator acted in submission to "love": but if "loue is the [parodic] fulfilling of the lawe"[50] for Bellingham, for Winthrop such a conjunction expressed the millennial, juridico-utopian aim of the Bay Colony's project. In theory, the law used love to provide and insure linkages between collective and subjective life—both through public display and the operations of conscience. In the next section I will lay out Winthrop's theory of the spirit and of interpretation, the "death" of which is one of the main passing events in *The Scarlet Letter*.

For the Love of Law: Winthrop's A in The Scarlet Letter

John Winthrop is not "in" *The Scarlet Letter*, exactly. His presence is never witnessed, just felt. Appropriately for a novel structured around a riddle of paternity, he is an absent father, a "departed" and "triumphant pilgrim" (150) whose only gesture is his death, and who leaves only a "radiant halo . . . an inheritance of his glory" (150) as his material trace in the text. Winthrop provides a new context within which to gloss the A, heretofore the sign of the unsaid, the obscenity that Hester and Pearl embody. For his death creates the first split within public definitions of the letter, between Angel and Adultery, signifying the heavenly and earthly body. This first split, in "The Minister's Vigil," sets the stage for the semiotic chaos that follows. In the following chapter, "Another View of Hester," the narrator notes that the people "refuse" to read the A as the ministers decree, defining it instead according to their own self-interested readings of Hester's place in the community. While the death of Winthrop and the release of the A might point to a breakdown of the law and of the rhetorically coercive power of the ruling ministers and magistrates over the public, it also might signify a breakdown that already exists within the law, one revealed by its magnification "on the cope of heaven. A scroll so wide might not be deemed too expansive for Providence to write a people's doom upon" (155).

What would it mean if the law were broken down? The idea of law relies on an assumption of its theoretical univalence: in the Aristotelian view of civil polity, for example, the patriarchal family generates the clan and the state; these are homologous, symmetrically totalized structures, produced by the same force, "the law," also called the law of nature. For Augustine, in contrast, this same "law of nature" founds civil law, but fallen man cannot see fully the natural law, and he needs a government to regulate his depravity.[51] In Puritan legal theory, which uneasily conflates the Aristotelian view of man's natural participation in civil life and the Augustinian view of depraved man's need for civil regulation, the singularity of the law's force is attributed to its origin in Scripture and in God's will.[52]

John Winthrop is, according to both his contemporaries and subsequent historians, the exemplary theorist of the practice of this law:[53] notably, his three speeches "A Modell of Christian Charity," "Arbitrary Government," and "On Liberty" are widely considered the ideological touchstones of legal and political theory in his age.[54] In particular, these discourses theorize an ideal relation between the individual subject and the civil polity, wherein natural law is modified by a regenerate civil law that regulates the passions of the individual subject but attributes the individual's desire to be so regulated to the light of his own reason.[55] The law is enforced not only through formal codification but also through a juridical apparatus that operates "inside" of the individual. By a principle called "synteresis," conscience becomes the trace of prelapsarian man's unimpeded access to the Law of Laws, that which contains both the law of nature and of reason—for before the Fall, these were the same.[56] Conscience, "the lawgiver," controls the individual's private acts, the ones to which formal and external social controls have no access. Along with writing formal, positive law, then, Winthrop legislates the terms of conscience and so constitutes the "inside" of the individual subject as an "outside," making the private self subject to the law's jurisdiction; he does this by harnessing the discourses of natural and civil law to a metaphor of the body politic, a body that can fulfill itself only through the practice and experience of love.

In suggesting that Winthrop's death generates an A, Hawthorne uses Winthrop strategically, to indicate that the master text of Puritan law provides the terms of *The Scarlet Letter* itself. Winthrop was the master of the system of signification and of law whose technology—the scaffold and the scarlet A—governs the novel's representation of official discourse; the shifting meanings that characterize the theory and activity of civil, ecclesiastical, and natural law are also at some level constituted by his discourse, to the extent that he codifies conventional political ideas in his own formulations. That the law itself might be always already "broken down" would be a new observation neither for critics of *The Scarlet Letter* nor historians of Puritanism;[57] but the particular resonance of the language of law as it is reproduced in and produces this novel has not been examined. In this section I will argue that the stress within the A, in its inability to control the variety of interpretations it called forth, was theorized and intended by Winthrop. His use of the language of love and the body is thematized not only in the novel's love plot[58] but also in its investigation of the relation between the construction of official discourse, collective identities, subjectivity, and the body. In the case of Bellingham, government by love signified the possible excesses of juridical discretion available to Puritan rulers and ministers. Winthrop's government of love is less literally sexually loving, and yet it too raises questions about the slippage between the (public) love of law and the (private) law of love. The empowerment of this love to transfigure individuals into conscience-bearing citizens is not only the condition under which participation in the polis takes place but also that in which the individual becomes reborn as a self-policing and desiring agent of the law—at least in theory.

Winthrop's use of the language of love in his construction of American Puritan ideology self-consciously traverses the ground of the secular and the spiritual. "Charity," in "A Modell of Christian Charity," refers to alms as well as to "love, the concept contained in the Greek word *agape*, translated *caritas* in the Vulgate and rendered as *charity* in some sections of the Geneva and King James

Bibles. . . . To him and his generation love to God and man was not just the English translation of some New Testament Greek, but a real, vivid passion in which *agape*, *philos*, and *eros* were all combined."[59] Thus when Winthrop asserts that "the Apostle tells vs that this loue is the fullfilling of the lawe," (288) he refers to three kinds of love: material charity—we should give to poor people beyond our means, we should forgive loans if the recipient absolutely cannot pay (286–88); economic and political charity—in "cause of Community of perill" we must act as if we had no private property and treat everyone as we ourselves would be treated; and the charity that comes from love of God, which impels us to give up narcissistic self-love and through love of Christ to love all men. "The ligamentes of this body which knitt together are loue. . . . Noe body can be perfect which wants its propper ligamentes" (289). Having established the dangerously resonant power of love, the discourse extends to a discussion of man's "marriage" with God, a contract which obligates us to uphold the covenant(s) of grace, of church, and of society. The body of the covenanted subject (all subjects are covenanted, though only some attempt to fulfill the terms of that covenant) is central to the ideological and discursive apparatus of Winthrop as Puritan exemplum. Entered into "marriage," the desire of the subject is translated into its most spiritual form; from this form all other earthly covenants—notably the social and the marital—are made sacred. So while the body itself in its materiality is not monumentalized—we can see this in the use of torture in the Puritan penal system, physical pain that signified jurisdiction over the subject's conscience[60]—it is still necessary to the metaphorical legitimacy of Puritan law that the covenant of grace both begins and ends with the body, whose behavior signifies the individual's status in the covenants of marriage and society because of its transfiguration through regeneration.

The law of love, then, is shored up by Winthrop's "reflection theory" of the relation between the individual, the social apparatus, and the Lord. Not only does the Puritan state reject the idea that private desires constitute a (post-Romantic) individual whose rights are its property, transcending the needs and claims of the law, but it legislates that these desires be brought into harmony with those of the state and therefore of God, in the scheme of providential history. The speech "On Liberty," given by Winthrop after his acquittal in impeachment proceedings in 1645, uses the same marriage metaphors to describe intrastate relations but substitutes "liberty" for love; "liberty" in his terms is, like love in "A Modell," the privilege of the disempowered to gain strength through subjection to the powerful; by analogy,

> the woman's own choice makes such a man her husband; yet being so chosen, he is her lord, and she is to be subject to him, yet in a way of liberty, not of bondage; and a true wife accounts her subjection her honor and freedom, and would not think her condition safe and free, but in her subjection to her husband's authority. Such is the liberty of the church under the authority of Christ, her king and husband. (341)

The "love" that founds secular and sacred marriage is the "liberty" to be subjected to the "husband": these analogies are conventional, and yet in the context of Winthrop's defense of his own discretionary power as a member of the magistracy, they constitute more than a reiteration of the discursive subtext of Puritan life in regenerate New England. At stake in this speech is the continued sacralization of the social covenant, without which the two kinds of "marriage" would have little valence in the citizens' consciences. The intended effect of these analogies is to monumentalize Puritan hierarchy:

> Therefore when you see infirmities in us [the magistrates], you should reflect upon your own, and that would make you bear the more with us, and not be severe censurers of the failings of your magistrates, when you have continual experience of the like infirmities in yourselves and others. (340)

The government of love requires the individual citizen to sublimate desires for the promotion of self to the interests of the state—which are also the interests of God, and thus ultimately of the individual as well, under the reign of free grace; likewise, should the citizen feel that a magistrate is inadequate, he should not question the hierarchical arrangement (this point dominates many of Winthrop's public pronouncements) but should improve *himself*. Conscience is enlisted to bring the discontented back into line; like a woman and like the church, the citizen needs to see that his position in the scheme of things brings with it certain responsibilities and certain rights, all of which, paradoxically, are privileges. Failure to fulfill the terms of this covenant will surely cause revolution in the sphere of all covenants: for, minimally, we all have access to "natural liberty"—"I mean as our nature is now corrupt" (340)—in which we are free to do evil as well as good and in which we will probably do more evil than good. "The exercise and maintaining of this liberty makes men grow more evil, and in time to be worse than brute beasts: *omnes sumus licentiâ deteriores*" (341). Adherence to Winthrop's conflation of the covenants—"civil," "federal," or "moral"—brings the subject under the sign of love and of liberty, in which "you will quietly and cheerfully submit unto that authority which is set over you . . . for your good" (342).

Conscience here brings the discontented individual in line with the ideal marriage, the state, God, and all law outside of corrupt nature. Yet in Winthrop's discourse on "Arbitrary Government" (1644), that same conscience does the work of nature in harnessing the potentially runaway discretion of lawmakers. While "On Liberty" sees the covenanted body as subject to an essentially transpersonal conscience, "Arbitrary Government" suggests that the conscience of individual judges ought to be considered safeguard enough against the natural lapses of their imperfect natures (478). Even while maintaining the hierarchical structure that he always promotes (in which authority and interpretation is the privilege of the upper classes and liberty that of the lower), Winthrop encourages citizens to resist a law or a penalty that goes against their own nature and conscience. This shift is most clear in the extract from the *Summa Theologiae* of Aquinas with which Winthrop amended his discourse.[61]

There is a difference in emphasis between the discourse on liberty and that on arbitrary government, in that the former justifies the power of lawmakers, while the latter valorizes a government of laws more than of men. These two discourses thus operate according to antithetical logics: either the judgment of individual, nonsacralized men is superior to the interpreted letter of the law or it isn't; either the law is inviolable or it isn't. What brings these divergent tendencies together is the role of conscience in fulfilling the inadequate structure—man or law. In "On Liberty," conscience corrects the natural Adamic imperfection of the individual subject, while in "Arbitrary Government," it works more mystically (according to the light of nature) to correct structural juridical imperfections. How does Winthrop, or Puritan discourse in general, justify these slippages within the founding terms and analogies of its theory?

At this point it would seem unwise to argue that the Puritan mind is rigid, unable to assimilate the play of interpretation represented, for example, by Hester Prynne's A.[62] Instead, we can see a historical explanation for the Puritan ability to accommodate this stress within the doctrine. The Puritan system of signification inscribes difference in the fundamental laws of its very consciousness: "the oneness of *allegoria* and *littera-historia*" in the Puritan automachia, according to Sacvan Bercovitch, "as well as the interchangeability of private, corporate, historical, and prophetic meaning" broke open traditional exegetical rules and allowed the rulers of the American project a new control over signification, one commensurate with the newness of the project itself.[63] What the fathers hoped to do was to legislate the range of references brought into play by a redeemed discourse, one that would always legitimate the hierarchies of scriptural and patriarchal law in the world-historical and providential-historical context of the Bay Colony. This desire to bring discursive play into the law—without objecting to the play of meaning itself—was, according to Perry Miller, characteristic of Ramistic thought.[64] The way in which the fathers imagined this was to repress the narratives of local, personal, and historical memory and replace them with what one might call an exegetical memory—a synchronic *langue* realized only in discrete *paroles*.

For example, the letter A itself has a history (how it got its shape) but it has no etymology. Thus the sign of the law, A—which is the law of language as well as the law of law—can be assigned meaning according to the requirements of the context. Because of the A, Hester is always the "text of the discourse": but over the course of her life and of the narrative, the discourse changes, and so the meaning of the A changes as well. And while in sum the collectively held meanings of the A exist in mutual contradiction, the exegetical memory, located "inside" of providential history, erases previous or contradictory significations if what the narrator calls the "self-interest" of the interpreter is served by a new gloss or interpretation.[65]

I have suggested that in the scheme of *The Scarlet Letter*, Winthrop signifies the stress within the A, and in the context of this discussion the *theory* of this split might be summarized as follows. In its desire to break down the boundaries that deform a traditionally "fallen" civil polity, the regenerate state uses language in its most "dangerous sense,"[66] relying on its resonances to maintain patriarchal jurisdiction over all facets of life, visible and invisible. In particular, "love," by leashing the body to the corporate civil and ecclesiastical lexicon, replaces the individual's personal historical memory with the regenerate state's exegetical laws. As a consequence, conscience—which can work either for or against the law, but always works in terms of it—is left to mediate between personal and public experience, acknowledging the claims of both and attempting to maintain their symmetry, their analogical relation, in the light of the laws of nature, reason, and the state. The law constitutes love, and in turn, love reconstitutes the law. But this mutuality of love and the law—which serves the utopian function of unifying divergent sites—is not "natural" here: it is an operation imagined by the state that understands the centrality of *desire* to faith and to civil discipline.

The Scarlet Letter plays out the implications of the Puritan love plot by literalizing the metaphors Winthrop provides: the citizen as woman, love as a quality of the body that contains the purest light of nature as well as its most depraved, unnatural darkness, conscience as the most powerful of juridical forces. Thus while it is plausible, as some have suggested,[67] that the governor functions in the text to illuminate Dimmesdale's corruption by contrast with his majestic virtue, the opposite reading is also possible: that Dimmesdale's condition with respect to the law, to love, to conscience, and to the sickness of the body is symptomatic of the kinds of stress Winthrop's version of the law responds to and reproduces.

In particular, the letter of the law erases historical memory, and brings to a crisis the relation of conscience to memory, since the *mode* of the Puritan juridical sign is to erase historicity and to install a juridical present tense. The iconography of the letter incorporates not only the birth of Pearl but also the rebirth of the letter's readers as they too become new subjects of a new letter of the law. This infantilizing mnemotechnique decenters and destabilizes the conscience-bound subject by overcoming the former law (in this case, that of the "fallen" polity): and this true subject, in adapting to the New Law, *in theory* will experience the New Law as solving the crisis of lawlessness the transition has itself created. And so Hawthorne's desire to produce an aesthetics of national fantasy—through displaying the mnemotechniques of the National Symbolic—is in part "predicted" by the transfiguration through law (via the motive of love) theorized by the Puritan fathers. The A is modernity, the performance of the present tense of collective identity, here a juridical present tense, since it is law that effects the shift between one configuration of one time, space, and meaning and another. But because this formal transfiguration of citizens into the juridico-utopian public sphere slights the scene of everyday life relations and consciousness, that scene ultimately provides the material for a counter-memory among "the people" which is individual, familial, collective, *and* historical: the libidinous ground on which Hawthorne's critical nationalism is founded.

THREE *The State of Madness: Conscience, Popular Memory, and Narrative in* The Scarlet Letter

THE PSYCHOPATHOLOGY OF PURITAN LIFE IN *THE Scarlet Letter* emerges in the disjunction between the citizen's identification with the state or "official culture" and her/his ongoing vocabulary, memory, and body. This competition between different modes of history and identity is experienced by social actors differently, according to their divergent social positions. The previous chapter staged the elaborate logic of juridical discourse in the novel from the point of view of the state's intentions and the state's political and libidinous contradictions. There, I argued that in the theory of affections put forth by John Winthrop's political science, "love" is a technical term designating a form of social control. The state's need for subjects who love the law, thereby loving the covenant, stands behind its periodic use of juridical spectacle to transfigure individuals into "collective subjects" of civil law. Juridical spectacle works to install a New Law by harnessing two different temporalities: first, that of New Testament eschatology, which places the Puritan colony within the time frame of God's providential "calendar," and second, that of the duration of the legal spectacle itself, which places the citizen in a present tense defined by the parameters of the legal "event." While the New Law of providential time is "experienced" only through faith, the New Law of juridical spectacle is installed periodically, in public celebratory and disciplinary moments: the citizen's participation in the collective Puritan project depends on her/his availability for transfiguration into these supra-everyday-life experiences of time.

The citizens of the New Law are thus reborn within a structure of memory, a vocabulary, and a feeling of obligation to the state and the scriptural law that founds it. Conscience is the moral link between the law and the citizen; in theory, there is neither a private part to which the state is not privy, nor a thought outside of the state's affairs. This means that, in the social theory of the Puritan conscience, the subject's personal identifications—bonds of family, class, race, ethnicity, gender, or nation—are subsumed under the more pressing project of acting in the colony's providential, political interests. Relations of space, of contiguity, are revised into orders of time in the Puritan utopian mnemotechnique. The citizen's portable memory of juridical magnificence takes the place of prior history and identity and casts the present tense as the shadow of the citizen's future obligations.

For Hester Prynne, Arthur Dimmesdale, and Roger Chillingworth, the installation of the New Law is a conversion experience, "a new birth" (80), revising not only their everyday life relations but also the meaning of their own memories, their abiding desires, and their very bodies. And still *The Scarlet Letter* also represents limits to the state's guardianship of subjectivity. "Official" memory involves the reproduction of the discourses that represent the dominant, hegemonic formations of the public sphere: and we have seen that the Puritan magistrates relied on the successful installation of juridical consciousness in the collective and individual "people" both to assure the loving coherence of the community and the privilege of the legislators. Yet the "people" at large, like Prynne, Dimmesdale, and Chillingworth, seem also to possess a "counter-memory." Counter-memory, and the historical narratives that represent it, does not oppose official memory but exists alongside it, recording information about the dominant culture without situating it as the only important site of activity and meaning. Counter-memory can be said to address the same time and place marked by official memory, but here the traditional state and public apparatuses appear as dominant elements *among many* that provide structures of identity for the citizen/subject. By this I do not mean to say, as other readers have, that Hawthorne is a populist, a lover of "the people's" consciousness, which is antagonistic to that of the dominant culture:[1] simply, here, that he represents the Bay Colony as constituted by a popular dispersal of interests, identities, knowledges, and memories that amount to multiple senses of the person, the law, and of history.

In *The Scarlet Letter*, the "genealogical"[2] task of representing the interests of counter-memory in a language and a space other than that of the public sphere is given to "the body," the material vehicle through which individuals become subjects of the law. The body, a privileged index of historical meaning, does not gain value and significance because of its origins or its traditional authority: nor does it efface the political and institutional problems with which we have been heretofore concerned. Rather, the articulation of "descent" or history on the body, in Foucault's view, is the culmination of the "stigmata of past experience . . . desires, failings, and errors." In *The Scarlet Letter*, the body is more than the mind's mystic writing-pad, where pathological symptoms appear to speak for the subject's unconscious. Bodies show the traces of the descent of history and desire as shared elements between collective and individual identity. We have seen this in the previous chapter, where I suggest that the state's theory of the body as a locus of social control runs into internal contradictions within dominant culture itself, when patriarchal authority is betrayed by the self-regulatory incapacity of official men over their symbolically empowered bodies. We can also see the body's adjudication of official, popular, personal, and historic meanings in the scarlet letter. A third space between the body's "inside" and its surface is constituted by the accretion of *kinds* of meanings of the A: the play of popular and official imagination on the "public body" spatializes meaning the way a palimpsest does, equating the significance of thoughts half-erased with more explicit and official utterances. I suggested in the last chapter that it is in the interests of official culture not to acknowledge the ongoing ambiguation of the A's meaning, so that its clarity as a sign of the law's power and necessity might be maintained. But the very fact of these less official, yet publicly embodied thoughts is crucial to the novel's imagination of how social resistance or social change might happen: the letter of the law provides, in more than one way, the material for counterculture. It is this material, which designates nonofficial modes of individual and collective experience, whose constitution and narrative fate is the interest of the present chapter.

In particular, at the moment of the law's initial display, it successfully transfigures the social and symbolic consciousness of the mob and of Hester Prynne. But the state of law also engenders superstition among the "people" and in popular discourse, which involves a kind of magical thinking that eludes full containment within the law and religion. For Prynne, Dimmesdale, and Chillingworth, magical thinking takes on new forms of unreason: the state of law is a state of madness, in which juridical transfigurations of the body and the mind induce species of insanity. Moreover, their derangement emerges *precisely* at the moment at which the apparatus of the state displays itself to its public and to the reader of the novel. Unreason, in *The Scarlet Letter*, occupies the crucial moment of the installation of proto-national consciousness in America.

The spaces beyond reason occupied by magical thinking and insanity are, in part, images of how the law itself works to establish a certain reign of reason that locates reason's antipode. But they are also forms of counter-memory: heterotopias that break up the perfect "sphere" of Puritan theory not by opposing it directly, but by skewing or distorting it, providing new contexts for its meaning. But why should the persistence of multiple modes of experiencing the law create these particular mystic forms of surplus consciousness? In the first chapter, the cases of Bellingham and, partially, Dimmesdale stood in for the ambiguous relation *within* the law between saturation by legal ideology and the eruption of "antinomian" forms of private discretion. The conflation of arbitrary and discretionary power within the dominant hermeneutic suggested that juridical excess was simultaneously within the letter and spirit of the law and beyond the proper ken of the individuals who administer it. But the citizens whose cases I will address in this essay are all merely subject *to* the law: within its symbolic order but outside of direct control over its legislation. These citizens' bodies are not protected by the law that administers to them; these citizens' minds are not fully engaged in support of the state's manifest legislation. Their "distortions" follow from the ambiguity of being a subject of and subject to a law that recognizes neither their historical existence nor their complex identifications, outside of the framework of the colony's New Law in America.

One other locus of distorted juridical subjectivity will be addressed throughout the chapter: the narrator. In the previous chapter, we have observed his consistent and harsh censure of patriarchal Puritan juridical logic, seeing it as a self-serving, mainly false utopianism. But the narrator is also saturated by the law, moved by the allure of its rhetoric. Despite the narrator's (historically locatable) ridicule of Puritan forms of social control, the spectacle of antinomian behavior—which he sees *everywhere*, and not just in the novel's main characters—is the primary site of social and subjective crisis for which his text is an "answer." It is not an unambivalent answer, however, as we will note in his association of sexual difference both with the law's shame and with its utopian attraction.

The narrator manifests a crisis of faith in the law, because its necessary address to the body produces unmanageable configurations of power and desire. It is here, in the intersection of desire and the law, that the nineteenth-century narrative finds its "national" linkage to the Puritans: the narrator desires to represent and to reinstall in his citizen/readers a proper attitude toward the law, which includes a belief in its necessity and a repression of its disciplinary excesses. A number of different but related operations enter into the narrator's reclamation of law as an entity in itself and as a structure of national memory, identity, and embodiment. Foremost is a rearticulation of the relation between law/the state and gender. While the Puritan/American project is united, in the novel, by its historical reliance on juridical ideology for the production of lawful bodies, subjectivities, and collective formations, gender's centrality to legal legitimation has produced, over the same span of time, a distinctly powerful, eroticized atmosphere. The law/gender nexus incorporates, in the narrator's view, both a politics and a fantasy of collective identity.

In demonstrating the various ways counter-memory operates within the Bay Colony, I will argue in this chapter that the aim of *The Scarlet Letter* is to separate, to transform, and so to preserve the law and utopian impulses (here figured as erotic, as well as theoretical projections) as modes of national self-identity. The activity of counter-memory within both official and popular consciousness provides the motive for the narrator's rescue of the *idea* of law from its intimate embodiment, its erotics, unreason. I will suggest that while *The Scarlet Letter* first represents patriarchal Puritan law as tragically failed utopian theory, the law emerges in the end not in full patriarchal bloom but as *necessary* for the colony and American history itself. Patriarchal law becomes the public *form* of collective life, invested in monumental male bodies without erotic presence. In addition, on behalf of affirming the symbolic linkages that have always motivated American collective identities, utopian

thought is revalorized at the end of the book: but this time in the bittersweet and depoliticized mode of private, "feminized," quasi-erotic fantasy. Men remain in symbolic power but, as "fathers," no longer carry sexual charge; women are recontained in the private sphere but there preserve the link between erotic and utopian desire. This is the solution that *The Scarlet Letter* offers to the problem of linking local bodies, abstract states, and diverse historical moments in post-utopian America.

Another View of Hester

The privatization of national fantasy in *The Scarlet Letter* is structured in the narrative's periodic return to the scaffold, its formal/juridical hallmark. I suggested in the last chapter that the repetition and reformulation of these scenes signal the centrality of social "position" to the novel, in its aim to map out the construction of the subject, local, and national identity. These configurations of social position also provide, for the narrator, some founding images with which to construct the American National Symbolic. Three times in the course of the novel the scaffold becomes a central "agent in the promotion of good citizenship" (55), a space for the transformation of subjects in their relation to the state, the civil, and the ecclesiastical laws to which they are obligated, and by extension to their fellow and sister occupants of the public sphere. And three times this condition of change, affecting both the subject of the law and the law itself, provokes a peculiar kind of linguistic disassociation that is characterized by the narrator as madness.

In the first instance of such a transformation, Hester Prynne fulfills the part of her sentence that calls for a three-hour exposure on the scaffold to the piercing eyes of the state and of "the public." The state goes out of its way to gather such an audience for the fueling of the Puritan penal machine: even an uncomprehending "crowd of eager and curious schoolboys" (54) has been given a half-holiday to join in Hester's spectacular torture. For most members of this audience, such a public spectacle constitutes their only positive participation in the political life of the Massachusetts Bay Colony. Even under the most liberal estimate of the percentage of citizens eligible to vote and to serve in the town and provincial governments, a large fraction of the crowd Hawthorne represents discoursing on and enacting the law have no formal say in its construction, reproduction, and enactment. The heavy emphasis on the women in the crowd, in this earlier scene, augments the representation of "the people" as exterior to the government and governors who ostensibly "represent" them, since women did not have the franchise.[3] Thus the avidity with which the townspeople stage such dramatic public scenes reflects in part its uniqueness in their own experience of the public sphere of power.

We are prepared for Hester Prynne's entrance into representation by the narrator's enumeration of diverse subject-positions whose purpose, in the narrative, will be to provide different kinds of judgment of Hester. The design of chapter 1, "The Prison-Door," in this light, is to establish the narrator's position as a historian and moralist who interprets according to the values and the symbolic logic of natural law, law of the sovereign heart and human nature.[4] Chapter 2, "The Market-Place," returns to the scene of the punishment within the *public's* "eyes intently fastened on the iron-clamped oaken door" (49). The activity of the public gaze signifies the operation of collective subjectivity: the political and juridical collective scenes with which the novel begins and ends reveal subjectivity to be a function not of self but of historical location and social position.

This "historical" and often ideologically interested set of differences structures significantly the "context" in which the discussion of Hester takes place. Against the Puritans' excessive seriousness of "demeanour" the narrator posits the "degree of mocking infamy and ridicule" that would be produced "in our days" (50). He himself is suspended between these two kinds of "demeanour" toward authority: although severely critical of the self-inflated Puritan juridical sensibility, he prefers the Puritan respect for the law to that of his own historical moment. The Puritans "had none of the heartlessness of another social state, which would find only a theme for jest in an exhibition like the present" (56). Here, as elsewhere, the narrator manifests his interest in reinstating the dignity of the law, both according to its own demeanour and in the people's "stern regards" for it (58). As it is, excess is always the mode of the American public's reception of the legal display, regardless of the century: throughout the novel's first six chapters, in which the narrator lays out the effects of the A on Hester and on the town during the three years after her punishment, such shuttling between gravity and ridicule, "its mingled grin and frown" (85), dominates the public response to the law/Hester, as well as the narrator's own.[5]

In addition, a supernatural aura immediately permeates the popular reception of the juridical spectacle. This aura seems to extend directly from the intensity with which the clergy (Reverend John Wilson, most famous for his role in persecuting Anne Hutchinson) makes Hester into a text: the more a text is glossed, the more aura it has. "So forcibly did he dwell upon this symbol . . . that it assumed new terrors in their imagination, and seemed to derive its scarlet hue from the flames of the infernal pit" (68–69). The negative, hell-focused supernaturalism of Puritan ecclesiastical-legal discourse is the verbal version of the visible spectacle that "impressed" (in a Lockean as well as a military sense) the minds and eyes of the spectators of the civil law. "It was whispered, by those who peered after her, that the scarlet letter threw a lurid gleam along the dark passage-way of the interior" (69). This suggests that the supernaturalism that characterizes the Puritan world view, in *The Scarlet Letter*, is itself a transfiguration of the law, its extension. This affiliation of law with the "mystic" is of course part of the intentional apparatus of the Puritan utopia (87). A "supernatural source" of representation was said to be the mark of the "Providence" God's elect participated in, in their City on a Hill (154–55).

But the glorious energy that transforms the A into God's nationalist handwriting is also inverted into the "lurid" association it gains as the Devil's mark (87; 242). Finally, the juridical/providential referent of the A is obscured in the way the popular mind transfigures it, through "a hundred false or exaggerated rumors" (246), into an autonomous agent of otherness, supernature. The A becomes the foundation for a discourse that does not refer simply to God's or the state's law, but also circulates among the people, becomes a vehicle for its imagination, a site on which a local collectivity emerges through a common (mis)use of language. This elasticity of the signifier is, as I have argued, crucial to the Symbolic power of civil authority. Juridical supernaturalism marks the popular fantasy about Hester's negative power for a short time after she leaves prison, and resurfaces whenever juridical spectacle creates a "contagion of her dishonor" (118) in the public sphere, such as in the novel's closing moments (246). But, for the Puritans, the potential cleavage between the official and the popular A was an impediment to the state's desire and intent. The brief duration of the A's disciplinary power indicates that Puritan symbolic law seems to stick only in the short-term memory: a fact of the novel's image of that law to which we will shortly return.

Finally, crucial to the narrator's construction of public subjectivity in its relation to the law is his persistent theorizing of the law's gendered nature. Early on, the narrator designates the judges' maleness as the main reason they cannot properly judge "an erring woman's heart" (64). The prisoner, in turn, "sustained herself as best a woman might" under the burden of the law's stern gaze (56–57). The male spectators in the crowd apparently sympathize with the magistrates' stern but merciful actions: they too refer to Hester as "woman," seeing her as the type (and perhaps the truth) of her sex (52; see also 61–63). The utopian rule of law constructed in the Bay Colony and addressed by official history is here exposed as a problem of rule by "men," but the not generic sort. In contrast, the problem posed for the law by subjectivity is manifestly figured in both the generic and the actual body and mind of woman (those unfortunate enough to be in the sphere of woman's influence—Chillingworth and Dimmesdale—might be said, in the narrative logic of the novel, to be "forced" into "subjectivity"/secrecy by their common penetrations of Hester).

I have argued that Hester becomes, by her likeness to Winthrop's image of the citizen as wife, a type of the citizen herself:[6] and given the earlier discussion of the franchise, we can see that the conflation of "subjectivity," "woman," and "citizen" is based not on "official history" but on a history of figuration. Within *The Scarlet Letter* this complex trope extends from the Puritans to the narrator (and to Hawthorne, in "The Custom-House"), in part through official metaphor, through literary/biblical referents, and in the set

of local allusions that mark popular discourse. The tradition-bound assignment of genders to these differently powered social positions has implications relevant to the narrative strategies of *The Scarlet Letter*: one, that the obstacles to displaying a man in a submissive pose extend from the patriarchal law's customary control over public representations; and two, that the mutual articulation of woman, privacy, and political submission is a central configuration of American national identity.

The political crisis of authority staged in the opening chapters by the narrator's repudiation of the patriarchal magistrates is also paradoxically figured as a gender crisis *created* by women and "woman"—although, as the women's responses suggest, the law allows many postures of submission to its patriarchal authority. The collectively held responsibility for self-policing designated all of the colony's subjects as guardians of the law. This is the foundation for the ethic of autonomous female jurisprudence that marks the female gender in *The Scarlet Letter*. Harsher by far than the magistrates, these women, with the exception of one "young wife," express rage and horror at the leniency with which the young, beautiful Hester is treated. This young woman, through proper submission to wifehood and maternity, seems to understand by choice the pain of punishment that is Hester's forced lot: she knows that the "heart" will always "remember" the trauma taken by the body, like a conscience that proclaims the necessity of the law (51). But the other women, not represented in maternal or spousal submission to the "discipline of the family" (91), do not occupy the space of subjectivity wrought by the loving pain of the law. Rather than assuming the affect of obedience, these women assume the sovereignty of their interpretation—customarily a magistrate's role. Although not full subjects within Massachusetts law as such, these "not unsubstantial" women (50) are more saturated with law than the law itself: their own individual senses of law seem to them more just than that practiced by the patriarchal judges.

But to the narrator, female jurisprudence differs in kind from that of the magistrate. The women's opposition to the magistrates is attributed to their "interest" in preserving the virtue of their gender by an insistence on theoretical purity: "Is there not law for it? Truly there is, both in the Scripture and the statute-book. Then let the magistrates, who have made it of no effect, thank themselves if their own wives and daughters go astray!" (51–52). The women's "interest" in preserving the written law is a major factor in the narrator's attribution of coarseness and vulgarity to them. Female jurisprudence operates "through that alchemy of quiet malice, by which women can concoct a subtile poison from ordinary trifles" (85). Even in Dimmesdale's exhortation to Hester that she reveal the name of the father, he says to her that *her* silence serves to "tempt" and "compel" him "to add hyprocrisy to sin," and hence denies him the relief of full confession (67). Female jurisprudence is blamed for its lack of interest in the delicate problem of adjudication that confronts the legitimate, patriarchal law: the "engine" of woman's juridical power is, like Chillingworth's over Dimmesdale, her intimacy with pain, and the subjective (i.e. "feminine") reflection on pain—the *poena* of punishment.

Not only do the women not display a proper attitude toward the law, their very presence in the public sphere violates the narrator's sense of propriety. The narrator repeatedly suggests that female publicity is both a symptom and the cause of the crisis in law that confronts the colony: "The age had not so much refinement, that any sense of impropriety restrained the wearers of petticoat and farthingale from stepping forth into the public ways, and wedging their not unsubstantial persons . . . into the throng" (50). Hester burns at being discovered "with a whole people, drawn forth as to a festival, staring at the features that should have been seen only in the quiet gleam of the fireside, in the happy shadow of a home, or beneath a matronly veil, at church" (63). The narrator remarks of her house that "A clump of scrubby trees, such as alone grew on the peninsula, did not so much conceal the cottage from view, as seem to denote that here was some object which would fain have been, or at least *ought to be*, concealed" (81; emphasis mine). The narrator's declaration of the desire to reenclose woman—even within representation, as in his negative conflation of Hester within the papist image of "Divine Maternity" (56)—prefigures his other aim, to relegitimate patriarchal law. If "woman" becomes the manifest, public problem of order and law, both by too much and too little legalism, then her containment solves the problem of contagion that has seemed to leak onto the magistrates' garb.

In short, "woman" has a labyrinthine relation to the law, in this text: in the scene of patriarchal excess of pomp, "demeanour," and privilege, "she" becomes the negative mirror of the law by producing an excess legalism of another sort. "Her" passionate belief in the letter of the law is a sign of its efficacy, and indeed the first six chapters of the text reveal the woman's/women's juridical ability to intensify Hester's pain and negative exemplary power. But "woman's" disbelief in the discretionary power of the magistrates makes her dangerous to their interest in maintaining the reigning hierarchy. Her fealty to the theory of the letter as opposed to its patriarchal embodiment diminishes her, making women appendages to, rather than foundations of, the Colony's utopian project.

Finally, the politically threatening juridical presence of woman as represented here has only a muted analogue in the historical conditions under which the Puritans lived, compared to the variety of male subversives. Two "historical" women represent the gamut of public female political activity in *The Scarlet Letter*. Anne Hutchinson, who has been ably explicated within the novel by Michael Colacurcio and Amy Lang, provides a model of the exceptional martyr to the law: threatening the mental and institutional sovereignty of the official men with her theoretical and practical acumen, her gender provided the magistrates with a logic for and a language of social discipline and sexual scandal.[7] But for all of Hutchinson's symbolic and historical resonance, she is a disembodied allusion in the novel, the mnemonic of a previous time of Puritan juridical/gender excess.

Ann Hibbins, in contrast, circulates ostentatiously through the text and the colony. Like her brother, Governor Bellingham, she is a site of comic estrangement, supplementing the serious sentimentality about the Puritan/American legacy that dominates the narrator's tone with the other major mode of historical knowledge through which Puritans survive in the American historical imagination: the stereotype. Hibbins is a parodic "witch" figure in many senses. She speaks the cliché necromantic language of Devil covenants, black books, fiends of the air, and so on. She disparages the visible sanctity of the colony's leading classes by reporting their cavorts in the forest, "when Somebody was fiddler"; she understands her special knowledge to be gendered, noting that ordinary depravity "is but a trifle, when a woman knows the world" (241). She also threatens Hester's composure constantly, much as Bellingham does Dimmesdale's, by asking precise, knowing questions about what constitutes Hester's "proper" identity; indeed, according to some sources, Hibbins was put to death simply because she displayed too much wit.[8] In the Colony and the novel Hibbins represents not nearly the threat to Puritan patriarchal political and intellectual hegemony of Anne Hutchinson: but her inclusion as a ridiculous version of public female institutional discourse, a figure not of dissent but of discomfort, emphasizes the banality of the violence political patriarchalism enacts—not just on the woman's/citizen's "person," but on the woman's/citizen's body itself. The novel suggests that it is one thing to recognize Hutchinson as a political threat and scandal: quite another, and laughable in a painful way, to understand that the Puritan politics of gender policing have been not simply discursive but fatal, in an ordinary sort of way.

Thus the juridical force of woman in the colony is largely the narrator's fantasy: a critical one, in its explication of patriarchal national/juridical excess, but repressive in its refusal to represent, positively, public female political dignity.

This discussion of popular subjectivity, supernaturalism, and the narrator's fantasy of woman demarcates the different discursive spaces within which Hester Prynne assumes her subjective identity as the public embodiment of the proto-National Symbolic. A figure of excess who is an agent of the law, her tenure in the Symbolic order depends on the letter's ability to control, to speak for her as she receives the law and as she operates in excess of it (both positively and negatively). Thus far I have enumerated the different sites on which the transfigured Hester/A stands in public, and suggested ways in which the immediate revelation of the A transfigures the collective and individual "popular mind" (57) of the spectators. But how does this excess of law, of subjectivity, of magical thinking affect and reflect on her own consciousness and mediate her representation to us in this first scaffold scene?

Hester Prynne's response to this scene manifests itself in her body, in ways she can barely repress. The stern attitude of the crowd, the "heavy weight of a thousand unrelenting eyes" (57) leave her no relief:

> under the leaden infliction which it was her doom to endure, she felt, at moments, as if she must needs shriek out with the full power of her lungs, and cast herself from the scaffold down upon the ground, or else go mad at once. (57)

The implosion of affect that marks the torture of her public exhibition provokes images in Hester of self-destruction. She feels suffocated by the pressure of the mass gaze, which seems to take up the space she inhabits. Hurling her voice and her body through the crowd to pierce the solid wall of public acrimony would be one way of establishing a space for herself, but this act of violence, easily appropriated in the civil and ecclesiastical apparatus, would only bring further torture and self-immolation.[9]

Her strategy of self-possession, if we can call an impulsive will-to-survive a strategy, is to go into her archaic memory, the one in theory erased by the "realities" of the scarlet letter (59). As with the "popular mind," the power of the law transfigures Hester's subjectivity into a supernatural machine. Even at this moment of despair, she turns toward the "imperfectly shaped and spectral images" that come, preternaturally, alive (57). Her memory is not a formal, monolithic object with a determined content or mode of representation. Indeed, the narrator, characteristically, formulates Hester's memory twice, to signal the fracturing of her identity under the pressure of the law.

In the first instance, the "phantasmagoric forms" of Hester's memory allow "her spirit, to relieve itself." But this relief is morally problematized, despite the narrator's generally sympathetic tone in this chapter. Hester's first memories on the scaffold are "trifling and immaterial" scenes of fun, irresponsibility, and pleasure: "passages of infancy and school-days, sports, childish quarrels . . . " (57). These "little domestic traits" of "her maiden years" are "intermingled with recollections of whatever was gravest in her subsequent life." The narrator leaves these engraved scenes to the reader's imagination: but surely among the memories of her post-maidenhood are graven, idolatrous images of the words, feelings, and sexual acts that constitute her repressed love story, and her entrance into motherhood and the law. In short, one censored image must be Dimmesdale's. In any case, the narrator seems to think that Hester is as yet shameless: for one "picture" within her memory is "precisely as vivid as another; as if all were of similar importance, or all alike a play" (57). Hester is constituted, at this point, by memories of private, intimate pleasure. The world of pleasure is supernatural because it honors no hierarchies, no duration, no boundaries between one image/pleasure and another. There is no law there.

"Be that as it might," writes the narrator, Hester next reverts to the scaffold's "point of view" (58). This, the point of view of the law, reveals a much different autobiography to Hester—not involving images of her pleasure, but of the fateful emergence of her guilt. This time she witnesses her chronological life history, seeing her natal nation and parents on the "track" to the present moment. In addition, she "saw her own face, glowing with girlish beauty, and illuminating all the interior of the dusky mirror in which she had been wont to gaze at it." This is much like the mirror in which Dimmesdale finds his own guilty subjectivity (145); but here, her narcissism isn't scandalous, but properly private and feminine. Hester is shocked by this virtuous version of her biography: its disjunction from her ignominious position within the law's present tense is so severe that she loses her name, imagining "all the townspeople assembled and levelling their stern regards at Hester Prynne—yes, at herself . . . " (58). How does Hester's memory operate here, fully saturated by the point of view of the law and by a personal, intimate semiotic?

The effect of the punishment, which ultimately leaves Hester in a "half-frenzied" "state of nervous excitement" (70), is to cleave the external "Hester Prynne" into two "persons," conjoined by one body. She first experiences on the scaffold the power of her mind to preserve her personal history, identity, and pleasure, which become alternative foundations to that which the New Law now offers her, in the present. In addition, motherhood provides for her a notion of "rights" that do not derive from the state. It also provides activity (the pleasure of sewing for Pearl, for example) that feels illicit and joyous. Her mind's recall of pleasures in her present and her past frees her to exceed the New Law, proving that she is not, in a way, "Hester Prynne." Her denial of the public transfiguration of the meaning of her name is, perhaps, one reason she does not hear "her" name when Reverend Wilson calls it, "more than once" (64). The dangerous potential of Hester's discovery of the sphere of counter-memory becomes manifest after the second scaffold scene.

On the other hand, as "the figure, the body, the reality of sin" (79), Hester gives her body and "her individuality" (79) over to the law, and to textualization in the public sphere. In her power to enable and to reproduce the law Hester's authority rivals Winthrop's: he, too, produces, represents, and interprets the law, and like Hester's, Winthrop's body/individuality is given entirely over to it, the A the sign of a complex (and loving, libidinous) politics of conscience. Yet it is in the realm of judgment that they differ: as magistrate and governor, Winthrop's love of the law is enforced through the legal apparatus and through "official memory," while Hester's judgments are largely personal and ineffectual ("I hate the man!") (176), because they exist only "within the sphere of theory" (164).

In submitting to this role, Hester's mind also becomes permeated by the pillory's point of view. Supported, as well as imprisoned, by the law's "cunning" and "*his* iron arm" (85; 78; emphasis mine), every fibre of her being is infused with a sensitivity to the presence of sin: the law in her produces a negative narcissism that reveals resemblances of her sin everywhere. It is as if, as the negative pole of the law, she reorganizes the "private sphere" of the town around its widespread sin. It is significant, given the text's argument about the general depravity of women, that Hester mainly recognizes sin in women, only occasionally feeling the burning feeling around "a venerable minister or magistrate" (87).

From the point of view of the state's intent, the colony is organized around positive law, through love, justice, and mercy. But just as the "utopia" to which the narrator refers must needs have produced a graveyard and a prison, so too, the positive law here coexists with, *and is not negated by*, its own negative. The language of "spheres" in *The Scarlet Letter* exemplifies the paradox of these coexistent forces. The scarlet letter is said to enclose Hester "in a sphere by herself" (54), and indeed the "comparative remoteness" of her cottage "put it out of the sphere of . . . social activity" and "the sphere of human charities" (81). But we have also seen that Hester's enclosure by the A's boundaries is in the conditional tense: it is "as if she inhabited another sphere. . . . She stood apart from mortal interests, yet close beside them, like a ghost that revisits the familiar fireside" (84). In Hester the sphere of positive law coexists with that of the negative: each is the vehicle for true revelation; each is a supernatural-like source of delusion and madness.

Although her social position makes it seem that she "communicated with the common nature by other organs and senses than the rest of human kind" (84), Hester's visible body radiates clarity: she is the negative image of positive law. But the narrator represents her mental life as fraught with ambiguity and ambivalence. We hear, for example, that she is fully lawful: the fact that she teaches Pearl truths about "the human spirit" found in the New England Primer and the Westminster Confession (111–12) shows that she still acts according to orthodox notions of piety. We also hear that Hester is "in a dismal labyrinth of doubt" (98–99) concerning the same Heavenly Father about whom she teaches Pearl. This contradiction is never explicitly addressed or resolved.

Moreover, the narrator repeatedly represents gaps between what Hester subjectively "knows" and what is "objectively" true about her motives, opinions, and desires. The narrator's tendency to represent and to undermine Hester's self-knowledge becomes more extreme as the narrative progresses. Although, in these moments after the first scaffold scene, he claims to show that "all was not corrupt in this poor victim of her own frailty, and man's hard law" (87), the narrator demonstrates numerous half-intentional "self-delusion[s]" (80). He delegitimates her efforts to be pious; he says that Hester "sinned anew" because she feels a rush of relief on being seen by Dimmesdale (86). Fractured by a mixture of self-knowledge and self-delusion, Hester's subjectivity becomes, in the narrator's view, entirely unreliable: not only is the meaning of her A indeterminate, but her mental and moral authority are called into question as well. And, as we have seen, this indeterminacy of authority "had provoked her to little less than madness" (113). She is unmanageable, and therefore, in his view, *non compos mentis*.

In sum, Hester struggles. But it is important to remember that she struggles under the double law of two territories: that of the Puritans and that of the narrator. First, she gives her body over to the Puritan law's clarifying activity in order to support the development of "conscience," consciousness of obligation to the law, in the minds and bodies of "the people." In the three years after her shame is displayed in the market place, her "official" body becomes the living embodiment of a number of discrete things: sin, law, conscience, collective identity, social hierarchy. In being so situated, Hester is not different in kind from her fellow and sister citizens. For they too develop genealogically, according to the production of official, popular, and intimate histories at the site of the "subject" and the subject's body. They too negotiate the proximity of and the disparities between the dominant discourses of the public sphere and the knowledges generated from places other than the state.

But Hester is unique, in this novel, in the way that she makes herself available for the other voices that express themselves through her. In her silence, in her decision not to make a "claim" for herself in public (160), she chooses a kind of madness, which is popularly interpreted as her supernatural power. This madness develops as she stops speaking in public: she occupies the gap between language that works as a system of meaning and language seen as a collection of signs with no relation to meaning. Hester decides to find comfort in this disjunction, using her muteness to provoke interpretations of her, letting the state and the public absorb her into their divergent fantasies, while occupying the silence of subjectivity "as if by her own free-will" (52). In so using her muteness to provoke lawful interpretation, however, she develops—in the narrator's view—a wild and revolutionary subjectivity.

Hester's state of madness, which at first has looked like a predictable response to a demand to submit her body/identity to the regulation of a New Law, and which repeats a popular tendency to associate the law with excess or supernatural power, comes to seem like a deliberately subversive act, in the chapter "Another View of Hester." But the events surrounding the second scaffold scene suggest that the text's determinations of Hester Prynne's wild consciousness also bring into representation a displaced concern: the scandalous, suppressed proto-American politics of patriarchal transgression. The novel initially registers the enigma of citizenship by figuring a complex antagonism between female experience and objective forms of patriarchal activity. But the second and third scaffold scenes bring into view the subjective experience of the patriarchal law by the *men* who are the law's agents. The male body, which provides the linkage between masculine sexual privilege and social, patriarchal power, turns out to be the major stress point in the social order: the latter two scaffold scenes explicate the origins of the stress and "solve" the problems masculinity poses for collective/national identity, which has traditionally relied on patriarchalism to provide intelligibility for dominant forms of power.

The novel's "solution" to the problem within the hegemonic is not, however, to banish patriarchalism from the public sphere. Instead, the chain of associations between the law, lawmakers, the gendered body, and sexual excess serves to displace political analysis onto the forms of psychopolitical trespass unique to patriarchal subjectivities. While we have addressed the way in which Hester Prynne takes on the burden of keeping this system coherent and effective, even as it distorts her own private relation to power, we have not yet examined how the paradoxical relations between official memory and counter-memory devolve on the text's other main theorist of collective identity: Arthur Dimmesdale. An analysis of Dimmesdale's ascensions to the scaffold will reshape our previous impression of how gender, subjectivity, citizenship, and the law are embodied in *The Scarlet Letter*.

A Minister is Being Beaten: Patriarchy and the Body of Law

An important shift takes place in the narrative when it addresses the subjective reception of the law by men: men publicly cast as patriarchs, heads of states and families. The patriarchal analogy is a divinely inspired theory of political legitimacy, although its forms have historically had diverse implications for the actual operations of states. In *The Scarlet Letter*, the transmission of legitimation from God to the individual male body also works in the other direction: male sexual desire is established as central to the political divinity of the patriarch. But adultery strains the alliance between sexual and political privilege: if the family is a central site of the translation of patriarchal authority to the individual man (which includes control over both familial sexuality and property, exemplified by the system of entailment), adultery by individual men threatens the very substance of patriarchal authority. In the counter-genealogy of the male body Hawthorne constructs, there is no simple alliance between male symbolic political and sexual power: indeed, it is the friction between these contiguous formations, symbolized by Adultery, that founds the narrative's manifest scandal.

The operation of the linkages between the male body and sexual, and political privilege has been metonymized as the transfiguration of the "penis" into the "phallus":[10] *The Scarlet Letter* too engages in an analysis of how the symbolic, public distribution of male power intersects with the private activity of masculinity, and further, how each of these positions relies on the "fact" of the penis and its possession by husbands and fathers. When Hester Prynne takes on the official external apparatus of Puritan law, she is brought from the sphere of domesticity to the public sphere, and is then made into a prosthetic phallus, a representation of the patriarchal symbolic order.[11] The aim of the law's symbolization of Hester is to create a collective juridical conscience and to transform Hester's own conscience into a place saturated by the law. Her doubts and her madness, recounted in the last section, emerge from the disjunction between her official self and her counter-memory—the archaic and private identities she holds, which represent the excess unavailable to juridical containment. But when the question of the interaction of the symbolic order and subjectivity is raised with respect to Dimmesdale and Chillingworth, a new set of problems arises. These men, as we will see, are already immersed in juridical identification: intimacy with the law is an a priori condition and privilege of masculinity in this novel. Adultery forces them to face the fact of male counter-memory: that *within themselves* which is "outside" or in excess of the law that founds their authority and self-identity.[12]

The crisis of this confrontation reaches its greatest intensity in the second scaffold scene. But the chapter directly following Dimmesdale's self-exposure, "Another View of Hester," supplants the appalling display of Dimmesdale's weakness and self-delusion with the narrator's invective against Hester's gender-based lack of love for the law. He does this, in my view, in order to exculpate the patriarchal position from its own symbolic inadequacy. He effects this rescue by exploiting the semiotic slippage between "sex" and "gender": he blames the sexual transgressions of men—in which, to continue the symbolization, the "phallus" becomes merely a "penis"—on women, who do not respect the order of law enough to maintain, in private, the logic of its representations.

The example of Roger Chillingworth is instructive here. Simply because he has been "intimate" in the sacred way of marriage with Hester (118), he feels he has the right to inflict pain on his structural replacement. Already "misshapen" and "in decay" from a life dedicated to philosophy and science (112, 74), Chillingworth embodies the deformity of patriarchal-juridical license and its power to deform as well. But because he is a man, a married man, a church member, a philosopher, and a scientist, he conceives of his own *ressentiment* as a component of the juridical power appropriate to his positions in history and in the state.

> He had begun an investigation, as he imagined, with the severe and equal integrity of a judge, desirous only of truth, even as if the question involved no more than the air-drawn lines and figures of a geometrical problem, instead of human passions, and wrongs inflicted on himself. But, as he proceeded, a terrible fascination, a kind of fierce, though still calm, necessity seized the old man within its gripe, and never set him free again, until he had done all its bidding. (129)

Chillingworth's proximity to the law transfigures his body and mind, and distorts his relation to his will, much as such juridical intimacy had done to Hester, Dimmesdale, and Bellingham. He has already been slightly deformed by his privileged position, but faced

with Hester's desecration of *his* name (Prynne, presumably) he takes on the *nom de plume* of negative law, seen now from the point of view of a certain version of patriarchal self-interest. He is "fascinated" by the object of righting the wrong done to "him," but not by "the gripe of human law" (75): "Then why—since the choice was with himself—should the individual, whose connection with the fallen woman had been the most intimate and sacred of them all, come forward to vindicate his claim to an inheritance so little desirable? He resolved not to be pilloried beside her on her pedestal of shame" (118). Note that "shame" here stands for "law." Elsewhere, "consummation" of the minister's punishment stands for "justice" (260). Appropriately, "fascinated" is from the Latin *fascinare*, "to enchant, bewitch, from *fascinus*, a bewitching amulet in the shape of a phallus."

In the sphere of libidinous legitimation that devolves from the patriarchal analogy, cuckoldry calls into play the "institution" of phallic poetic justice, and Chillingworth acts out the patriarchal animus of the state enraged by obstacles to its authority. He plays out the libidinous energy behind the law, when its "phallus" is denied or degraded. Thus Chillingworth is not anarchical or technically antinomian. As the narrator frequently says, he is Satanic, replicating and inverting the forms of positive law: "The victim was for ever on the rack; it needed only to know the spring that controlled the engine . . . " Chillingworth perverts as well the supernatural aura of the scene of juridical torture, imagining "a thousand phantoms . . . all flocking round-about the clergyman, and pointing with their fingers at his breast!" (140). Having "made the very principle of his life to consist in the pursuit and systematic exercise of revenge" (260), Chillingworth represses his counter-memory—his prior identity and personal history—and dedicates his tremendous talents to bringing the other outlaw into his jurisdiction, which is delimited by the rights of husbands.[13] Like the other subjects in this novel whose literary representation and social status is emphasized and elaborated by their identification with the law, Chillingworth becomes a hideous figure of juridical excess, deformed *because* dedicated to the law—but deformed differently from Hester, because of his intimate and unique proximity to phallic privilege.

The physician is "outside" of civil law by virtue of his lie and the "lock and key" of Hester's silence (118); but, as with both Bellingham and Dimmesdale, Chillingworth's access to power enables him to veil his use of it, and to rely on its penal forms. By the end of *The Scarlet Letter*, Chillingworth's Satanic lunacy, his "unhumanized" (260) transformation into a species of negative law, deforms him so thoroughly that the scaffold, the legitimated public space of partiarchal discipline, is the only place on which Dimmesdale is invulnerable to his machinations. At that moment when the two men confront each other, each with his own pain and each with his own privilege, Dimmesdale's "triumph" over Chillingworth is a victory for the patriarchal state's rule of law over the phallic-libidinous activity that has historically flanked that law. At stake in this split within the patriarchal—where the forms of law come to diverge from the body of the man—is the future intelligibility of national identity, as I will argue below.

But the narrator's observation that the men were "mutual victims" suggests another ongoing agenda in *The Scarlet Letter*. This strain of narrative argument attempts to displace onto women/citizens responsibility for the men's sexual abuse of the juridical ground of patriarchal legitimacy. The famous passage in which the narrator theorizes about the nature of "passionate" love and hate, and whether they "be not the same thing at bottom," describes, not heterosexual relations in the novel, but rather relations between the two men (260).[14] Indeed, the narrator fantasizes about "transmuting" the "hatred and antipathy" women create among individual men into "golden [man-]love" (261) that will transpire in "the spiritual world" (260–61). Given the narrator's prior representation of male patriarchal excesses, what are we to make of this eruption and validation of homosocial desire?[15] While the "triumph" of the historical-patriarchal state is an important aim of *The Scarlet Letter*, the narrator's dream of a utopian world of men invests the male gender (but *not* the male body) with another, purer kind of power. The madness of the law is due to its libidinousness: but in a world without women, men will not need to "regulate" alien subjects. Note that there are two alien subjects requiring discipline here: women and the male body. In utopia, love will reign, transfiguring *men* into their ideal, disembodied, "spiritual" relations.

The conditions of the homosocial utopia, in which male power and pleasure is emancipated from the body, suggest a strategy for understanding the psychopathology of patriarchal juridicalism. Hester Prynne's proximity to the law transfigures her body into a public monument. She acceeds, in silence, to the state's pedagogical appropriation of her body: not only because her release from the "problem" of the body liberates her mind (as in the homosocial utopia) but also because giving up claims to autonomy and independent agency is a route to social legimitation. Female activity, then, is legitimate only when it displays submission to the law—that is, when the woman paradoxically acts by giving up control and agency to the law, not to her inclinations. Female sanity is possible only under the same self-negating conditions, when counter-memory is fully dedicated to juridical service.

Chillingworth's case, however, reveals that the protocols of the body are entirely different for the man. The public, professional male body is also a pedagogical tool, like a scaffold: but male legitimacy depends on the appearance of professional mastery of, not submission to, the law. The public authority of the master and the order he represents depend on his ability to occlude the activity of his private body: no private impulse, no scandal of counter-memory, can break through to the public scene without undermining the symbolic authority of the patriarch. As a doctor, Chillingworth seems professionally committed to curtailing the body's public display of private stimulus: however as a wronged husband, he is committed to torturing into public the nonofficial impulses that threaten the very ground of male symbolic power. In this way he brings into representation the stress within the patriarchal analogy. He shows that the body of the male that materializes the lines of power must be veiled in order for those lines of power to take on transhistorical, symbolic force. Thus, crucially, male embodiment itself threatens to collapse the public authority of patriarchy: the eruption of male counter-memory or negative law degrades the symbolic power of the public male body, turning it into "flesh," which is involuntary, libidinous, unmastered, and therefore unmasterful.

From this point of view, Dimmesdale's self-combustion can be traced to his need *to not know* that he has a body: his proximity to the law, his life-long expectation of the legitimacy that comes from professional mastery of the soul and the spirit, occludes knowledge of the body, and most importantly occludes his understanding of *how* the male body works as the point of contact for its social power. This paradox about the male body's place in patriarchal authority results in the minister's confusion about the meaning of his acts: for the fully lawful man there is neither a split nor a fantasy of a split between his official and his private self. His relation to the law is his subjectivity; his intimate desires and practices powerfully inform his public discourse about the soul and God's law. He is an exemplum, and he is self-exemplified. The tryst with Hester changes all this. By revealing to Dimmesdale the role his body plays in founding his intellectual and spiritual power, illicit sex *creates* a counter-memory that destabilizes fundamentally his assurance that he justly masters the law. Acting against the law while being its agent creates two Dimmesdales: the "minister," whose very discourse represents and reinforces the law of the father(s), and the "untrue *man*" (145; emphasis mine), constituted by a silent and "dim interior" (130) that represents the sensual material of his consciousness and his body unmanageable by the law, the truth he also "loved" (144). The relation between these two "men" is a matter of much speculation.

The narrator constructs a genealogy of the minister's identity by exposing disjunctions between his public reception and his private and official self-representations. In designating multiple paths of his pathology, the narrator shows how the patriarchal will-to-not-know has involved both the minister's own eccentric relation to his body, history, and the law, and a variety of public codes that affirm certain strategies of patriarchal empowerment. Five paths in particular cross over Dimmesdale's ravaged body and mind: one, the Puritan juridical construction of private identity through the double operation of official spectacle and personal conscience; two, the collective political discourse of love which, through a typological rhetoric of the loving body, overemphasizes the role of affect and desire in the dissemination of the law; three, the Puritan theory of history, which, in providing a utopian providential context for actions taken in the present tense, enables Dimmesdale to "suspend" the meaning and judgment of his historical actions; four, the participation of his public in the same achronic discourses, which leads them further to disable literal meaning and the present tense as possible signifying contexts. The fifth determining factor is of a quite different sort: the narrator links the minister's disorder to the obstacles facing the construction of a truly accurate American national memory. These are mutually determining forces that mark the minister's character: the chapters "The Interior of a Heart" and "The Minister's Vigil" map out the private and public implications of the patriarch's disorder.

The splits within Dimmesdale's relations to systems of law and justice are marked not by his silence, as it was for Hester, but by a strange, shrieking utterance: the shriek that threatens to explode from Hester on her judgment day (57) appears as well within the minister, who actually enunciates it on the scaffold. His psychological strategy for negotiating the antagonism between his political/symbolic and sexual desires and meanings is to produce madness and an incapacity for action that affirms the law and his love for it—despite his repeated transgression of its local principles. Twice on the scaffold, Dimmesdale experiences a crisis of intention that both moves and paralyzes him. In the first instance, his relation to his own speech (that is, his intentionality) is disrupted; in the second, the reliability of his vision is called into question.

The night Dimmesdale chooses to disclose himself on the scaffold is the negative of the one on which Hester Prynne was displayed: so foggy that Dimmesdale is invisible, and therefore "[t]here was no peril of discovery"; so damp that Dimmesdale's tenure there is suicidal, should "the dank and chill night-air . . . creep into his frame, and stiffen his joints . . . and clog his throat with catarrh and cough" (147). The variety of bodily self-negations the minister engages comes to a head when his voice transfigures him into a negative space:

> Without any effort of his will, or power to restrain himself, he shrieked aloud; an outcry that went pealing through the night, and was beaten back from one house to another, and reverberated from the hills in the background; as if a company of devils, detecting so much misery and terror in it, had made a plaything of the sound, and were bandying it to and fro.
>
> 'It is done!' muttered the minister, covering his face with his hands. 'The whole town will awake, and hurry forth, and find me here!' (148)

Moved to laughter, torment, and impulsive shrieks, Dimmesdale wondered "if he were going mad" (150), for his sounds "were uttered only within his imagination" (151). The fantasy of being consumed by the law is a fantasy of powerlessness. By standing on the scaffold, Dimmesdale loses all control of his free will, his reason, and his body. No power over movement or restraint emanates from this pilgrim: erupting with mirages of his own activity, his loss of reason makes him *non compos mentis* by his *own* lights. Such inadequacy releases his responsibility for his past: it "proves" that in the light of law, only insanity motivates him to immoral acts and immoral speeches.

We have seen, in the cases of Chillingworth and Prynne, that such madness comes from being oversaturated with law: the very act of lawlessness creates a psychological dissonance so huge that the subject ceases to be, in some fundamental way. Hester, for example, is said by the narrator to appear "like a mask; or rather, like the frozen calmness of a dead woman's features; owing this dreary resemblance to the fact that Hester was actually dead, in respect to any claim of sympathy, and had departed out of the world with which she still seemed to mingle" (226). Dimmesdale, too, carries the etching of his fractured subjectivity on his body. He too becomes a "ghost" (190), "a shadow, or, indeed, ceases to exist" (146). Were this dissolution actual, the problem of the body for Dimmesdale would be solved. The sign and the vehicle of his lawlessness would be eradicated. But the minister's disembodiment is psychic and figurative, not material or public. Indeed, his public duties sustain his body and perversely transform his incorporeality into a sign of virtue.

Dimmesdale suffers greatly the pull of his ambition against his self-revulsion. But, in the public sphere, the minister's sin manifests itself as a greater authenticity of the soul. As a result, he achieves "a brilliant popularity in his sacred office" (141). The phenomenal spiritual power he has over his parishioners derives not from what distinguishes him to himself—his love of law, of knowledge, and of rhetoric—but rather from that of which he must remain unconscious, to retain his mastery: his emaciated body; the tonal affect of his language. His parishioners come into the church not because the light of reason and nature have been revealed to them through his mouth but because his *affect* speaks of yet a deeper experience within the conventional Puritan frame of reference.

Therefore, for the purposes of the church and state, Dimmesdale is an effective conscience, or more accurately an affective one: for he brings people into the church and into the law not by a traditional reliance on reason or the light of nature, but according to the seduction of tone, the labial activity of the "Tongue of Flame" (142). The narrator uses his editorial apparatus to affirm that at the base of Dimmesdale's attractiveness is an erotic appeal enhanced by religious affect—the chapter in which Hester and he revivify their love is, for example, called "The Pastor and His Parishioner." In contrast, the aged patriarch Reverend Wilson is represented as outside the circuit "of human guilt, passion, and anguish" (65). Dimmesdale embodies for the public the New World utopian law of love, wherein the covenant is seen not so much as a duty but as the proper container for the desire, the "passion" of the citizenry.

The other pastors also administer the love that binds individuals to collective spiritual uplift. But the parishioners' passion for Dimmesdale goes dangerously beyond "reverence" for his sovereignty over interpretation of the soul's obligations to the law. Significantly, the minister seems to be the only young man in town, so that along with his dissemination of the law of love, his performance is sexually charged for the members of his parish. "[B]looming damsels, spiritually devoted to him" (125) were "victims of a passion so imbued with religious sentiment that they imagined it to be all religion, [bringing] it openly, in their white bosoms, as their most acceptable sacrifice before the altar" (142). His vocal seductions of the audience dangerously confuse patriarchal symbolic and sexual authority. Placed in a central position by the ubiquitous political hegemony of patriarchy, powerful due to the erotics of his proximity to the law, Dimmesdale is nonetheless unselfconscious about the derivation of his power. He thinks he should feel special shame because of his hypocrisy but never seems to make the connection between his affair with Hester and his usual execution of his vocation.

Dimmesdale's desire to maintain his fame and power translates into a disgust at "his miserable self" (144). But where does Dimmesdale locate his potential emergence from this "self"? Not in language: the narrator has shown us that his very rhetorical mastery allows him to delude his parishioners and himself about his own spiritual practices and intentions. Because his language speaks his desire in ways he cannot control, Dimmesdale relinquishes his faith in it. To manage his spirit the minister can therefore rely solely on the comfort of the visible, the material action, gesture, and image: the "interior" of his own heart is revealed to him only in his mirror-image and in the procession of images "reflected" in the mirror before which he keeps his nightly vigil (145).

Just as he confuses official and sexual power, Dimmesdale interprets the "prick and anguish of his daily life" (141) as a call not to rethink his epistemological mastery of the body of Christ/the Church, but to materialize and to transfigure his own, earthly, "impulsive" body. Seeing bodily discipline as a route to policing the soul, the minister thus appropriates and internalizes the law's mnemotechnique. His unceasing speculation exposes the impurities in his soul, yet in a strange perversion of sacred rituals of introspection. The litany of acts: scrutinizing himself in the mirror, watching the procession of hallowed figures in his diseased life (as Hester impulsively does, on the scaffold, to relieve herself of the pressure of the mob's gaze—but here he performs the ritual privately, fetishistically, *to relieve himself of himself*), fasting, bloodying himself with his own private scourge, "until his knees trembled beneath him, as an act of penance" (144). But this is simply the simulacrum of penance, because it is produced sensually to kill the "untrue man" produced by his renegade sensuality.

While acting outside of the law by virtue of an "impulse," by the "lock and key" of Hester's silence (118) and the "lock and key" that closets his self-flagellation (144), the minister's body remains the locus of his "bondage" (197) and his "pleasure" precisely because it is so intimate with the law.[16] In short, he literalizes the machinery of conscience—the abstract memory of the juridical apparatus—burned into the mind of every citizen; he assumes the positions of judge, jury, and victim. His mad laughter on the scaffold—or the laughter that possesses him—uncannily reproduces the bitter laugh he generates by self-flagellation (144).

At stake in the construction of conscience then, is the effect of the law, its affect—ultimately the repression of laughter and the body in favor of patriarchal reason. Dimmesdale's conscience is thus the site of a political confrontation within the Symbolic order. It emerges from the confusion of the penis and the phallus, from the eroticization of patriarchal power that locates its pleasure, when it can, in performance—both vocal and sexual. Dimmesdale's mind, body, and voice appear to be totally and wilfully saturated with the law, motivated by orthodox desires, and representable within the conventions of reason. But under the pressure of his troubled conscience he reifies the dialectic between image and text that has heretofore characterized the public expression of the law: in fetishizing the image of the self as icon, Dimmesdale refuses to submit to what the Puritans called "discipline," the application of the rule of law to local events. This is, of course, the very same discursive "discipline" he produces for his parishioners.[17]

But images serve Dimmesdale no better than the language he has repudiated as the vehicle for his atonement. If the first moment of his mad/lawful laughter expresses his loss of control over internal signification, the second deranged event points to the implications of Puritan semiosis for collective subjectivity, as it is condensed in Dimmesdale's broken mind:

> a light gleamed far and wide over all the muffled sky. . . . So powerful was its radiance, that it thoroughly illuminated the dense medium of cloud betwixt the sky and earth . . . with a singularity of aspect that seemed to give another moral interpretation to the things of the world than they had ever borne before. (153–54)

The narrator suggests that this uncanny bright light, bright like the apocalyptic "light that is to reveal all secrets," is simply a meteor "burning out to waste" (154). But, he notes, this event can serve as an emblem both of Puritan collective subjectivity and the semiotic heritage of the American National Symbolic: "We doubt whether any marked event, for good or evil, ever befell New England, from its settlement down to Revolutionary times, of which the inhabitants had not been previously warned by some spectacle of this nature" (155).

These two historical constructions—Puritan culture and pre-Revolutionary America—comprise a crucial part of the novel's staging of Dimmesdale's subjectivity and his conscience. The minister himself reads the blazing light as the A he does not display on his breast. To explain this, the narrator does not rely on the Puritan habit of reading "natural phenomena" as "so many revelations from a supernatural source" (154). Instead, "it could only be the symptom of a highly disordered mental state, when a man, rendered morbidly self-contemplative by long, intense, and secret pain, had extended his egotism over the whole expanse of nature, until the firmament itself should appear no more than a fitting page for his soul's history and fate" (155). In other words, the narrator sees Dimmesdale's narcissism as a violation of the collective nature of public signs.

The celestial, supernatural blaze of collective political identity has mainly been transmitted through the visions of individuals: "Not seldom, it had been seen by multitudes. Oftener, however, its credibility rested on the faith of some lonely eyewitness, who beheld the wonder through the colored, magnifying, and distorting medium of his imagination, and shaped it more distinctly in his afterthought" (155). This is one of Dimmesdale's central functions in the colony: to use his "official" imagination to generate the utopian light that will transform the historical present tense into the mirror of a glorious future. But the narrator here characterizes such prophetic interpretation as distortion: he implies that the utopian interpretation of natural signs is a politically sanctioned practice of misreading. The construction of the minister's role as bridge to the future thus works in an ambiguous way, for here the psychopathology which we have heretofore described as his personal response to the law must be articulated within the historical heritage of the Bay Colony and the nation as well.

In the most diagrammatic sense, this scaffold scene maps out the complex lines of patristic inheritance that found the future of the colony/nation. Just as Governor Winthrop's death is revealed in the narrative (as opposed to "in the sky," which happens soon after), Reverend Wilson walks by, a "luminary" "surrounded, like the saint-like personages of olden times, with a radiant halo . . . as if the departed Governor had left him an inheritance of his glory" (150).[18] This demarcation of patriarchal authority is further complicated by Dimmesdale's characterization of Wilson as *his* "professional father," since it is Wilson who previously suggested that all Christian men "hath a title to show a father's kindness" toward Pearl (116). The image of entailment we receive here is engendered by the elasticity of paternal metaphor within patriarchal/juridical semiotic hegemony: while "mother," in this text, is a unique and nonmetaphorical relation, "father" can be said to engender a multiplicity of paternities. The dispersal of the position of "father" is necessary to the authority of Puritan law and the legitimacy of the Puritan state, for it provides the collective and individual conscience with a reason to hold sacred all men, as if by an alliance of blood. Dimmesdale, the "father" who is also the "son" in this hierarchy, is the site of intersection between all of these various patriarchal positions. But this overdetermination is also one motive force behind Dimmesdale's lunacy, for signs of his disparate fatherhoods are, truly, written everywhere. In addition, the blazing A reveals to Dimmesdale the presence of Chillingworth, who is also physically and morally revealed by the light (he stands on the street in front of the scaffold). It is as if the illumination of the letter (what "discipline" and criticism should do) reveals all the fathers to us, in their alliance and their apocalyptic configuration.

Thus Dimmesdale's contiguity to the death of Governor Winthrop provides a new context within which to understand the minister's disease—not simply as an individual formation, but also as a general quality of patriarchs. The narrator also reveals that the astral A refers to the semiotic habits that distingish the Puritan collective imagination. At the moment when the governor's death is coordinated with the release of "an immense letter—the letter A—marked out in lines of dull red light," the narrator comments that only Dimmesdale's perverse mind would see the celestial formation as an A. "Not but the meteor may have shown itself at that point, burning duskily through a veil of cloud; but with no such shape as his guilty imagination gave it; or, at least, with so little definiteness, that another's guilt might have seen another symbol in it" (155).

If the narrator is right, then the colony/nation itself is mad, for another's guilt does *not* see another symbol in it—the town, too, sees the A, although attributing it not to the guilt of an Other but to the virtue of Winthrop, whose passing was heralded by the Angel A as it made its way up to heaven. Thus the passing of a governor, "the Governor," is a scene of the law's reinforcement in the popular mind and also is symbolically the death of law: a scene of proper reading and of a disintegration of perception that marks the onset of social anarchy and psychological madness. Here Dimmesdale is exemplary—each of Dimmesdale's breakdowns, after all, takes place on the occasion of a transition in the governor's office.

Besides the marks of Puritan patriarchal semiotics that cross over Dimmesdale's body and mind, Dimmesdale (ideally) makes coherent the temporal fantasies of the colony, extending it into the future. This activity too has its subjective costs. As "a professional teacher of the truth" (153), Dimmesdale is called to be the translator of local history into the logic of Providence. Puritan discourse, as I have suggested, relies on the elasticity of the juridical sign to merge diverse social positions into a linguistic and political identity—the mental space of collective and ultimately national life. In theory and by all appearances, this letter of the law is clarity itself, but we historically mediated readers apprehend it as a hieroglyph. Thus, paradoxically, in order for the juridical signifier to seem a priori and uncontestable, it must simultaneously be a route to knowledge and an act of forgetting.

This is why the state of madness, in *The Scarlet Letter*, erupts when the law displays itself in state ritual or in changes of the figures who represent it. The political display of utopian semiotics makes the state's discursive and juridical practices vulnerable to interpretation, revelation. A citizen might actually *see* the apparatus of memory and forgetting embodied in the emergence of a new political exemplum. Thus, crucially, Hester's centrality to the state as the executor of its symbolic apparatus works in particular to create an *aura* of tradition. She installs the New Law on her own body, but by her patriarchal embroidery effaces the law's newness (82). Therefore the installation of the new New Law is itself a moment of lawlessness. I have earlier suggested that the juridical practices of the state fathers, which rely on the construction of a dialectic between public images and commentary, efface the temporality of the historical event, replacing it with a new event, a New Law, a scene of sacred/juridical reading. This merging of "historical" and "hermeneutic" time (not at all an a priori distinction, but an operation of sacred and political allegory) dissolves the formal and customary apparatuses of social and linguistic meaning.

The minister is unable to submit to the discipline of the letter, *because he is its master*. He cannot submit because he *remembers* the strategies of the letter in the service of merging civil, ecclesiastical, and natural law.[19] Thus the complexity of his hypocrisy.

Dimmesdale speaks falsely about himself by exploiting the typological space of the dominant disciplinary languages; but this bad faith is his official function, insofar as he is supposed to represent the inevitability of the collective future. The overdetermination of the minister's intention creates a split in his consciousness that mirrors and enacts the rules of the dominant Puritan semiotic. The minister internalizes the law's confusion of context and event. He hears himself speak the truth of his fraudulence; he hears himself speak falsely while the soul's truth nonetheless finds its way to his parishioners; he hears himself speak, and then it turns out that he hasn't spoken at all, or that he has half-spoken. All the while he is warden of patriarchal law (his library is "rich with parchment-bound folios of the Fathers, and the lore of Rabbis, and monkish erudition" [126]). He has mastery of it and also is its most abject failure. Such perversions of the law create an "inextricable knot, the agony of heaven-defying guilt and vain repentance" (148). This knot is embroidered by the law's election of Dimmesdale, and in part reconfigured by his own narcissism; but it is also foundational to the American project, whose future is signaled feebly within the frame of the novel proper.

In implicit contrast to Dimmesdale's tortured "soul's history" (155) the narrator posits the public history of the nation, a history later "wasted" again, like the meteor, by the utopian claims of the Revolutionary War times that have obscured history's bright lights.

> It was, indeed, a majestic idea, that the destiny of nations should be revealed, in these awful hieroglyphics, on the cope of heaven. A scroll so wide might not be deemed too expansive for Providence to write a people's doom upon. The belief was a favorite one with our forefathers, as betokening that their infant commonwealth was under a celestial guardianship of peculiar intimacy and strictness. (155)

This suggests that when *The Scarlet Letter* speaks of the self-obsession of a public man, it describes Dimmesdale as a unique person, an exemplary Puritan dignitary, a metonym for collective psychopolitical practices in the Bay Colony: it also implicates postrevolutionary American culture for its own narcissism and historical amnesia. American revolutionary culture, by claiming the special privilege of the patriarchal analogy—from "celestial guardianship" to "our forefathers" to, presumably, "us"—obscures the scene of history by constructing "a people" within a pan-historical, utopian space of power, a wide "scroll." For the Puritans this utopia is manifested in the "intimacy" with which the colony submits to the "wholesome" discipline or "strictness" of the law, as if members of a family (91).

For the postrevolutionary nation, utopia is signified by America's liberation from the seventeenth century—its brand of "forefathers," utopianism, government by sacred law. The narrator implies here that the positive, progressive forms of postrevolutionary history, which are simply alien to the often supernatural forms of Puritan national expression, constitute not "true" memory but rather compensatory mystifications for a repressed and "doomed" past. Law, supernaturalism, madness, revolution: these become ways of talking about memory loss, which is a personal, a collective, and a national tragedy. Such a tragedy, so painfully wrought in *The Scarlet Letter*, might provoke desires for counterrevolution, counter-memory, or the return of the (sexual) repressed: yet the tendency of revolutionary theory and practice to produce the *erasure* of history, identity, meaning, and the body—for individual subjects and for the nation—provides the opportunity for a crucial moral lesson in the novel's second half, as we will see in the next section.

Revolutions in the Sphere of Theory, Thought, and Feeling

The death of Winthrop and the display of Dimmesdale fundamentally transfigure *The Scarlet Letter*. Winthrop's letter, writ larger than life, is the formal "master-word" of the Puritan semiotic (93) and collective identity. His death seems to create and to reveal a vacuum in the symbolizing (and therefore juridical) power of the state, which is also, ultimately, a vacuum in the construction of conscience and historical memory. Dimmesdale is the embodiment of this symbolic and political crisis. But his failures are not due to a flaw in juridical technique: the minister is saturated with all of the laws he has broken. Rather, the formal apparatus of collective order is called into question by the very potency of the Puritan mnemotechnique, and by the irony that memory of and fealty to the law requires the conquest of the citizen's counter-memory, collective identity, and will. Almost immediately following his materialization on the scaffold, Dimmesdale forgets that it really happened: "so confused was his remembrance, that he had almost brought himself to look at the events of the past night as visionary" (158). Such amnesia comes to Dimmesdale because he cannot face, in daylight, his inadequacy to the law/truth he loves. He cannot face the fact that the law's clarity of representation is a sign of its unreliability: then, his illiteracy with respect to the Letter would extend to himself as well. And perhaps he also experiences a memory lapse because the very operation of the Puritan-utopian hermeneutic, which relies on the panhistorical efficacy of patriarchal alliance, itself requires the lawful citizen to leave the material historical event for the sphere of theory and interpretation, where colonies, bodies, minds, and souls are translated to their ideal relations.

This collective and individual crisis in meaning and memory takes place seven years after the novel opens. Seven years is the term of enslavement that marks the legal contract of a bond-slave (104); heralded by the death of Winthrop, this span of years seems to delimit the general efficacy of the law as well, including its ability to legislate memory. For directly after Hester witnesses Dimmesdale's disintegration and abasement the narrator proclaims an epochal shift in the very ground of *The Scarlet Letter*. It is not only that "Hester Prynne did not now occupy precisely the same position in which we beheld her during the earlier periods of her ignominy" (160). The very meaning of the symbol, "or, rather, of the position in respect to society that was indicated by it" was "transfigured" along with Hester (163). Hester occupies one "position," the A another, and their mutual articulation yet a third, and all of these are now different points on a new map of the colony. The politics of conscience, staged in the representation of the divergent identities that mark the public and private spheres of the colony, once again emerges as a *question* of intelligibility that the narrator feels obliged to clarify. Topographical instability resurfaces in the narrator's descriptions of identity; the popular imagination and the imagination of the state are brought back into play as indices of the hermeneutic and political overhaul. But why should Dimmesdale's public abasement be, as Pearl herself senses, cause for "a sense of any trouble or impending revolution" (228)?

Hester Prynne is the conventional sign of the law, and also of the law's failure to deter, regulate. Accustomed to the public display of her impropriety, Hester has long been the limit of what representations the law can abide of its *inability* to prevent transgression. But Dimmesdale's release of his crime into the public sphere of representation dissolves the patriarchal law's display of sanctity and authority. Publicly staging his own inadequacy to the law and to the Symbolic Order he is ordained to sustain, the minister violates what has heretofore been the narrator's taboo against the explicit representation and analysis of patriarchal transgression. Bellingham is constrained by Hester's embroidery, and contained within a web of discreet narrative allusions, while Winthrop merely materializes symbolically, a rhetorical and alphabetical ghost: both protected from a critical gaze by the privilege of the patriarchal control over

public display. Dimmesdale, in contrast, humiliates himself, Puritan law, and the future nation in exhibiting his own inadequacy to the law and the law's inefficacy with respect to its own.

In the chapter "Another View of Hester," which follows the minister's ignominious display, the narrator joins Hester in horror at the public show of the minister's dissolution and likewise feels "a responsibility . . . in reference to the clergyman" (159). But here the interests of the narrator and Hester diverge in ways that fundamentally transform the novel. The responsibility Hester feels is to reempower the minister, to return to him control over language, the law, and his own body, so ruthlessly taken away from him by their engagement in a "link of mutual crime" and negative law (160). But the narrator's mission, following Dimmesdale's self-exposure, is to rescue the law from its humiliation, to eradicate the amnesiac technology of the state, and to make Puritan culture "safe" for the future identity of the postrevolutionary nation.[20]

The narrator effects this rescue by a twofold operation. First, he dislodges from the center of the text the crisis of juridical indiscretion that has plagued the colony. No longer are we concerned with the ethics of the state's juridical and patriarchal practice. Instead, in "Another View of Hester," we are reenclosed within the spaces of counter-memory—that is, of the individual and collective identities that accompany, but do not originate in, the official discourses of the public sphere. Second, the narrator couples the new hegemony of counter-memory with an ascendant female gender. Substituting "literary" for "historical" evidence—he says, for example, that but for the domesticating effects of Pearl, Hester "might have come down to us in history" (165)—the narrator nonetheless imagines, in this new chapter, the historical emergence of a *female* order of law. We might parodically call this a Female Symbolic Order, since it is a fantasy of how "woman" would discipline social formations—states and bodies—in the absence of patriarchal law. While one might argue that this chapter simply traces Hester's unique juridical psychopathology, the narrator's fixation on questions about the meaning of "woman" suggests that here he understands "Hester Prynne" mainly as the intersection of a historical subject with a transpersonal sex/gender system. *He* raises the discussion of Hester to the level of generic, gender discourse: this is the new vantage point for the "other" view of "Hester."

Why does the narrator's response to Dimmesdale's insufficiency take the form of a gynocratic fantasy? As in all that relates to the law in this novel, the narrative critique of woman pertains to a suspicion of women's fundamental antagonism to patriarchal law and to patriarchal law's inadequacy with respect to its subjects. But prior to Dimmesdale's spectacular failure, this crisis has been played out within the proper boundaries of official representation: all public behavior has referred to the state law as its master-text. Starting in "Another View of Hester," patriarchal law is no longer the origin of the colony's dishabille. Instead, from this "other" point of view, the exhaustion of patriarchal authority is traced to the deliberate activity of the Female Symbolic. In the process of shifting blame, the narrator takes up the mantle of male alliance to deconstruct the claims of woman. Once again, however, this critique reflects not only on the value of the woman but also on problems within patriarchal law itself. In the following paragraphs I will elaborate the postulated new regime of female law, the narrator's critique of it, and the implications of that critique for the political imagination of *The Scarlet Letter*.

The textual appearance of the Female Symbolic is an uncanny version of *The Scarlet Letter*'s founding event. Quite simply, the narrative of "Another View of Hester" repeats the strategies of the novel's opening chapters, beginning with the narrator's use of the politics of public space and the pulse of the popular imagination to highlight Hester's usurpation of the authority previously owned by the men of law. He then evaluates the "effect of the symbol . . . on the mind of Hester" herself, just as he did during her occupation of the scaffold (163). The Female Symbolic thus has narrative kinship with patriarchal law's production of collective and individual subjectivity, of physical transfiguration, and of supernatural thinking: it is the law's mad wife, who is full of "so much power to do, and power to sympathize . . . with a woman's strength" (161).

Each of these juridical categories, the patriarchal and the feminine, is marked by a different logic and a different language. Hester Prynne's feminine law reproduces the formal structure of legal representation without the attending aim of public or self-discipline or submission to the law. She still transports the hegemonic A of juridical law: but seven years after the A is invested with the negative power of church and state, the state's intention for it to be a portable penal machine—pillory, prisoner, text, and commentary rolled into one complex body—is simply now one of many coexisting but not competing definitions of the letter.

One "office" of the scarlet letter was to become a nodal point for the construction of collective identity: and indeed, as the narrator canvasses the town, we see that the A fulfills this office still, but only formally. Its originary meaning has been transmuted into its opposite: the adulterer's A assumes the sacred aura of the cross on a "nun's bosom" (163), and it organizes the translation of hatred into love, marking no internal condition of ambiguity or ambivalence in the process. In so acting, the letter retains the transfiguring power the state intended it to wield, but does not hierarchize or evaluate the various contents produced from within the disparate social positions brought into contiguity through the A's sociality. Each "meaning" of the A carries with it its own logic, according to the unique "interests and convenience" of the various populations that interpret it (160).

The "public" is the first entity to register that the state has, after seven years, lost control over the A's and Hester's meanings, and therefore over collective memory and identity. Because Hester never expresses her desire in public but "submits" to public interpretation in a way that she never submits internally to the law, the narrator feels that she exploits "human nature" (160). She plays on its "despotic" tendency to love the abasement of the powerful and the selflessness of the abject who have acknowledged the hegemony of the public judgement (162). Likewise, "men of rank" and "individuals in private life" (none of these positions is mutually exclusive—men of rank are also individuals in private life, as the novel starkly shows) also experience the historical process of transfiguration and inversion. They domesticate Hester's iniquity according to different schedules: the "rulers, and the wise and learned men of the community" relax "[d]ay by day," while private individuals have already "forgiven" Hester her "frailty," seeing the A as a sign of "good deeds" performed since 1642 (162). Hester's place as public disciplinarian is, seven years later, generally attributed to her sacred and virtuous womanhood, which is defined by the "woman's" uncomplaining and willing submission to constant pain. Even though "men" *remember* and tell tales about what the A's original signification was, the letter has lost its repulsive negativity in their *eyes* as well, and taken the form of sacred purity, spotlessness, invulnerability (163).

In short, the founding principle of the Feminine Symbolic, in the narrator's rendering of it, is negative: it dispenses with *intention* and constraints on the free play of desire and interpretation. It is a law without "right," "justice," and telos (162). It releases conscience from abstract "obligations." The female affirmation of dispersal and multiple interpretation horrifies the narrator: like the public, he attributes these qualities to the interaction of the juridical law, the law of gender, and Hester Prynne herself. But this interaction has different meanings for the "people" and the narrator. In public, her actions come to "mean" her intentions. To the narrator, Hester's body is an obstacle to understanding what her true meaning is, and its opacity is complexly subversive. He counters her growing public legitimation by attacking her body—her sex and her gender—and locating the "real" Hester only in her mind, "within the sphere of theory" (164).

The paragraphs in which the narrator explains Hester's political theory are confusing and confused. The narrator asserts, "The world's law was no law for her mind." But he proceeds to show that, in England and Europe, there is no "world's law": there, state military and juridical authority is being contested by "[m]en of the sword." Moreover, "the whole system of ancient prejudice" [and] "ancient principle" has been "overthrown and rearranged" by "men" with "emancipated" intellects (164). If this "freedom of speculation, then common enough on the other side of the Atlantic," is not the "world's law," even though it has overthrown traditional systems of legitimation and knowledge, then what is?

Even as revolutionaries, these bold and heroic "men"—soldiers, politicians, philosophers, "forefathers" all—were distinguished by their engagement in the historical struggle for political hegemony that has marked Western culture's "official" narratives. The men fight with each other in war and in politics. They fight with their ancestors through usurpations of textual and hermeneutic authority. But in the Female Symbolic, these traditional realms of authority are essentially irrelevant to visionary thinking. The legitimation that would come from simply engaging with and usurping the traditionally male spheres seems not to be of interest to Hester. Perhaps this is the "world's law" she breaks: "[l]ittle accustomed . . . to measure her ideas of right and wrong by any standard external to herself" (159), she simply refuses to submit to the law of inevitability that has made the patriarchal part of law either "nature" or "its long hereditary habit, which has become like nature" (165).

Instead, Hester conceives of the world from the point of view of "the whole race of womanhood" (165). The interests of "womanhood" are rather simple, in contrast to the vast and complex regulatory apparatus that sustains patriarchal political and sexual privilege: Hester seeks the idea that will enable all women "to assume what seems a fair and suitable position" (165). One "position" Hester does not imagine as a foundation for gender justice is motherhood. Hester herself not only envisions killing Pearl to spare her the ignominy of womanhood (166), but does not imagine that the family hierarchy, with its patriarchal heritage, can provide the basis for the utopian transfiguration of social relations.

Three steps are necessary for the public, historical installation of the Female Symbolic. The first is that

> the whole system of society is to be torn down, and built up anew. Then, the very nature of the opposite sex, or its long hereditary habit, which has become like nature, is to be essentially modified. . . . Finally, all other difficulties being obviated, woman cannot take advantage of these preliminary reforms, until she herself shall have undergone a still mightier change; in which, perhaps, the ethereal essence, wherein she has her truest life, will be found to have evaporated. (165–66)

Hester imagines no community of love here. Nor does this tripartite blueprint for the installation of a new society repeat the vision of sentimental feminism Hawthorne would have recognized in his own culture:[21] Hester's utopian speculations in the book's final chapter more directly repeat those, with their commitment to the moral discipline of female sexuality through the categories of virginity/sin. In "Another View of Hester," however, Hester's views are radically materialist. She senses that the structural discriminations of society are prior to the construction of individual and collective consciousness; men and women will be redeemed only after the material forms of social life originate from a new and unimaginable (or simply unrepresentable) source. The unrepresentable and the nonpatriarchal merge, in the Female Symbolic. As a result, the feminine law is itself impossible to imagine—note the vagueness of Hester's formulations. This is perhaps why she shuttles between thinking utopian thoughts and thinking of suicide (165–66).

In short, the paradox of the Feminine Symbolic is that it exists as the unthinkable possibility of history. This is a fundamental element of utopian discourse. Jameson writes, "Utopia's deepest subject . . . is precisely our inability to conceive it, our incapacity to produce it as a vision, our failure to project the Other of what is."[22]

But while proclaiming Hester a social traitor for occupying the realm of theory, the narrator undermines the force of her speculations. He might have undermined them by commenting on their vagueness, their insufficiency as theory. Instead he characterizes them as species of *ressentiment*, a female complaint. He proclaims the feminine law a simple antipatriarchal phantasm, an acting out of the desire for male negation.[23] By constructing what appears to be a tawdry and libidinous motive for Hester's social thought, he defines the strategies for his counterpolitics. Delegitimating Hester's utopian theory by addressing, interpreting, and disparaging her body, he turns the possibility of postpatriarchal social thought into an advertisement for abstract citizenship in the liberal political public sphere. This is why, to counter her thoughts, he deconstructs her gender.

Hester considers herself a woman, theorizing on behalf of women. But it turns out—according to the narrator—that her long proximity to the law has vaporized her femininity: "the light and graceful foliage of her character had been withered up by this red-hot brand, and had long ago fallen away. . . . Even the attractiveness of her person had undergone a similar change" (163). The narrator cannot decide whose fault Hester's intimacy with the law is: "She was self-ordained a Sister of Mercy; or, we may rather say, the world's heavy hand had so ordained her" inadvertently (161). No matter: the narrator views Hester's deportment under her quasi-official "ordination" as a crime she commits against the law of nature and of the state. In particular, her crime is to have "turned, in a great measure, from passion and feeling, to thought" (164) and thus to have "evaporated" that "ethereal essence" that kept her intelligible as a woman (166; 165).

Hester can not speak for woman, because by dedicating herself to a life of thought about women, she has unwomaned herself. Moreover, a "woman never overcomes these problems by any exercise of thought" (166). The narrator takes on the eradication of this negative space (she is not a man, just a not-woman) as his mission: "She who has once been woman, and ceased to be so, might at any moment become a woman again, if there were only the magic touch to effect the transfiguration. We shall see whether Hester

Prynne were ever afterwards so touched, and so transfigured" (164).

The first instance of such a transfiguration in this text, however, turns out to be a feminine ruse. The operation of the Female Symbolic is such a perversion of the familiar affective authority of the woman, that it transfigures woman herself into her monstrous likeness. For instance Hester, "unsexed" by her embrace of thought, becomes luxuriantly a "woman" again, in the forest rendezvous with Dimmesdale. But this "woman" is a Satanic simulacrum who transforms time, space, and the body:

> There played around her mouth, and beamed out of her eyes, a radiant and tender smile, that *seemed* gushing from the very heart of womanhood. . . . Her sex, her youth, and the whole richness of her beauty, came back from what men call the irrevocable past, and clustered themselves, with her maiden hope, and a happiness before unknown, within the magic circle of this hour. (202; emphasis mine)

The "woman" Hester here becomes is not a real "woman." Her embodiment of her maidenhood, restored to its prehistorical plentitude, takes place at the cost of negating the fact of the past—which for Hester means the voiding of her discipline within patriarchal time. Her self-transfiguration at the expense of juridical memory signifies that here, lushly feminine, she is nonetheless immersed in her "unwomaning" law. Her body is a fraud; her conscience is "estranged" (208). Contrast the authentic "woman," in little Pearl: at first, she is "a *creature* that had nothing in common with a bygone and buried generation" (134–35; emphasis mine), who needed "a grief that should deeply touch her, and thus humanize and make her capable of sympathy" (184). Pearl's "humanization" is powerfully linked to her ascension to proper "womanhood," via her acknowledgment of Dimmesdale's paternity. As her tears of recognition and forgiveness "fell upon her father's cheek, they were the pledge that she would grow up amid human joy and sorrow, nor for ever do battle with the world, but be a woman in it" (256). For Pearl as for all Puritan proto-saints, in the redeemed world there is no past, and the present tense is just a pledge to live lawfully in the future. Recognition of the father symbolizes simultaneously submission to the juridical law and the law of gender. Feelings of humanity are the privilege the obedient subject enjoys, so that submission to the father's law will be felt as freedom.

In short, the narrator concludes: female authority is located in passion and feeling and not in thought; sublimating feeling to the world of thought unwomans the woman, transporting her to a politically and semiotically liminal space that is both self-deluding and culture-threatening; and, nonetheless, no rigor of thinking will protect the woman from her transfiguration in the sphere of discourse, which includes the public sphere and the narrative text. Pearl's ideological *menarche* reveals that the real "woman" is a "creature" who "pledges" herself to the patriarchal law—its hierarchies, history, and collective identity—lovingly and painfully, not under constraint, nor after great thought.

When the narrator announces that the "scarlet letter had not done its office," (166) he is usually taken to imply that Hester has proved impossible to discipline through legitimate means. But this judgment, though it comes after an extended display of Hester's revolutionary thinking, does not reflect simply her personal danger to Puritan/American dominant culture. Counter-memory occupies an ambiguous space, registering personal and culturally shared materials and experience. Thus, from one point of view, the "difference" signified by Hester's gender stands in for the way the material of counter-memory devalues the law: in the sense of undermining and weakening it, and also of deconstructing its claims to transhistorical authority. "Woman" here in either case figures as a locus of privatization that dissolves the forms of public authority, threatening to substitute a regime of reckless subjectivity. But another kind of juridical metonymy operates as well. At first transfigured by the letter's power as the law's sign, Hester turns the A into her own monogram. This semiotic transformation erases the possibility of a solely political explanation of the letter's inadequacy to the duties of its "office," which are to legitimate the state apparatus by managing the structures of conscience and public memory. The narrator thus also makes the case, through the Female Symbolic, that the suturing of (any) gender and the law is the origin of its indiscretions, its maddening and its disfiguring effects. For gender is always linked to the sexed body as well as to political forms.

So far in this chapter I have described the variety of ways in which subjectivity derived from proximity to the law creates two kinds of excess in *The Scarlet Letter*. In one, madness and supernatural thinking were "normative" responses to the investment of social material by the law. The other effect of the law was to produce, by negation, a counter-memory in the individual and collective subjectivities of the colony. This counter-memory, which includes the materials of everyday life, personal memory, shared folk-knowledge, and love not motivated by the law's desire for proper citizens, provides the materials for three kinds of social transformation. The first and most ordinary is in the construction of collectively held meanings derived from private conversations but taking place technically within the public sphere of discourse: from this we see the extraordinary production of the A's meanings over time. The second potential of counter-memory is to destabilize the system of patriarchal legitimation signified here by the law: Dimmesdale's confusion of the official, the libidinal, and the private reveals both a structural and a subjective fissure in the way patriarchy thinks about the body of its privilege. The third use of counter-memory is in the deployment of its materials for utopian ends. This is the radical impulse behind Hester's political theory, as we have just seen. The narrator sees the first two developments of counter-memory as a sign of the inadequacy of patriarchal law; and the third, the feminization of utopian political thought, as an argument for patriarchy's necessity. Such are the paradoxes brought to light in the forest scene. Here, Hester acts as an agent of the Female Symbolic: the narrator fights her New Law with his own peculiar jurisprudence, authorized by natural law. As with the other juridical scenes in this novel, the emergence of a New Law is designated by an explicit manipulation of space: the space of feminine law is a "dark labyrinth," an "insurmountable precipice," "a deep chasm," in "wild and ghastly scenery" (166).

It is as if "Another View of Hester" revealed in Puritan New England an entirely new and exotic landscape. On passing through its forest wilds, Dimmesdale, the tourist, catches glimpses of what appears to be post-patriarchal life—even though the manifest purpose of Prynne's actions is to animate his patriarchal prowess through "love," just as Governor Winthrop might have ordered. For Hester, the "native," antinomian wanderings in the theoretical wilderness of revolutionary spirit are considered the usual thing; but for the minister, the spectacle of counter-law makes irrelevant his interior struggle to both master and nourish his self-abjection. He thus experiences "a revolution in the sphere of thought and feeling" (217). Dimmesdale's transportation into the mentality of the New Law reveals an uncanny collaboration: proximity to radical female law makes him insane in a new way. His libidinal psychopathology emerges into the daylight and is no longer contained on the scaffold. It also liberates him to produce utopian social theory on behalf of the patriarchal state.

What is the meaning of this paradox, that the application of revolutionary female political theory leads to the release of male libido and state-utopian discourse? For one thing, this causal relation reconfigures Hester's law as a conventional type of Puritan utopian thought. The novel draws a new map in the forest scene, in which the world of Hester's jurisdiction is explicitly located among a plurality of utopian spaces. On one side of the forest, the debased post-utopia of the Bay Colony; on the other, John Eliot's Praying Towns, Christian utopias (soon to be annihilated as well) dedicated to the spiritual and social transfiguration of Native Americans.[24] The narrator's concurrent allusions to Eden (202–3) and to Sodom and Gomorrah—as "the minister departed" the forest, "he threw a backward glance" (214)—suggest that the revolutionary space of Hester's imagination is also profoundly a commentary on the utopian energy that circulates in the Scripture that authorized the colony. The novel here reinforces the coupling of utopian theory to bodies and political formations. It shows that these paradisal desires, which refuse a priori categorization into "the personal" and "the political," are ongoing impulses behind both progressive and depraved activity. It proposes too that just as the complex and fragmentary nature of personal desire must be acknowledged even as it is disciplined, so too the utopian impulse behind social life must be acknowledged as a desire integral to the subject and given a "fair and suitable" political form.

While the novel as a whole links the formal and subjective incarnations of the utopian impulse, its thematic interest directly after the forest scene is to adjudicate the psychic form of the minister's submission to the Female Symbolic. Seven years earlier, the law-crossed lover had self-"consecrated" his activity. When he did this, and begat Pearl, Dimmesdale simultaneously initiated a new law (recognizable as law only because of its philological relation to scriptural codes), and shielded himself behind the privilege and the logic of the orthodoxy.[25] Chillingworth's effect on the minister's mind and body, at the juncture of patriarchal privilege and discretionary license, is merely an intensification of these contradictions. "Its result, on earth, could hardly fail to be insanity, and hereafter, that eternal alienation from the Good and True, of which madness is perhaps the earthly type" (193). According to the narrator's reasoning, the Good and True and the law do not noticeably converge. The minister's insanity is thus, as I have argued, both personal and culturally emblematic, maintained by a structure of hypocrisy in which the man's guilty conscience helps legitimate his symbolic authority and social position.

But "the same minister returned not from the forest" (217). Wherein lies the difference? The chapter "The Minister in a Maze" reflects structures of madness—"a fortunate disorder in his utterance," for example (219)—very similar to those registered in Dimmesdale's first scaffold scene. But under the regime of the Female Symbolic, the minister is no longer constrained by his prior submission to legal *appearances*. "[B]ewildered as to which may be the true" minister, his "mind vibrated between two ideas" (216, 217). This suggests a transformation in his mode of doubleness. Earlier, he saw his "true" self in the negated, self-fetishizing subject suffering in the mirror; now he occupies the gap between the true and the false faces he wears, having lost his control over the different representational codes he develops to manage his guilt and his hypocrisy. Earlier, he occupied Hester's position on the scaffold as Hester did: silently, passively, egoistically. The forms his temptation now takes reflect his structural privilege in the colony as a man and a patriarch, whose "interior kingdom" had undergone "a total change of dynasty and moral code" (217). He wants to torture patriarchs, widows, and young virgins with blasphemous assertions about the "truths of Scripture" that have provided them the most "consolations" (218) and him the most power. This is, no doubt, why the narrator characterizes him as motivated by "the whole *brotherhood* of bad" impulses (222; emphasis mine).

However the narrator makes it clear, on the renewal of Dimmesdale's and Hester's vows in the forest, that Dimmesdale is not to be allowed to take complete responsibility for his action.

> Were such a man once more to fall, what plea could be urged in extenuation of his crime? None; unless it avail him somewhat, that he was broken down by long and exquisite suffering; that his mind was darkened and confused by the very remorse which harrowed it; that, between fleeing as an avowed criminal, and remaining as a hypocrite, conscience might find it hard to strike the balance; that it was human to avoid the peril of death and infamy, and the inscrutable machinations of an enemy; that, finally, to this poor pilgrim, on his dreary and desert path, faint, sick, miserable, there appeared a glimpse of human affection and sympathy, a new life, and a true one, in exchange for the heavy doom which he was now expiating. (200)

The failure of conscience to "strike the balance" is especially symptomatic of problems within the structure of Puritan law, which relies so heavily on the juridical force of conscience to forge an analogy between personal and social covenants. Since civil law has no access to the interior of an unwilling heart, the narrator usurps the law's privilege, establishing his own version of the "legal" situation of the conscience and making his "case" for Dimmesdale's relative innocence. His juridical consciousness is explicit: "what plea could be urged in extenuation of his crime?" The narrator is the attorney for the pathetic minister, and the passage above is like a final plea to the jury to consider extenuating circumstances, with all the attendant forensic slickness: note that the minister must choose between fleeing as a criminal and being a hypocrite, and apparently can entertain no thought of staying and revealing all.[26]

Why does the narrator wish to argue the minister's case? Certainly the forest scene and the walk through the town Dimmesdale takes shortly after he leaves Hester's space testify to his unworthiness: "[W]herefore should I not snatch the solace allowed to the condemned culprit before his execution? . . . The decision once made, a glow of strange enjoyment threw its flickering brightness over the trouble of his breast. . . . 'Do I feel joy again?' " (201). Yet his renewal of his "fall," the experience of the "burning" feeling we have associated with the presence of sin, the "revolution" in his personal body politic, does *not* reveal the minister's *intent* to digress: "In truth, nothing short of a total change of dynasty and moral code, in that interior kingdom, was adequate to account for the impulses now communicated to the unfortunate and startled minister" (217).

The words "unfortunate and startled" provide one key to the narrator's desire to rescue the man from blame for the renewal of the love plot: while Hester "had habituated herself to such latitude of speculation as was altogether foreign to the clergyman" (199), the minister "had never gone through an experience calculated to lead him beyond the scope of generally received laws; although, in a single instance, he had so fearfully transgressed one of the most sacred of them" (200). The minister's impulsive passion, in other words, has left him without free will, whereas Hester's "mind of native courage and activity" could not possibly have missed the implications of her act (199). Thus, we are prepared to see Hester fall anew and to be judged as entirely guilty for it. Dimmesdale's unconsciousness, on the other hand, releases him, in the narrator's view, from responsibility for his own sin. She blithely transgresses Law itself, while he "so fearfully" disobeys "one." These different standards of competence are crucial to the novel's closing "revelation" of yet another new New Law for the colony and the nation.

In so gendering the politics of intention, the narrator of *The Scarlet Letter* demonstrates the momentous struggle Nancy Armstrong describes, in *Desire and Domestic Fiction*, to transform the meaning of the modern political subject from a collective "person" with always social interests into a subjective individual with no proper or essential interest in politics. Two kinds of transition were necessary for the production of this modern subject, an "individual" who saw her/his authenticity not as hereditary or institutionally conferred, but as founded on emotional, affective, psychological sovereignty. In one, post-Enlightenment middle-class culture needed to pass through the body of the woman, in the "sphere" of her affective forms of proper activity, to produce new, psychologized definitions of what motivates political behavior: not class—but self-interest. Yet, secondly, it was necessary that the emotional authenticity of the woman of modern middle-class culture not generalize to her enhanced political power in the middle-class public sphere.

To discipline "the woman's" private prestige, and thus to preserve the political public sphere as a male domain,[27] was to demonize her sexuality. In "Another View of Hester" and the forest scenes following, the narrator displays precisely this emergent political psychology and its concurrent sexual disempowerment of female gender authority, aiming to separate Hester from the implications of her political thought through a wild diversity of gender representations. In "Another View of Hester" she embodies the public, feminized image of collective virtue and emerges as a not-woman who has ungendered herself by virtue of private political thoughts; in the "forest scene" with Dimmesdale her radical subjectivity is displaced entirely into a praxis of sexual subversion. And yet, as we will see, the narrator does not "win" this struggle to depoliticize Hester, nor to transform politics into a crisis of male sensation: his consciousness of patriarchal political pathology, which is both affective and institutional, forbids the conclusive authorization of male political subjectivity and the elision of pragmatic political interests. *The Scarlet Letter* attains its productivity as critical representation by continuing to the very end to shift between the registers of public and private forms of legitimation both for men and for women. In this sense the novel moves beyond both the narrator and "the middle-class novel" as Armstrong represents it.[28]

The miscegenation of desire and the law central to the operation of the Puritan/American utopia has been carefully orchestrated, in *The Scarlet Letter*, to have originated in a number of different sites. The colony's legal fetishism, its reliance on affective codes to bribe citizens to affirm the state's proleptic expression of "their" desire, its utopian promise of perfect justice (individual and collective) is successful, in that the centrality of law's letter to social position and all forms of consciousness remains the main fact of Puritan and proto-American "historical" experience. I place "historical" under erasure because the strategy of the official Puritan hermeneutic is to efface political subjectivity, knowledge, and memory by the blinding light of providential fulfillment, a time held in trust by God's covenant with "the people."

By the same "token," the demands of juridical iconicity produce different types of counter-memory. In itself, counter-memory is a politically neutral category of knowledge and experience: supernatural thought, for example, both directly reflects the popular reception of the law and provides a mode of speculation and a vernacular that circulates freely within the public sphere of discourse, with little regard to legal matters. Likewise, the madness created in individuals whose passionate loyalty to the law's appearances comes into conflict with their counter-memory does not necessarily unravel or deface the manifest fabric of social life. However, when the law's control over the reality of the appearance breaks down, when ornamental embroidery starts to look like revolutionary graffiti, then it becomes apparent that the materials of counter-memory are always available for the purposes of social disfiguration. It is important to note that this threat is as much to the law's utopian promise as it is to its structural hegemony in the patriarchal state.

Finally, the narrator posits "the body," brought into history and representation by its gender, both as a source of and a resource for the production of law, collective identity, historical consciousness, and the discipline of wayward citizens and the political imagination. But the very power of the body to produce linkages between distinct social positions is the source of its negative, uncanny power. And while sexual difference becomes the narrator's vehicle for exploring the different operations of the body's lines of force, the narrator does not simply locate in the sexual circulation of bodies the "problem" of law in *The Scarlet Letter*. Indeed the indiscretions of law on bodies are as powerful as the excesses of bodies within the law's jurisdiction. The body, counter-memory, and official discourse are thus not separate sites of knowledge or history in this text, but are mutually articulated elements that provide the *materials* for the production of identity, consciousness, and historical knowledge, the three contiguous areas of political and semiotic concern from the very opening(s) of *The Scarlet Letter*.

To uncross the tangled lines of desire and power that produce the different deformations of the law in *The Scarlet Letter*, the narrator stages the *dis*articulation of utopia and the law, a process that makes manifest the historical and, in his view, essential tensions between them. To merge these two categories, to assert their mutual inevitability, was the Puritan dream.[29] One can read their separation in the novel as the end of utopia and the victory of a negative, disciplinary, or simply symptomatic pragmatic politics dressed up in idealism; or one can read it, as I do, as an attempt to envision the preservation of utopia's link to politics despite the disfiguration of personal, collective, and national fantasy that has resulted from their relation. The narrator preserves utopian fantasy and the patriarchal state; he also constructs a narrative record of their "historical" failures. He effects this rehabilitation by installing yet a third new New Law, in the third scaffold scene. In its return to the marketplace for a third affirmation of the state's Symbolic Order, the narrator also produces a new distribution of desire, reconfiguring the body within a newly safe sphere of historical/national consciousness.

"The New England Holiday" and "The Procession" differ from the novel's first two chapters in that state and collective identities are here even more elaborately symbolized and dispersed over the common scene of political display. The "cultural work" of the governor's "procession" is to transfigure the historical quotidian into the time and space of a new political reality:[30] "the custom of mankind ever since a nation was first gathered," is to reaffirm ritually the hope that "a good and golden year were at length to pass" over the colony, due to the rule of "a new man" (229). In the meantime though, the public is depicted as simply milling around and playing, waiting for the parade of state to bring it into line with the new governor's regime, to install a new tone to public life, and redefine their meaning as a "people."[31] The parade itself is sensually more complex than Hester's spectacle was, heralded by music that imparts "a higher and more heroic air to the scene of life that passes before the eye" (236). The sumptuary masquerade of the law is now embodied in different costumes: Hester's official hegemony of ornament augmented by military dress and weapons. The crowd is more explicitly composed of different classes, ages, races, and nations. Likewise, Hester's A operates both to make her invisible, in the usual way, and to embody her painfully, as if freshly applied. Thus here, as elsewhere in the novel, the defamiliarization of the subjects present to see the law and to hear the commentary that theorizes its implications is a central technique of the public construction of collective identity.

To provide this commentary is Dimmesdale's role. Since the state holiday is also the occasion of his return to the patriarchal public sphere, it is is tempting to read his majestic (and entirely orthodox) performance of the Election Sermon, and then his variously received scaffold confession, as affirmations of the novel's early critique of the formalism of Puritan legal theory and practice for its violation of historical truth and consequent deformation of subjectivity. For again Dimmesdale goes out in a blaze of glory by exploiting the paradoxical meaninglessness of the "actual" word. The narrator ridicules the public for its uncomprehending and manic joy after the Election Day speech; but they read Dimmesdale as he has trained them to read him, as a purveyor of the Tongue of Flame whose great power is in his transcendence of earthly "meaning" for the sublation into spirit and inspiration.

> The eloquent voice, on which the souls of the listening audience had been borne aloft, as on the swelling waves of the sea, at length came to a pause. . . . [Next] His hearers could not rest until they had told each other of what each knew better than he could tell or hear. (248)

When Hester listens to the minister, she also hears him strangely, selectively:

> Muffled as the sound was by its passage through the church-walls, Hester Prynne listened with such intentness, and

> sympathized so intimately, that the sermon had throughout a meaning for her, entirely apart from his indistinguishable words. (243)

Instead of words, Hester hears the "undertone" of "sweetness and power," the "plaintiveness," "the anguish,—the whisper, or the shriek," the powerful "cry of pain." The narrator comments, at the end of these remarkable passages, that "It was this profound and continual undertone that gave the clergyman his most appropriate power" (244). Likewise, when the minister assumes the scaffold he speaks of himself as "I," "me," and "him," and so maintains the self-allegorization that has always obfuscated his agency. As official language rolls and thunders over the heads of the people in the marketplace, making "one vast heart out of the many" (250), they are designated as citizens, educated to read the discourse that calls out to them: it is here that the proto-national "consciousness" is installed and—from the point of view of subsequent historical amnesia—eradicated in America.

The Election Sermon should not be seen as Dimmesdale's only official act; his personal confession must be read as equally "official," equally a public commentary on the new regime. On the pulpit he officially affirms the conjunction between the state's utopian promise and submission to the law, and so does a service for the patriarchal status quo. The minister also does a service to the state by simply appearing scandalously on the scaffold. Insofar as he is "saved" there, he reiterates its awful potential to extend the state's interests onto bodies, an important though negative fact to be known. And while his scaffold confession does not adequately expose his sin (as it cannot, because the Puritan semiotic marks the subject's public, official identity as the point of reference for any of its other manifestations), he nonetheless "comments" directly on the legitimate power of patriarchal law by publicly describing and assuming *Hester's* repulsive self as the "truth" of his own body. "He bids you look again at Hester's scarlet letter! He tells you that, with all its mysterious horror, it is but the shadow of what he wears on his own breast . . . " (255).

The "truth" of his body reflects, as always, on the complex state of juridical, patriarchal, and private authority that he, as an "official man," negotiates. In its most vulgar incarnation, Dimmesdale's defiled body joins with Chillingworth's progressively "withered" and "shrivelled" body (260) to display the repulsive effects of violating the alliance that constitutes and legitimates the patriarchal analogy. Like Bellingham, who violates the alliance among the Fathers to regulate themselves according to the laws they represent, these two men exploit their social proximity to the law by transforming it into a private, discretionary apparatus that has the privilege of "consecrating" its own acts. Their public profaning of the patriarchal analogy, which threatens the institutions and customs that organize social life, appears on their impotent bodies as an expression of their internal perversion, but also crucially as a reinforcement of the symbolic "father" over his embodied counterpart. The men thus become the sign of the necessity to erase the individual patriarchal body from the set of patriarchal "necessities"—the penis subtracted from the phallus. Even the deaths of Dimmesdale and, later, Chillingworth mark them as derelict with respect to patriarchal authority. Patriarchs live on, in *The Scarlet Letter*, as monuments, as "names," as "allusions" in the National Symbolic. Dimmesdale and Chillingworth fail to ascend into iconicity, because they are "mutual victims" of the solipsistic desires and "rights" of the *individual* male body. As Hester's body has provided the law (and its agent, the narrator) with its figure of legal transgression, the men's bodies provide the allegory for political corruption. The scapegoating of their bodies (especially the minister's) allows corruption to be symbolically expunged from the corpus of the community and the state, but without actually changing the proper regard for the patriarchal forms of power that constitute the state's law.

In contrast, the monumental collection of Mount Rushmore-like forefathers—"Bradstreet, Endicott, Dudley, Bellingham, and their compeers"—has no private body, counter-memory, little "brilliance" or "activity of intellect" (238), and so displays none of the qualities that have made other official men dangerous and unreliable. Patriarchal iconicity comes, in the text's final moments, to imply a condition of "not desiring." The suppression of desire's play is what the A was supposed to do to Hester. But the lawmakers from whom she received her letter were already animated by self and by desire their rhetoric could not acknowledge or authorize. As a result, Dimmesdale, Chillingworth, and Bellingham "forgot" themselves, in exploiting the discrete privileges of their symbolic and sexual power. The novel's fantasy of the exhaustion of the masculine sexual animus envisions arresting the proliferation of indiscretions performed by official men, acting officially.

Indeed, the collaboration of their monumentality and the narrator's rescue of the idea of patriarchy suggests that in the new literary-national order men will "be" and not "do." When Hester shoulders the "responsibility" (159, 170) for the debility of both fathers, she also inherits the activity of public collective "imagination" that used to be one of the Fathers' great strengths and passions. Her subjectivity, the cause of so much trouble in the novel, comes to be crucial to its preservation of the utopian promise of national identity. It provides the materials with which *The Scarlet Letter* images a space beyond the negative contours of Puritan culture—the falseness of its utopian juridicalism, and the dangerous, self-undermining "nature" of patriarchal nations.

The utopian "promise" is sheltered, for the Revolution and beyond, in the diminished, private "region" often called Hester's "feminism." No longer embroidering to earn her bread, no longer a dangerous supplement to the law, Hester makes prophecy her commodity: but this time her vision of the future extends from a revision of the "story" that has defined her relation to the law, the public, her own desire, and the novel. Now the tale of Hester and Dimmesdale, a political scandal, is reduced to a mere love plot, and she to "one who had herself gone through a mighty trouble." From within this new narrative history, a place with its own moral and literary (not political) laws, Hester is shown to have "comforted and counselled" the love-ravaged people of the town—"Women, more especially,—in the continually recurring trials of wounded, wasted, wronged, misplaced, or erring and sinful passion" (263). She "assured them, too," that "in Heaven's own time" the "ground" of gender relations would be replaced by something better, happier, and asexual. A woman unburdened by "sin," "shame," or "sorrow" will reveal the way to be "happy" through "ethereal . . . joy" rather than in the expression of any kind of erotic desire (263). In so prophesying Hester gives the love-crossed no hope for relief from their current misery.

Hester resorts to a discourse of religious sentimentality to "remedy" an insidious and symptomatic political problem, and mainly addresses women—whom, as we have seen, are the traditional figures for "the governed" in the language of Puritan politics. Because "woman" refers both to a gender and a position in a legal hierarchy, the meanings of love and gender in this passage extend to other vital areas of desire and social association as well. First, Hester's "rediscovery" of America is marked not by the hegemony of state law but rather by the citizen's voluntary application of the discipline she had been previously impressed to perform. The monumental patriarchs, like the law's letter, exist mainly as points of reference for citizens seeking to know the law under which they operate—and here is the origin of the National Symbolic, whose inheritance of the A's function will be addressed in the next section, on "The Custom-House." But social discipline is transformed, at the close of *The Scarlet Letter*, into an effect of autobiographical example and personal persuasion. Thus Hester's language of sacred love transfigures the official rhetoric of love's obligations.

Second, her shift to sentimentality can also be read as the assertion of literary law over that of official culture. The law of literature is no less textual than the state juridical apparatus—still circulating around Hester's A, in the popular imagination. It is hardly less patriarchal, as we see in the litany of adjectives describing the general tendency of female desire to damage and to be damaged. The distinction of literary law from the law that has historically demarcated the public sphere is in its preservation of the category of the utopian, which has been vanquished from "history" time and again, in its inevitable disappointments. Preserving the utopian in *The Scarlet Letter* means preserving the hope that ethics and politics might merge—at least in the textual instance of political fantasy the novel donates to America. The utopian is also the discourse that protects the dignity of sexual desire—but here by keeping the erotic out of the public sphere altogether. Juridico-ethical standards and sexual desire were the two related areas of vulnerability in early Puritan culture: on Hester's return they appear to be only immanent categories, future projections of private interest, not patriarchal tools. This difference between Puritan and the narrator's rhetoric and values is apparent throughout the novel, but only in this final moment does the narrator obliterate and erase the "realities" of the other mode.

In "Another View of Hester" Hester imagined a post-apocalyptic world as the foundation for justice, although she could not say what agency would bring about this transfiguration. Now she again learns that love is the Word. But this is a different love. She is no longer interested in theorizing justice but rather imagines "a surer ground of mutual happiness." She no longer imagines society but instead speaks abstractly, about an indistinct future moment brought about by a "lofty, pure, and beautiful" female individual. She no longer convenes collective identity within the public sphere of discourse and exchange (the marketplace), but rather convenes in the home's safe space atomized subjects possessed by individual sorrows. Only the state's laws occupy the public sphere; the "people" has been disbanded and reconstituted apolitically as victims and agents of thwarted desire. Significantly, each of these spaces is homosocial, unerotic, disembodied into distinctions between the "heart" and the "law."

The disciplinary effect of Hester's domestic activity is nonetheless to preserve the idea of law, to repress the potential eruption of female antinomian energy, to encourage women/citizens to read the present tense as their reality, fundamentally invulnerable to historical time. On the other hand, these conversations within the home are, at the end of the novel, the only remaining places where historical narrative and social fantasy might be transmitted. As lovers, in this novel, women are uniquely literate in the ways of private affect and popular vernacular. As "citizens," women transform this female material into the popular form of utopian speculation. This speculation, while originating in love-talk, becomes in Hester Prynne's voice a fantasy of a future collective existence. We have seen this pattern, in which official history merges with folk-knowledge in the minds of female storytellers, as a paradigm moment of cultural nationalism in *Seven Tales of My Native Land*. This female-popular-private source of national narrative is also central to *The House of the Seven Gables*. It is, and is not, necessary for the maintenance of patriarchal law; it is, and is not, an instance of autonomous female political theory. But as the guardian of desire and hope for future justice, the domesticated institution of women's consciousness is crucial to Hawthorne's critical revision of American national identity.

Finally, the recuperation of the State in *The Scarlet Letter*, which starts with the judges' inadequacy and ends with affirmation of the state and its representatives, takes place through its symbolic translation in the novel's love plot, a plot that serves both to expose the corruption of the law and to preserve that law from the anarchical tamperings of its desiring agents—ministers, needleworkers, physicians, and judges. Playing politics in the language of love allows the narrator to inscribe the "outline" of his story on the body, separating it from the law and scapegoating it, so that the individual characters suffer and die while the state, flawed as it is, might continue as a realm of theory through which circulates the utopian desires of individual and collective subjects.

At the end of the novel, after the government celebrates its own reinstallation (yet again), the narrator shifts his attention to another potentially political scene—the death of Dimmesdale, followed by the figurative and real death of Chillingworth. Yet the termination of the fathers' lives does not produce joy on the narrator's part. Instead, in conclusion, he embarks on a meditation on the body, insisting that the citizen's body must be available to the law, in an intimate relation of desire and violence. The moral he puts forth, that to be "true" is to "[s]how freely to the world . . . some trait whereby the worst may be inferred!" exhorts the citizen/reader to donate her/his body to public intelligibility (260). From the point of view of this maxim, the narrative aims to install a memory of the consequences that persons, citizens, and states suffer when the subject insists on her/his physical and psychic opacity or autonomy from the community. Dimmesdale and Chillingworth finally join Hester by bringing their bodies into the public gaze as registers of the law: after the narrator sees the scarlet letter perform its offices, he turns to his own body as well.

> The reader may choose among these theories. We have thrown all the light we could acquire upon the portent, and would gladly, now that it has done its office, erase its deep print out of our own brain; where long meditation has fixed it in very undesirable distinctness. (259)

Throughout the novel, the narrator has taken strategic positions on behalf of staging a national memory that understands historically the vexed relations between utopia and the law. He has critiqued the excesses of patriarchal, political, and personal desire that have marked the Puritan/American project, while preserving the utopian impulse that motivated the juridicalism of the colony and the nation. Central to his critique and to his identification with utopian fantasy is the "problem" of the body. It requires protection from violation, and it requires discipline. He has made observations about how to adjudicate these different claims but is never observed participating in the political "necessity" for which he argues—in contrast to the way other Hawthornean narrators of this period materialize in their texts. But at the end of *The Scarlet Letter* the narrator inscribes himself within the time and space of the text and therefore of the nation. He does this not as an abstract citizen but by embodying his ungendered flesh.

The status of this body is ambiguous, for all we "see" is the "brain" that has meditated on the "portent." One might argue that the narrator's brain is a mere abstraction, like the great "heart" of humanity. But its painful materiality suggests that the "brain" is the narrator's body, and the agent of his social practice. Specifically, the body's sensual memory here registers the narrator's affiliation with other national subjects. Physical proximity to Hester Prynne and to the tattered A centuries later, produces a burning feeling that links disparate persons sensually together, even as it signifies the boundaries or limits of their bodies. The confluence of official and counter-memory, through the synchronous sensations of different bodies, invokes the "simultaneity" of national existence over time and despite the shifting boundaries of the American map.[32] Thus *The Scarlet Letter* moves beyond a Revolutionary War model of American citizenship that requires historical amnesia and the repression of the body. The narrator's revision of the National Symbolic foregrounds discomfort, (self-)consciousness, and a feeling of physical intimacy with the other subjects whose memories and dreams derive from the same collective knowledge. By calling the A a "portent" the narrator installs *The Scarlet Letter* itself as a utopian fantasy, which is also deeply physical, social, and national, as in the utopian speculations of Dimmesdale and Prynne. Americans, like lovers, occupy a self-consecrated space: like utopia, this space is personal and abstract. These likenesses, in their "electric chain" (153), provide an argument for seeing knowledge, memory, and critical consciousness as metonyms for the "body" with which citizens, affiliated in the abstract, must learn to know their nation.

FOUR *The Nationalist Preface*

THE SCARLET A IS NOT *THE SCARLET LETTER*, AND THE
properties of one can not be assumed to characterize the other. When the scarlet A is "elected" to fulfill an "office," it is chosen because of the magistrates' and ministers' belief in the force of bodily inscription to recast the person as citizen. To the state, the A represents the crime and the punishment not only for the criminal herself, but also for the readers of her body/text, who are themselves conscripted into conscience by the sight and memory of the letter. Thus, as I have argued, while the criminal experiences punishment directly on the body, the state theorizes the proper citizen's "body" as an abstraction constituted by a certain configuration of knowledge and memory, as in the case of the narrator's "brain" (259). We have seen that the A creates sensations and memories wherever it goes, eventually adulterating the public "imagination" (69) in excess of what the law intended. Whatever ambiguity of content the A comes to embody, however, the letter's formal function is always to represent the possible confluence of the juridical and the utopian impulses of civil life.

But *The Scarlet Letter* opens out onto a post-utopian field. The terrain of the Puritan community, marked by the monuments of death and crime, testifies to a crisis in the state's mode of authority: while official symbolic forms of juridico-political life have become the "realities" of conscience and collective identity (59), the unsanctioned materials of archaic, affective, and popular knowledge—which I condense in the category "counter-memory"—are exiled from value, though not from activity, within the political public sphere. The narrator of *The Scarlet Letter* charges that the Puritan fathers were hypocrites in their management of this material: for by repudiating the nonofficial consciousness of the person, "the people," or the "folk," the Fathers constitute counter-memory as such as a threat not only to the state's authority, but also to the political-utopian linkage that the Puritan state promises. The condensation in "*s*carlet *l*etter" of both the "*s*editious *l*ibel" tatooed on the Puritan dissenter William Prynne and the A stitched to Hester is one of many ways the novel reveals a connection between erotic, political, and utopian urges. But because the Puritan fathers can not "know" themselves except as they appear officially—on behalf of a juridical

politics of "love"—the ongoing needs, desires, and memories that motivate them personally *and* politically remain undisciplined, and threaten to undermine the Puritan paradise of law.

In order to imagine the preservation of the political-utopian promise, *The Scarlet Letter* anatomizes the Puritan state, tracing the law's theoretical failure to its reliance on the discretion—the political and erotic self-discipline and self-knowledge—of the patriarch. In the end, the narrator imagines a realm that separates utopian fantasy from political activity, preserving textually their centrality to collective identity while nonetheless reconstructing them as separate strands of social life. Utopian fantasy (both personal and corporate) is exiled to the world of female counter-memory; politics is limited to the patriarchal world of "government by law, not men," where masculine affect is suppressed in order to preserve patriarchal political authority.

But the novel's mode of resolution aims not to provide a literary remedy for the Puritan inability to forge a positive link of the utopian and the political, thus prescribing for the present tense a new utopian-American "law." Nor does it merely propose a genealogy of the way the citizen's body has been gendered/regulated on America's behalf. The investigation of Puritan political identity in *The Scarlet Letter* establishes both techniques and precedents for understanding the modern American citizen—as s/he adjudicates official and private forms of historical memory and the utopian impulse toward intimacy that marks both erotic and political desire.[1] But now many official and unofficial historical horizons implicate the citizen's consciousness and loyalty. These are the lineaments of Puritan culture and the Revolutionary War era, each marked by the claim that it is the temporal and ideological "origin" of America. Each of these "American origins" has produced, by the time of "The Custom-House," its own symbolic and practical political conventions, and each sanctions a mnemotechnique that valorizes specific values. The fact of this double historical heritage creates a crisis for Hawthorne: we have seen, in *The Scarlet Letter*, the complexities of constructing citizenship within one dominant logic of collective identity, and in "The Custom-House," citizenship is so much more multiply determined. In Hawthorne's mind, the Revolutionary War dominates the symbolic sphere of official American culture, circa 1850, while Puritan history is now, ironically, retrievable only through counter-memory. Thus here as elsewhere Hawthorne does not set up an antinomy between a public/political sphere and private/autonomous existence. The A that circulates memory and amnesia, sensation and disembodiment within and between "The Custom-House" and *The Scarlet Letter* makes fantastic maps from such distinctions. It would, then, seem unlikely that these two political-utopian American "spaces of time" might converge in an intelligible national identity, and yet in "The Custom-House," as in *The Scarlet Letter*, Hawthorne uses the copresence of transitional historical moments as foundational national *topoi*.

As "The Custom-House" represents American history, the modern national memory is marked more by lack and discontinuity than utopian plentitude. The "man" of 1850 (Hawthorne does not theorize *la citoyenne* here, an absence to which we shall return) spans a number of contemporary spaces and systems (for example, the home and the workplace; federal and transcendentalist cultures) and inherits a variety of pasts, none of which are experienced by him as a "whole" context, either in the present tense or in memory. This signals a dilemma of national magnitude: for if America is unable to maintain a comprehensive political/symbolic space, then political affiliation and personal memory become merely localized formations.[2] Paradoxically, Hawthorne designates the Revolutionary War as a major source of the nation's faulty memory: this is paradoxical because the Revolution is seen conventionally as the historical fulfillment of the providential promise to unite the political and utopian in the nation. In *The Scarlet Letter* the ideological, historical, and semiotic shallowness of modern Americans is seen as an effect of the way Revolutionary War rhetoric produced national consent through the idea of American exceptionality, which justified collective egotism; in turn, "The Custom-House" presents the post-revolutionary elision of the Puritans as an empirical, not ideological, phenomenon. Hawthorne writes that many of the official documents of Puritan culture, which could have provided diverse commentary on the surviving anecdotes and images left to the nation by the Puritan "forefathers," were purloined by the British during the Revolution. This simple cause produces devastating effects on national culture. But as we will see, Hawthorne's credulous historiography sets up the reader for more subtle and savage analyses of the way post-Revolutionary War official culture misrepresents the national-utopian promise it has made to "the people."

The loss of the Puritan primary texts has two main effects on national memory. The first effect, as I suggested in the previous chapter, is that the Revolutionary War here represents not an event in the continuity of American history but a discursive rupture, a false beginning. In addition, the destruction of the archive means that the records of "our" Puritan heritage, of the law's efficacy and its trials, come mainly from nonofficial sources like custom, oral history, and journals. Americans are forced to glean prenational American history from the shifting eyes, half-ideas, and distorted memories of individuals and the traditions of "folk" history. Hawthorne himself suggests that only his personal heritage splices his consciousness to the pre-national past, and only tenuously at that: despite having himself inserted the "w" into "Hathorne," he still affirms the continuity of the patriarchal name, and the traditional habitation of Salem by the Ha(w)thornes as his only links to the Puritans, in the absence of official signs—that is, until he finds the A.

Two hundred years after its construction, the ragged A still has the power to make a political subject feel compelled to wear it, "involuntarily" (32). Like a Puritan, Hawthorne "seems" to be burnt by the A he assumes. But as a result of the A's supernatural power he loses control of his senses, his body: "it seemed to me, then, that I experienced a sensation not altogether physical, yet almost so" (32). He also loses his irony: "the reader may smile, but must not doubt my word" (32). He loses his patriarchal memory; he becomes newly embodied and abstracted. Yet the sudden collapse of his sureties shows that Hawthorne is also a post-Revolutionary War American, contained in a modern vernacular totally other to the patrifocal one he also owns as his "national" inheritance. The double consciousness we witness when the A destabilizes the pre- and post-revolutionary national identity Hawthorne carries is not simply a condition of contradiction. Here Citizen Hawthorne is the product of stress between technically and ideologically divergent modes of political-utopian discipline and desire.

While "The Custom-House" has been widely read as the self-expression of a person—an embattled artist or a frustrated politician—it can also be read as a study in the genealogy of national identity, as it discloses the variety of historical forms that descend on America, in 1850. In this chapter I will consider "Hawthorne" as the experimental "subject" of national identity.[3] He depicts on his own and on others' bodies the various logics of modern American citizenship: here, as in *The Scarlet Letter*, Hawthorne designates the citizen's body as America's permanent archive, a palimpsest that carries the (dis)figurations of the many "moments" past and present that converge on the modern subject. By establishing modern citizenship as a species of deformity and denaturalization, "The Custom-House" exhibits both a negative and positive nationalism. It aims to continue the genealogy of state indiscretion we find in *The Scarlet Letter*, by exposing the shameful official mechanisms or mnemotechniques of federal nationalism. The preface also continues the novel's focus on the state's effect on citizens—

especially "official" citizens, Americans who have made a profession out of being Americans and who therefore magnify and make public the popular operation of political ideology. As in *The Scarlet Letter* proper, these "official" citizens are men who enjoy the privilege of a patriarchal, homosocial sphere of political life.

But while the preface betrays the costs of national practices and forms of symbolic self-reproduction, it also tries to resurrect the utopian promise of "America." National identity, for all its limitations, liberates the subject from his otherwise hopelessly local affiliations, including the genealogical ties to space and time—to Salem, to the Ha(w)thorne family history there—that impinge painfully on his consciousness and his imagination. But there are limits to this path of rescue: if the crisis to which Hawthorne here responds is one where national amnesia, unconsciousness, half-knowledge, and state responsibility for these various incapacities characterize the effects of the National Symbolic, then the revised place of utopian projection must not simply liberate the subject from his local, practical, bodily, and familial experience and knowledge. It must not censor memory and the common forms of historicity that mark labor and domestic activity. America is theoretical proof that a political system might bring utopian standards into its historical realm; but can utopia be equally infused with the historicity and contradictions of politics and of everyday life? Citizen Hawthorne, struggling to remember his pasts and negotiate his current horizon, puts pressure on literature to render such a utopia for the American citizen at large—the "reader" with whose "rights" he is terribly concerned (4). Here he tries, as *The Scarlet Letter* differently tries, to install counter-memory within the consciousness of national culture. We will see, given his critique of the physical and psychic corruptions of national identity, whether the mnemotechniques of the utopian literary text can make an author a national hero.

I Pledge Allegiance to the Flag

As we approach the Custom-House, we are situated in a suspended landscape, at the intersection of modernity's gaze and history's inscription on the territory. This spatial suspension shares with

"Alice Doane's Appeal" and *The Scarlet Letter* a pedagogic function. In "Alice Doane's Appeal" the defamiliarization of the landscape was a strategic move on the narrator's part. There, he reconfigures the view from Gallows Hill over the vast expanse of Essex's domestic and commercial "prosperity" by finding that one undeveloped spot from which American consciousness could emerge anew while remaining in the realm of history. Here, we see the same landscape as in "Alice Doane's Appeal," but "with Gallows Hill and New Guinea at one end, and a view of the alms-house at the other" (8). Prosperity is no longer in the picture. While, as in the early tale, Hawthorne aims to give "a faint representation of a mode of life not heretofore described" (4), now the "life" here is more complicated, for there is no spot unsaturated with personal, regional, national, even international meanings.

Proximity to *The Scarlet Letter* leads, in addition, to a greater clarity about the cultural context in which Hawthorne articulates the citizen's national identity in "The Custom-House." We have shown that the novel opens twice, to establish both the variety and the noncoherence of the contexts in which we are to understand the relation of Hester Prynne and the law she configures: but the narrator of *The Scarlet Letter* depicts with great clarity the points of view he brings into the narrative gaze. In contrast, our Custom-House guide simply stutters as he leads our eyes toward the Custom-House:

> In my native town of Salem, at the head of what, half a century ago, in the days of old King Derby, was a bustling wharf,—but which is now burdened with decayed wooden warehouses . . . —at the head, I say, of this dilapidated wharf, which the tide often overflows, and along which, at the base and in the rear of the row of buildings, the track of many languid years is seen . . . —here, with a view from its front windows . . . stands a spacious edifice of brick. (4–5)

The building organizes our visual experience of the wharf. Like Hester and the A she wears, the brick house arrests the movement of our eyes, and of the guide's stuttering narrative. Its ocular power is reinforced as the point of view shifts within the passage, when our gaze is matched by the "view from its front windows." Yet while Hawthorne can see the Custom-House, he can barely describe it for the history it evokes. "A spacious edifice of brick" edifies us, if we can see it: as a victim of the periodic tides; a longtime site of commodity exchange; an expanse in which cultural contact between nations takes place officially, as Salem stands in for America in its capital interchange with Africa, South America, or India (6, 29); a regional home of federal hegemony; the narrator's politically abandoned home, and his newfound literary abode. Struggling to honor this cluster of meanings, the narrator's only clear statement about the House situates it in America's negative, post-utopian heritage: "[n]either the front nor the back entrance of the Custom-House opens on the road to Paradise" (13).

The Custom-House tests our competence at national consciousness. As the reader/tourist first approaches it, s/he is confronted by a generic "spacious edifice of brick" ornamented by different forms of the American flag, "with the thirteen stripes turned vertically, instead of horizontally," and we are supposed to know, without thinking about it, that "a civil, and not a military post of Uncle Sam's government, is here established" (5). Here, Hawthorne conjoins the technical operation of the national icon and its subtle creation of national subjectivity. In this trivial detail about the flag's position, we see the nation; we see that within the nation there is a civil apparatus and a military apparatus, mutually distinguished by the same flag; we "know" that certain positions of the cloth (its horizontal or vertical direction) are politically significant, whereas others (whether the flag "floats or droops") are not, and we feel casually familial with this information, in the way that we might with an uncle (5). There is nothing fascinating about this information: it is a priori to the national subject.[4] Thus the placement of this flag at the first internal post of this narrative formally transports us to the space of having "already read" the sign we encounter: this translation of the reader to the time and space of national identity is a major aim of the National Symbolic, as I have previously argued. And yet the implantation of national consciousness remains obscure, even as we experience its operation. The riddle of national consciousness takes on mythic intensity in

Hawthorne's self-characterization as a sybil, the enigmatic source of the national future whose truths were both crucial and inaccessible to the audience to which they were addressed.[5]

In contrast to this minor, banal, unconscious renewal of our formal acquaintance with the American flag, comes another invocation of a central icon: the American eagle. Constituted as the national bird at the formal inception of the nation (at the Continental Congress in 1782), this eagle also hovers over the Custom-House and thus over the narrative, but this time not as a benign site of national self-identification. Its malignity derives from a number of different sources. It has been widely noted that this eagle brings into the text a gratuitous, and therefore crucial, gender difference. Hawthorne asserts that he has been betrayed, seduced by this emblem: the kind of idolatry that encourages "many people" to seek "to shelter themselves under the wing of the federal eagle; imagining . . . that her bosom has all the softness and snugness of an eiderdown pillow" has also, at one time, characterized him. She is unnatural: "oftener soon than late," the eagle/mother "is apt to fling off her nestlings with a scratch of her claw, a dab of her beak, or a rankling wound from her barbed arrows" (5). Although we later learn that the patriarchal political patronage system is really the source of Hawthorne's political decapitation, Hawthorne here places the blame on American iconography itself. Figured as a mother and not a forefather, it seduces him into the comfortable fantasy that he belongs to a family (unlike his own parthenogenic patriarchal one, as he imagines it) that will embrace and nurture him with its immortality, which is also the immortality of the "nation" as constituted in providential history. Membership in this "family" also naturalizes his rightful and inalienable inheritance of state power.

In revenge, Hawthorne works to defamiliarize both the icon and the vast realm of iconicity, with its familial pretensions.

> Over the entrance hovers an enormous specimen of the American eagle, with outspread wings, a shield before her breast, and, if I recollect aright, a bunch of intermingled thunderbolts and barbed arrows in each claw. (5)

Hawthorne says that the Custom-House eagle holds in her talons both "thunderbolts and barbed arrows." Yet he indicates that he might not recollect the statue aright and, strategically, he doesn't—the "real" statue actually holds one bunch of arrows in one set of talons, and an olive branch in the other.[6]

The political icon typically operates as a stable signifier, one that generates meaning while standing outside the play of interpretation. The icon contains the history of its prior uses as a sign of imperial power—in Imperial Rome, say—but its form veils the history of its function. Moreover, no force of memory or misuse can make the American Eagle a generic eagle, because by definition "American Eagle" is a figure denaturalized in the service of political continuity. Indeed, the Eagle transfers to the nation its own translation from nature to artifice: as the bird's iconic value inheres in its promise of federal immortality, it demonstrates the "necessity" to extract the federal apparatus from history, its "organic" source. This process of abstraction, while not always involving the extrication of signs from Nature, is crucial to the effectivity of the National Symbolic. Likewise, the federal icon transcends local political oppositions (notably the contemporary Whig-Democrat struggle), and yet constitutes these struggles as well—for it represents the ultimate booty (the winner gets access to the icon's monumental power). But the omnipresence of the icon also provides reassurance that local squabbles take place, in a sense, inside the utopian-American domain, the fundamental sovereignty of which is immune to petty struggles over "representation."

This confusion of effects plays itself out on the "manly character" (39) of the "official" men made iconic by the hypostatizing power of the Custom-House, boring "one another with the several thousandth repetition of old sea-stories, and mouldy jokes, that had grown to be pass-words and countersigns among them" (14). Hawthorne's depictions of his fellow patriarchs are famously acerbic. But they are also sentimental. For as we shall see, the universal infantilization of these old soldiers in the bosom of the patronage system, where they reduce all language to the baby talk of military codes, marks them as citizen-victims betrayed by too great an identification with the political order they serve.

The Psychopathology of "Official Life"

General Miller, the aged and infirm Collector of the Custom-House, provides the most complex example of the effects of national service. Doubly immersed in the state's military force and its civil power, the general is completely caught in his own abstract national historicity, and at the same time reproduces a painfully parodic version of the play between memory, amnesia, and identity that marks the dominant national character, as filtered through the National Symbolic. As his body decays, his memory of his historical eminence petrifies him in his moment of glory, within the "evolutions of the parade; the tumult of the battle; the flourish of old, heroic music, heard thirty years before" (23). Miller's disability is not simply a function of old age. His national bond has apparently always sundered him into at least three "persons": in his civil role, he approximates the Puritan fathers' "stubborn and ponderous . . . integrity"; as a military man, "his spirit imparted its triumphant energy"; and "in his heart" he holds an "innate kindliness," even "a young girl's appreciation of the floral tribe" (22–23). Unfortunately, this "heart" has not had much "official" use: his patriarchal, state-identified, "masculine character" (22) has almost entirely "obscured" his counter-memory, the nonofficial aspects of his character that, Hawthorne surmises, might otherwise "impart resemblance" between him and other human beings (22).

In magnifying in his person the evisceration of the overcredulous national subject—"transfigured," like Dimmesdale and the other patriarchs, into a body with an "official" name, like an A—General Miller also embodies the futility of any citizen's attempt to merge in a seamless continuity her/his personal and national memory. Hawthorne likens the General to a fort, "Old Ticonderoga" (21–22). He has written a tale about this fort, titled "Old Ticonderoga, A Picture of the Past,"[7] which provides an important gloss on Hawthorne's reading of the general's painfully literal "national identity." This tale, like "Alice Doane's Appeal," addresses the problem latter-day Americans face of achieving a vital and vitalizing national subjectivity, once again using the distinction between abstract knowledge and sensual experience to map out the crucial sites for transfiguration. But in contrast to "Alice Doane," "Old Ticonderoga" does not involve projecting the national problematic of readership onto an inadequate female audience: here Hawthorne volunteers a semblance of his own consciousness as the object of experiment.

Once meaningful to the nation's preservation, Fort Ticonderoga now decays physically and in memory. The history-seeking narrator of this tale proposes that the analogy between physical decay and the decay of national memory can be attributed to two factors: the "veritable naming frenzy"[8] of American culture, which obscures the signs through which one might "know" the past, and the difficulty of reproducing historical "experience" even by physically occupying the landscape made sacred by prior cultural activity. But how else might one apprehend an event that has already happened? The always posterior position of the citizen who desires contact with her/his culture's infinitely receding scenes motivates visits to America's mnemonic "national" sites. In this particular instance, the visit produces a solution to national amnesia quite different than the recourse to monumentality that closes "Alice Doane's Appeal."

> Those celebrated heights, Mount Defiance and Mount Independence, familiar to all Americans in history, stand too prominent not to be recognized, though neither of them precisely correspond to the images excited by their names. In truth, the whole scene, except the interior of the fortress, disappointed me. Mount Defiance, one pictures as a steep, lofty, and rugged hill, of most formidable aspect, frowning down with the grim visage of a precipice on old Ticonderoga, is merely a long and wooded ridge; and bore, at some former period, the gentle name of Sugar Hill. (11: 186)

The narrator tries to bridge two gaps: first the discursive space between the Bunyanesque names whose power has attracted him to this spot and the look of the spot itself, and second the physical decay of the actual fort from its prior majesty. The mountains "Independence" and "Defiance" are like the "General": official names, motivated by historic events that transformed the "meaning" of the landscape, obliterate folk-names and the memories that would accompany a more "gentle" life. "Sugar Hill" is not pronounced a more authentic name than its military replacements: it is simply the sign of a prior history and a distinct discourse that refers to a different epoch—with which it shares, nonetheless, an inclination to neutralize other pasts by nominally revising the landscape, which is otherwise "too prominent not to be recognized."

Confused and startled by the landscape's inadequacy to "the images excited by their names," the narrator is further shaken by the fort's disrepair. A fellow tourist from West Point then verbally reconstructs the fort, providing "the meaning of every ditch, and . . . an entire plan of the fortress from its half-obliterated lines" (11: 187). The narrator is unsatisfied with the geometrical approach to reconstruction, even though it is probably more "accurate" than anything he might construct. Instead, he prefers to think, as many a Hawthornean narrator does, of "a series of pictures" (11: 190) using the historical material he carries around in his memory, involving the Revolutionary War efforts of Amherst, Burgoyne, and Ethan Allen. In short, in "Old Ticonderoga," a citizen's subjectivity, distressed and defamiliarized by the National Symbolic so fundamental to his map of the world, is consoled by the imaginative reconstruction of other American subjects (made "American" by their importance in the production of the national narrative), who are also depicted negotiating the deceptively accessible terrain of the "national." It consoles this narrator to think of "pictures" rather than monuments, personal names rather than place-names, and "poetry" rather than "mathematics" (11: 186–87), as the founts of national identity. Finding the real thing less iconic than he needs it to be, historic names and places enable him to rewrite "the lapse of time and change of circumstances" (11: 191) according to "the motives and modes of passion" (33) that make them resemble "private" individuals, like himself.

Yet at the end of "Old Ticonderoga," the narrator is wrenched out of his imaginative engagement with this consecrated spot by the tolling of a bell. This bell, "given by the steam-boat Franklin," forces him to return to the scene of his present "realities"—the word that also describes Hester Prynne's consciousness of her imprisonment within the law. And what are his realities? "The whole country was a cultivated farm" (11: 191). The narrator has been called back to the law of post-revolutionary America, by reminders of two of its forefathers: Benjamin Franklin (who made a famous military expedition to Champlain) and Thomas Jefferson, of the cultivated farm. The intensity of the nation's martial triumph has been eclipsed by its even more intense political merger of Enlightenment reason and utopian capitalism.

The monumental symbolics of American military activity are, in this tale as in "The Custom-House," vanquished by the subliminal omnipresence of American property and commodity interests (categories in which inhere our inherent "rights") "to return no more, or only at some dreamer's summons" (11: 191). Here we see the flexibility of the national mnemotechnique. As the land is named and renamed, in a partial reminder of a national past, as the courageous activity of a set of soldier-politicians comes down to the entrepreneurial presence of one "Mr. Pym" and the military theory of the West Point man, the consciousness of the generic national subject/tourist is the site of nationally induced self-erasure. Post-revolutionary America transfigures the very conditions of its own production, in the creation of a mass of decayed part-objects that stand in for the transhistorical whole nation.

General Miller, alone among the mass of Custom-House cretins, is a tragic figure: stubbornly immersed in the past, at the point when his identification with the nation was at its most intense, he acts in staunch loyalty to the idea of America while refusing its strategy of historical self-occultation. Thus it is not only the Revolutionary War that ruptures what would be the "natural" narrative continuity of American history and consciousness. Rather, by linking General Miller with "Old Ticonderoga" Hawthorne suggests that the "official" American practice of self-burial under an avalanche of names and "New Laws" is a fundamentally nationalist gesture, vital to constructing America and its political-utopian "present tense" (see chap. 1). This strategic use of temporal abstraction is also, as we have seen, something Hawthorne's contemporary society shares with the dreaded Puritans.

It is ironic that the practice of self-erasure on behalf of the national "realities" provides a crucial linkage within American culture, since it also causes the very shallowness that marks the minds of the Custom-House officials. Totally saturated by national memory, yet they have no sense of history: for this requires an ability to occupy both the past and present. Thus the condensation of the national subject into one or another kind of smallness of mind is simultaneously the "normal," inevitable effect of psychic union with the nation and, in Hawthorne's view, a pathological result of this alliance. In this state-sponsored fusion of the normal and the pathological the Custom-House men are akin to Dimmesdale and Hester, lawful and mad on the scaffold.

Hawthorne experiences the distressing linkage of national identity and pathology viscerally. Reading a moral in the body/text of General Miller and the other desiccated patriarchs, he "endeavoured to calculate how much longer I could stay in the Custom-House, and yet go forth a man" (39–40). Is the "man" here the abstract "human" citizen named by the Constitution or a gendered, embodied subject?[9] It has been argued that Hawthorne is most like Hester when he is an Author of Art;[10] but we can see that his corporeal experience of the law brings him closest to her. We remember that too close identification with the law exhausted Hester's femininity: the narrator says that years of toting the state's A has made her unintelligible as a woman (163–66). But this analysis of Hester's gender takes place not with reference to the sex which brings sexual difference into play, but rather in the narrator's discussion of Hester's traitorous political theory. Conventions of gender representation mark love plots in *The Scarlet Letter*, but also position subjects as citizens with respect to the Puritan state. This is to say that gender discourse works in the novel to link the body of the sexual subject to the body of the citizen, and thus provides important information about *how* individuals get caught up in collective affiliations, both of the romantic and political kind. By the same logic, official service, sexual difference, and subjectivity intersect in "The Custom-House" such that the codes and conventions of gender representation figure considerably in Hawthorne's anatomy of national citizenship.

Hawthorne's federally inspired loss of power echoes *The Scarlet Letter*'s depiction of what happens to Hester, when she relies on the law's "iron arm" (78). Hawthorne, like "every individual who . . . leans on the mighty arm of the Republic," loses his "own proper strength," "the capability of self-support" (38). This is the abstract language of citizenship: "individuals" lose their dignity by depending on the state. But quickly this relation of dependence leaks into gender codes. The "proper strength" of the official man apparently resides in his sex: just as Hester becomes a non-woman by her intimacy with and submission to the sovereignty of the law, so too Hawthorne fears devoted citizenship might unman him. Of course, such a release from the (gendered) body into abstract identity is, in theory, an emancipatory effect of national citizenship: the citizen's right to self-sovereignty is a priori, not a function of what an individual is or does. In Hawthorne's case, however, emancipation from the body into national identity produces potentially debilitating contradictions. First, his access to family and national history depends on his patronymic identification: by wanting to gain "public notice" like his male ancestors, he means to reproduce in his own time a semblance of their privilege, which was constructed by the cultural dominance of the patriarchal analogy in Puritan culture—but *in theory* this mode of disseminating power no longer obtains in a republican state.

Yet clearly Hawthorne's masculinity was a crucial relay to power in the American political public sphere. Thus, like Dimmesdale, Hawthorne confronts the contradictory demands of state patriarchalism, which locates political power in a male body, while in theory privileging abstractions like the soul or the self. According to the logic of "The Custom-House," the patriarchal analogy works something like this, in 1850s Salem: the Custom-House appears to be an objective institution that exercises power not over people but over commodities and money. But as an arena for patronage, the House is also a repository of the state's power, where deserving male "children" get their rewards. The family romance of the state is, however, constituted not by a desire to create a secure domain for its children but by a desire to use systems associated with the family (a closed economy, nepotism, inheritance) to manage the kinds of desire (greed and ambition) at play in the way it distributes its resources—its goods and its sanction. Hawthorne satirizes the nepotism of the state for equating sons with servants, and satirizes the men who treat their position in the national family as sanctioned by natural right. He also chides himself for having relied on the pseudo-natural family to fulfill its historical and conventional promise to take care of those who participate in its economy, its patrilineage.

The parthenogenic fantasy of the patriarchal nation finds its Other in the figuration of woman/women in "The Custom-House." Women, in the preface, are aligned with the stuff of the quotidian, with counter-memory: the "magic" skill of cleaning women (7), the "mysteries" of woman's needlework (31), and even the "miscellaneous good" activities of Hester Prynne (32), are at once banalized and constitute a realm of value outside the exhausted patriarchal "sanctuary" (7) of the Custom-House and, presumably, the "state" of value whose borders it protects. The additional fact that the state is represented by an unnatural maternal animal (who also remains outside the House, eagle-eyed) suggests that while female figuration exposes the limits of patriarchal practices in this preface, it only constitutes figurative material for the "revolutionary" disruption—not destruction—of the male hegemonic order, or utopian America.[11] Here, as elsewhere, what looks like female strength is only figural, exotic, marginal—not *political* in any material sense. As we will see, Hawthorne's utopian reformulation of the means of national identity retains an alliance among a "patriarchal body" of men, whose presence in the National Symbolic is a central fact of American self-intelligibility (12). Patriarchalism remains fundamentally American, even as its ideology is made archaic by republicanism, and even as its pathology is played out on the bodies and minds of its official citizens, the superannuated heroes who work with Hawthorne.

"But who can see an inch into futurity, beyond his own nose!"

Hawthorne's response to this display of national, political, and patriarchal infirmity is not to exile himself from America, in body or mind. The extrication of a "person" from her/his national identity is not, in this text, a psychological possibility. In addition, as Nissenbaum has argued, Hawthorne's departure from the Custom-House was not only involuntary but powerfully resisted by Hawthorne, who here underplays the degree to which his transfiguration into a "politically dead man" by patronage politics distressed him (43).[12] Neither seeing the possibility for non-national identity, nor desiring to disidentify as such with the nation, Hawthorne's desire to become, punningly, "unaccustomed" (12) to the world of the Custom-House results in the construction of a strategy about how to protect the citizen from the state's apotropaic and atrophying iconic regime.

Simply, to become unaccustomed, Hawthorne leaves Salem. We have seen such a move before, in *The Scarlet Letter* and "Alice Doane's Appeal": a crisis in cultural intelligibility leads to a spatial solution; the shift in the terms of Hawthorne's map reproduces the aesthetics and politics of defamiliarization central to the project of critical nationalism which, I have argued, is the central cultural work in Hawthorne's American novels. In this section I will outline the way "The Custom-House" imagines the recuperation of national fantasy on behalf of a critical nationalism. As in *The Scarlet Letter*, Hawthorne here emphasizes transfigurations of form, of the nationalist mnemotechnique, rather than revisions of iconic or ideological content.

While Hawthorne parodies patriarchalism in "The Custom-House" (12–25), the historical eminence of male authority remains not a benign fact of, but a key relay between the American present and its many pasts, both political and economic, public and personal. But in order to revise the National Symbolic, Hawthorne revises the meaning and structure of patriarchy as well. He locates national identity not in the public record, which features the activity of patriarchal officials, but in the descent of the paternal name. To Hawthorne, the family name is polysemous: consistent and self-contradictory. He uses this name to signify both his broken and unbroken ties to the national past (9–11). Hathorne, the Puritan family name (undesignated in the preface), conjoins local, prenational, political, and personal history, along with linking Hawthorne to the history of patriarchal privilege. Ha*w*thorne, the modern name, includes the history descending from the Puritans, but also marks his modernity, his difference. It is clear he "identifies" with his ancestors, of whom he writes that "strong traits of their nature have intertwined themselves with mine" (10): but his distance from some of their political actions and notions ambiguates the intimacy of this identification. Identification with his own family name becomes a formal fact that implies nothing about closeness, distance, love, or ambivalence. In addition, his attitude toward his own past stands in for a new attitude toward his other "family" name, "American." Earlier I noted Hawthorne's citation of a breakdown in the official annals of American culture, due to the British destruction of the Puritan archive: Hawthorne's patrilineage not only gives him a sense of personal inheritance, but his "boyish imagination" (9) provides for the nation another archive and another mode of knowledge from which to gain material for the production of a historicized *and* utopian American heritage. The "personal" source of national knowledge in Hawthorne's own case stands for the material of counter-memory that, I have argued, is central to Hawthorne's revision of America's modes of self-consciousness.

The history of the Ha(w)thornes in America is a history of cultural amnesia, although the modes of forgetting change over time and according to the nature of the things disremembered. The Puritan Hathornes appear in the narrative annals of American history as agents of state-sponsored patriarchal and religious brutality, and for this Hawthorne feels the "curse" of his origin (10). He also thinks official history has done them a disservice, for they performed "good" acts that haven't been remembered in the nation's annals—because "good" acts do not usually constitute national "news." Later generations of Hathornes appear in the national narrative not at all, again because their private money-making vocation at sea and their familial identifications at home rendered them invisible, at least in the context of the political public sphere. Whatever his forefathers "were" in life, he identifies with them by means of an occupational genealogy: Hawthorne's focus on what his ancestors did for a living is a part of his general recasting of national history in the material that circulates through daily life, despite the effect (and the intention) of America's "great man/great event" narratives to bury most of the culture's activities "as old houses . . . get covered half-way to the eaves by the accumulation of new soil" (10).

The elevation of popular knowledge and everyday life to the canons of national history does not simply refer, therefore, to the history of great men: it is not just America's "forefathers" who count, but "my forefathers," who are also his "race" and "my great-grandsires" (10). Hawthorne's use of this language establishes that "forefathers" are not only men in the abstract with abstract privileges but men with bodies, who participated in the culture's foundational and scandalous "historic" events, plus "unmemorable" activity in everyday life, and also: biological reproduction. It is significant that Hawthorne speaks of his emancipation from Salem in the same breath with wishes for "my children" and their futures (11–12): his counter-memorial to national culture is embodied in these kinds of reproduction, and in them situates the motive for reviving national fantasy. But there are still no women in this reproductive economy—even no inkling of Sophia Hawthorne. Contra the current criticism, which argues for the primacy of motherhood and of Hawthorne's real-life relations with women in *The Scarlet Letter*, the simultaneous embodiment and male self-containment of procreation here reminds us that Hawthorne's linkage of bodies and cultural reproduction does not promote heterosocial love per se, or the family, or any purely local or private formation, but rather aims to vitalize their place in the production of national identity.[13] Thus counter-memory becomes linked to the authorial body and what it produces: texts, money, children, readers, citizens, and visions of the nation.

In short, Hawthorne demonstrates here a strong desire to reconfigure the conditions under which his descent within the nation (and the reader's, whose "rights" are a central concern here [4]) might be imagined, and then prophesied, projected into the future. He sets up a structural homology between the reader and the citizen: the shared text approximates the textuality of the National Symbolic and enacts the process of identity construction central to national self-linkage. Accordingly, he creates a literary mnemotechnique of national identity based on the knowledge, consciousness, and affective material of counter-memory—through what he might call the materials of the *new* "law of literary propriety" (27). His literary aim is thus national-utopian, but not in a simple way. Hawthorne deploys textually what Jameson calls "an aesthetic of cognitive mapping" through which the territory and its inhabitants might pass to realize the productivity of nationhood and citizenship.[14] The text as "space" becomes another native land, or political "territory," which can incorporate materials the nation has already gathered—from Puritan and other pre-revolutionary war cultures, political and literary texts and discourses—and materials from everyday life, which are generated faster than history can record. The realm in which these all mingle is neither for domestic comfort, nor a national "homeland," though. Instead it is a place—a National Symbolic—where citizen/readers must periodically go to witness the ongoing historicity of the objects of their collective knowledge. Only through such voluntary displacement can the subject be protected from the manipulation of political icons; only through identifying with the noncoherence of collective and personal experience can the national as a nexus of public fantasy be *meaningful.*

I do not mean that "The Custom-House" is an argument for art's superiority over politics, history, or the material world.[15] Neither is it simply an affirmation of "theory" over "practice": this is the offense of the transcendentalist philosophical-utopian "soap-bubble" (37) he deflates in the text with a sharpness that equals his derision of the federal state. The equivalence Hawthorne sets up between transcendentalism and the Custom-House is based not on their apparent difference but on the logic of exclusion on which each operates, their mutual repression of difference according to the logic of "perfect" "integrity" (24). Literature, in contrast, functions here as an arena of inclusion, speculation, and defamiliarization. The literary text—like the citizen's authorial body—becomes radically the archive of incongruous kinds of social materials, different modes of knowledge and memory, and the multiply determined positions that make up "perspective" within the collectively shared discourses of American society. As Hawthorne says about his own desires, he wanted to "mingle at once with men of altogether different qualities" (25), to "imbue [him]self with the nature of the other" (36). He wants to refertilize "the dead level of site and sentiment" as well, by so revitalizing the elements and the technology of the National Symbolic. By dismantling the opposition between the political public sphere and everyday life, Hawthorne imagines a new mode of national identity, a new individual and collective relation to knowledge, and, as we will see, a new body.

The theoretical map on which the re-production of the National Symbolic takes place is the "neutral territory, somewhere between the real world and fairy-land, where the Actual and the Imaginary may meet, and each imbue itself with the nature of the other" (36). Hawthorne's "neutral territory" is an allegory of his own social sensibility, a place where literary intellect might create counter-forms to those that ornament and inhabit the Custom-House. He "invests" these forms—objects in his writing-room whose value is constituted by their domestic daily use (the child's shoe, the doll, the hobby-horse)—with "dignity" (35). (Note that these writer's implements are not pens, paper, and portraits of authors, but signs of the authorial body's circulation in other domestic realms of desire, where children are reproduced.) Hawthorne implicitly opposes the *unheimlich* dignity, the "strangeness and remoteness" (35) of the children's objects, to the domestic and naturalized deformity wrought by the dominant National Symbolic.[16]

Ordinarily, these imaginative transfigurations lead to the "emoluments" (8) of literary activity every "romance-writer" creates—writing for profit (35). But the literary profit gained in the neutral territory is in the currency of absolute value, a value that transcends the chaos of material circulation and philosophical speculation. Indeed, one can read in Hawthorne's initial desire to reside there, as in the Custom-House, a wish that he, the "bad half-penny" (12) would be taken out of circulation, only to discover his full value. In this sense he aims to become an icon himself, the individual-as-eagle. Here I reproduce the conventional critical wisdom about the neutral territory: that it is an apolitical place of escape from the violence of political existence, which is also, for official men, the violence of everyday life.

Yet "The Custom-House" does not depict the neutral territory as politically "neutral." For one thing, the very dream of its existence contests the hegemony of the political public sphere, along with calling into question its value as the nexus of national fantasy. It is not simply the general "materiality of this daily life pressing so intrusively upon" Hawthorne (37) that dooms his attempt to suture post- to pre-revolutionary America by narrating the stitching on Hester Prynne's A. The life that has robbed "an entire class of susceptibilities" (36) from other Custom-House officials has robbed him as well: and this is the life of the "official" American, whose relation to every object and thought he has is "opaque," shrouded by the absorption of "the substance of to-day" in the ahistorical iconography of America (37). We can see the damage wrought by the political public sphere in the way official bodies are marked: Surveyor Pue's official "frizzle" and "apparel" (30), the "stain" of witch's blood on his ancestor's surviving bones (9), the infirm corpses of the Custom-House men, and, crucially, the burning A on Hawthorne's own body (32) become, here, some canonical texts of national identity.[17] Hawthorne's early discussion of the ethics of autobiography asserts explicitly that the dignity of the body is a right the reader should expect and demand from any communication: the neutral territory Hawthorne constructs for the reader/citizen operates according to the play of surfaces and reflections in light, shadows, and mirrors. This strategy of indirection and unfamiliarity does not violate the form of the thing but understands and embraces its indeterminacy as an object of knowledge. I would argue that, consistent with the rest of "The Custom-House" and *The Scarlet Letter*, the neutral territory is not simply an author's fantasy of the imagination's ideal state. It is also a citizen's prophecy of a utopian political space that would derive its intelligibility from a collective hermeneutic that honors internal difference and historical temporality. Even the territory itself is unstable, not there naturally or even for the asking: Hawthorne strains himself, "striving to picture forth" the space unsaturated by dominant cultural practices (35). The "neutral territory" is thus a contestant in the struggle over the status of objects, the meanings of words, and the autonomy of the citizen, in opposition to the mind-garbling, body-penetrating mnemotechnique of the United States. But it is also an instance of an emergent "form" of national identity. A territory that, by framing objects, produces new knowledge: but the knowledge and the territory (images refracted off objects, like signifiers off signifieds) are not in themselves concrete, material, available for possession. In the new National Symbolic, objects are willed into meaningful existence and then, as it were, run out of meaning once they have regenerated the citizen's mind. The short half-life of the new national semiotic works in dramatic contradistinction to the operation of the brain-searing A we have witnessed in *The Scarlet Letter*.

Hawthorne inherits the struggle to create a new mode of national identity after finding the scrap of Hester Prynne's A left by his "official ancestor," Surveyor Pue (33). Hawthorne conjures Pue in the tradition of Hamlet's ghostly father: the surveyor tests Hawthorne's loyalty to and love for patriarchy, demanding that he act in "consideration of my filial duty and reverence towards him" by making public his "lucubrations" on Hester Prynne (33). In addition, Pue leaves Hawthorne the confusion of public and private interest from which the linking of dominant and counter-memory takes place, as his "private" papers collected during "official" times signify a yet unarticulated space of fantasy, labor, and identification. Pue transmits to Hawthorne the official, patriarchal sanction to profit from his own, "neutral" night thoughts. Hawthorne could write neither Pue's Puritan tale nor the work that would "diffuse thought and imagination through the opaque substance of to-day" (37) while using "Uncle Sam's letter-paper" (27): more evidence of his need to occupy a counter-space (psychically, physically, discursively) to that authored by the nation, while still addressing the need for a national semiotic.

In Pue's exhortation, literature, national identity, and the counter-hegemonic merge. The result of this merger is a revitalized "paper" continuity with the past, and more than that as well. While the revolutionary claims that have marked American (a)historicity have resulted in gaps of official knowledge—which serve the interest of the modern state in representing itself as the *summa* of historical process—American literary history will survive in texts treasured by the "few who will understand" the sibylline utterances of the author (3) and, most crucially (from the point of view of national culture) in the popular imagination at large, which will have extracted from the texts a common set of characters. Rather than relying on the federal eagle to create a collectivity based on the incorporation of its ahistorical-utopian promise (the promise of the nation to lift its people outside of everyday life), the literary memory Hawthorne constructs is only viable in conjunction with everyday life—not as it exists, but *as it will be.* The imaginary, utopian nature of these popular-national fictions distinguishes them from populist articulations as such: he demonstrates here not a love for "the people" as a mass, but a desire for "the people" as a nation.[18]

Hawthorne's representation of this new "state" here, as ever, turns to the body as its index. This time, though, it is his own body that articulates the productive possibilities of cognitive mapping. To give himself the utopian "body" that his political crisis forces him to imagine, he kills himself into figuration, becoming alternatively "Irving's Headless Horseman," a "decapitated Surveyor," and the author of "The Town-Pump." From within these figures Hawthorne constructs a new law of literary temporality. As a mortal author he can be obliterated in the machinery of circulation, and as a mortal politician he can be guillotined because of his very access to power, but as a literary figure he "lives" as a nodal point of national identity—so long as he is put to use by the popular memory.

Hawthorne's similarity to "Irving's Headless Horseman," for example, is assigned to his "longing to be buried, as a politically dead man ought" (43). But the analogy with the Headless Horseman goes further: suspended in the discontinuities of history, the Headless Horseman always returns to the place of his death in the hope of reuniting himself with his head. In Irving, as in Hawthorne, he is spurred on by the fantasy that it is possible to return to a complete body, unspoiled by history. Hawthorne does the next best thing in conflating himself with Irving's character (already itself an "American" master-text derived from folk sources): truly a "literary figure," Hawthorne no longer produces literature, but is a production of it, outside of the cycle of life, decay, and death. Like the Headless Horseman, the decapitated Surveyor will be kept alive not as a monument of history books or a mark in a church register, but in the ceaseless production of American folktales, allusion, and gossip—like the federal eagle, he is a self-proclaimed Original American text. Unlike the eagle, however, the decapitated Surveyor derives his new power through narrative circulation, while the American eagle's force derives from its transcendence of local history, narrative, and desire.[19]

Likewise, the fantasy of the "Town-Pump" with which "The Custom-House" ends represents its central object as a "neutral territory" of a sort, condensed into an image. But here too the object gains social and historic value not in itself but insofar as it is a nodal point around which social circulation takes place.

> It may be, however,—O, transporting and triumphant thought!—that the great-grandchildren of the present race may sometimes think kindly of the scribbler of bygone days, when the antiquary of days to come, among the sites memorable in the town's history, shall point out the locality of THE TOWN-PUMP! (45).

Hawthorne here refers to his tale "A Rill from the Town-Pump," a monologue spoken "through the nose" of a pump at the corner of Salem's two main streets.[20] This "nose" not only knows the past but is the horizon beyond which, as Hawthorne points out, the subject must somehow imagine futurity. By bringing into conjunction the pump's historic forms, daily uses, and its future "success" (9: 148)—presumably in providing a public outlet for a variety of thirsts—Hawthorne not only gives shape to the continuity of collective memory but stages a position from which modernity itself might be known as well.

"A Rill from the Town-Pump" provides a vision of collectivity from the literal ground up: it provides a genealogy of the pump itself, its line of descent. The town pump's "natural" product has always existed—it is "the unadulterated ale of father Adam" (9: 142). But its interest in this text derives from the "ale's" universal usage. Before it was a pump, it was a "spring" that bubbled for the "Indian sagamores," until European "fire-water" replaced it as the sagamores' liquid of choice (9: 144). Gradually taking shape as a pump (although buried for a while under civilization's dust), it quenched every thirst, including that of Winthrop, Endicott, and Higginson,[21] as well as consecrating the baptism of every child. As such, the pump intersects with all of the modes and apparatuses of power in the town—those of "official" and "counter-memory." As the pump sees it, he is the body and the essence of history and all local-historical citizens, the "person" of civil law, medicine, town treasurer, overseer of the poor, and constable (9: 141–42). His water is water, but also the soul, natural discourse, unmediated truth at its origin (9: 147–48). Moreover, his product is "free": "here it is . . . and not a cent to pay!" (9: 142).

But there is nothing "democratic" in the pump's activity, in the political sense: it is a "natural" point of convergence that attends not to political hierarchy or personal interest but provides a relay between the material and the moral worlds, the past and present civilizations that have occupied this spot, now called Salem. The perpetuity of such a spot enables Hawthorne to generate a discursive field out of the history of activities that have occurred there, the way Gallows Hill functions in "Alice Doane's Appeal." But in "Alice Doane's Appeal," the discursive field was itself a muted monument to a common shame (for which Hawthorne's text provided the "voice"): in "A Rill from the Town-Pump," the field is a site on which the variety of social positions it brings into conjunction are not merged or adjudicated, but simply (not politically) represented as the "fact" of collectivity, both past and in the present. And so the pump provides a position from which to project future social formations—or at least future forms the pump itself might take, in future societies (it wants to be "marble . . . richly sculptured" [9: 147]). This figuration of a collective future unoriginated by a state or national formation is the pump's utopian fantasy.

Hawthorne's fantasy of being known as the author of "A Rill from the Town-Pump," however, retains the national address of "The Custom-House" at large. He reveals a wish *to have already altered* the future form of the nation by the production of literary texts: he thinks in the "future perfect." Hawthorne's civic posterity will not only have "read" Hawthorne's tale and thereby witnessed the various rulers, drunks, lovers, and dogs whose epochs of activity have made up American life. They will also, unlike Hawthorne, have historical comprehension of their own material world by being in control of the objects through which they are represented to themselves. Thus the complex temporality of the pump's assertion that "The better you think of me, the better men and women you will find yourselves" (9: 145).

In sum, the critical National Symbolic of "The Custom-House" requires a radically philological collective understanding of the objects of national culture. Literature records that the town pump and the A accrue meaning by their "use": both objects work like texts in that their value rises as they circulate through the bodies and minds of their individual and collective readers. In the time and space of reading they create a utopian *and* a historical space for collective, sometimes national fantasy. For reading, in the fantasy of *The Scarlet Letter*, is not merely "academic": it is a species of social discipline and social reproduction that Hawthorne exploits to break apart the hegemony of dominant culture over politics, consciousness, and bodies.

But it would be a misreading of the tone of "The Custom-House," to see the familiar and the literary merged in a seamless present that contains the past and projects the future forms of the nation. The very hyperbole and artificiality of the preface's closing moments—spoken by a dead man, in reference to a personified pump—suggests that the critical National Symbolic, as Hawthorne imagines it here, will also resist the temptation to naturalize fully its images, thereby turning them into icons. His fantasy of the town pump does not abstract it from its context and its use, but situates it in the public consciousness. In contrast, the post-revolutionary eagle and the Puritan law aim to attain the demeanor of natural authority. It is such a demeanor that has served the interests of the Puritan and then the national "state" to obscure the historical process by which authority derives its simulacra of stability and its political legitimacy. As a result, the new/familiar regime of literary-national history retains the aura of "strangeness" central to the activity of all productive "neutral territories." The artificiality of literary form forges the space for a historically complex national memory. It also reminds Americans, as they conserve the utopian promise that has motivated a cluster of experiments within the nation's territory, that the nation is not the origin of utopian fantasy, but rather one historical claimant to its fantastic inheritance.

FIVE *America in Everyday Life*

THERE IS A MAGNIFICENCE TO NATIONAL EXISTENCE. The experience of "being utopian": this is the citizen's erotics, to feel infinite because abstract, and passionate, in collective self-transcendence. *The Scarlet Letter* feeds on this experience of political ardor, addressing its first four chapters to explicating the juridical spectacle that situates the novel, from its very origins, in an overcoming of daily life. But when the intense experience of political existence falls away, as it first does in Chapter 5 of the novel, what is the citizen left with? On leaving the prison, Hester is forced to invent a "daily custom" (78) and to experience the "daily torture" (86) of private and public life with the scarlet A. Immediately, the "ordinary resources of her nature" must be tapped (78), for they will be tried "[t]o-morrow," "the next day," and "the next" (79). The moment in which she reinvents daily life for herself is frightening: for Hester's submission to the law required that she relinquish control over time, and she had gotten used to having no agency.

One might conclude from this that in the novel "daily life" is in some opposition to "political life." Hester shuttles between these poles, living in a world of everyday relations organized around her work as a seamstress and a nurse, except when she is called, by periodic political and theological necessities, to occupy solely her symbolic, official meaning. These transformations of identity are experienced as temporal shifts: the "accumulating days" of unspectacular life transmute into the present tense of the law, which arrests workaday temporality to perform for the state its own mastery of time, space, and meaning. When released from the state's theatrical and symbolic domination of the public sphere, the citizen might be said to recede into a place much harder to represent, the mental and physical practices of "personhood," or personal life—not "private" life, for persons circulate through public as well as private spaces and relations.

Yet "The Custom-House" shows explicitly how deeply implicated the state is in the definition and construction of daily life itself. Complaining about how "official life" (14) violates his sensibilities, Hawthorne comments that "Uncle Sam claimed" only a "three hours and a half" as "his share of my daily life" (35). Three and a half hours is not very much: but Hawthorne's identification, as a laborer, with the United States of America, impresses "the materiality of this daily life" (37) so forcefully that only the deepest recesses of night offer a *potential* base from which a "realm" might be projected that in futurity might be "neutral," independent of national reference. This is to say that both the utopian and the practical operations of national existence hold daily life in hostage: and that daily life, in refracting the utopian and pragmatic strains of modern sociality, is the place where the historical uncanny and the future, unimaginable form somehow meet. It is, indeed, the place of anachronism. If we can say that collective political identity, in colonial and national "America," is in a crisis of meaning in *The Scarlet Letter*, we can also see from these examples that the crisis of political identity is experienced, in the novel, as a crisis of everyday life.

Theoreticians of everyday life—Agnes Heller, Michel de Certeau, Antonio Gramsci, Henri Lefebvre—designate the present tense as the screen on which power, resistance, and submission are negotiated.[1] Gramsci thus speaks of constructing a philosophy of praxis, which takes the everyday structures of common sense and develops a critical language and awareness from them. Without this development of "already existing [popular] activity," the "subaltern" element in the public sphere is doomed to "consider the present . . . with a mode of thought . . . which is often remote and superseded."[2] One of these anachronistic and alienating structures is national language, which to de Certeau "implies a distancing of the living body (both traditional and individual) and thus also of everything which remains, among the people, linked to the earth, to the place, to orality, or to non-verbal tasks."[3]

We have seen that this "distance" or abstracting, which is both a mode of political domination and a utopian mode of hope, coexists, in a relation of permeable boundaries, with the memories and knowledges of everyday life and language. Moreover, people are not naturally "the people" in their local affiliations: the "local" is an elastic concept, incorporating a wide range of political identities—national, regional, provincial—as well as the non-"political" experiences of social life in which categories like "the people" feel, mainly, irrelevant. I do not mean to be making simply generic observations about nationhood: for the "nation's" competition with these more experiential nodes of social and political relation was a crucial issue in the public adjudication of mid-century political identity in the United States.[4] While my reading of *The Scarlet Letter* has followed the novel's own historical perspective, in situating its contemporary moment in the 1850s as a vanishing point in a narrative that leads from colonial to national times, the novel also raises serious questions about the legitimacy of this narrative, and of the Providential position it secures for national identity, over local and everyday relations. Indeed, to take seriously the enigma of "native" political identity, one must read *The Scarlet Letter* not only as an "American" text, but also as an entry in a "war of position"[5] between the federal state and its internal Others, its rivals: the region, the "local" state, the community, the "everyday."

I have argued that Hawthorne had an interest in a kind of revisionary nationalist pedagogy. In his early work, *Seven Tales of My Native Land*, he occupies narratively the ambiguity of the word "native," which refers both to local and national identities, to forge meaningful links between different eras and modes of life that transpired within the different political spaces of New England and the United States. The purpose of such rear projection was not simply to teach the present about the past, but rather to break the frames that seemed to separate national modernity from the provincial, and thus to enrich how Americans, in the present tense, thought about the heterogeneity of the social formations, practices, and ideas that constituted what was intelligible about national culture. Hawthorne's pedagogy involves mining the past for facts and practices but is also an experiment in how to think—about the machinery of citizenship and political identity.

I have described how the surviving tales of this volume, which was burnt by Hawthorne in despair over the absence of an interested audience, all reproduce specifically a scene of historical transmission, a tableau in which information about the past emerges into the consciousness of a young person who inhabits this complexly "native" geopolitical space. This historical information, while narrated, and thus put in some sort of order, always appears to the hearers to be bubbling to the surface all at once, disordered, like a dream—for example, the dream of "An Old Woman's Tale," in which two lovers separately dream the same dream, which is a dream of late Puritan culture, and a dream about digging, perhaps for antiquarian valuables. I would not call this nativist work propaganda, however, nor even "thick propaganda," as Sacvan Bercovitch does, made on behalf of national hegemony or liberal consensus. For the history Hawthorne makes fictive has not only a defamiliarizing but indeed a potentially destabilizing function, which threatens the nation's status as the ultimate political referent.[6] So often articulated in the form of a mystery, his silences work paradoxically against a powerful politically sanctioned ideology of amnesia, in which national history appears best served by careful elision, or sanctifying anthologization in gold leaf editions left on the coffee tables of the literate.[7] In *The Scarlet Letter*, Hawthorne alludes to this elite arrogation of national history in the "we" that glosses Hester Prynne's observation, in Governor Bellingham's hall, of "a folio tome, probably of the Chronicles of England, or other such substantial literature; even as, in our own days, we scatter gilded volumes on the centre-table, to be turned over by the casual guest" (105).

In opposition to these limited modes of distilling national history, Hawthorne writes *The Whole History of Grandfather's Chair* (1841), a history book for children. Here the historiography has a deliberately familiar and a familial air. The collection, narrated by "Grandfather" to his several grandchildren, derives American history from "the substantial and homely reality of a fireside chair."[8] Grandfather owns and sits in the chair. He selects the stories he tells the children only from events that have significantly touched the chair: it has been made meaningful by a long history of use. The everyday life, "homely" setting of the patriarch's furniture, however, does not implicate national history in the artifacting mode of much material culture analysis, which casts the social practices of early Americans as quaint facts about primitive ancestors.[9] Grandfather's more central impulse is to oppose the way historians and politicians locate America in stories of landscaped places or public spaces made sacred by monumental political activity. He wants to leave his grandchildren, as an inheritance, an intimacy with the practices and the subjective experiences of public power of the past. He wants to displace, but not to suppress, the nation's great moments of public glory, which were readily available and oft-used signifiers in the living archive of cultural memory I have called the National Symbolic.

Thus, Grandfather's tale does not chronicle, as had Walter Scott's Scottish history *Tales of a Grandfather*, the battles that made New England and the United States possible. Indeed, Hawthorne's Grandfather explicitly refuses to tell his grandchildren the story of the battle at Bunker Hill. He says he is not that kind of historian. For knowledge of the battle, he takes the children, tourist-like, to see the diorama at the Bunker Hill monument, so magnificently and famously eulogized by Daniel Webster as a kind of early Statue of Liberty, dedicated to "OUR COUNTRY, OUR WHOLE COUNTRY, AND NOTHING BUT OUR COUNTRY."[10] Equating the "country" with "the truth, the whole truth, and nothing but the truth" to which any juridical subject must testify, Webster draws on his status as statesman and lawyer to imbue the collective exercise of memory with the obligations of law. He also speaks in the plural voice of the exemplary citizen:

> We come, as Americans, to mark a spot which must for ever be dear to us and our posterity. We wish that whosoever, in all coming time, shall turn his eye hither, may behold that the place is not undistinguished where the first great battle of the Revolution was fought. We wish that this structure may proclaim the magnitude and importance of that event to every class and every age. We wish that infancy may learn the purpose of its erection from maternal lips, and that weary and withered age may behold it, and be solaced by the recollections which it suggests. We wish that labor may look up here, and be proud, in the midst of its toil. We wish that, in those days of disaster, which, as they come upon all nations, must be expected to come upon us also, desponding patriotism may turn its eye hitherward, and be assured that the foundations of our national power are still strong. We wish that this column, rising towards heaven among the pointed spires of so many temples dedicated to God, may contribute also to produce, in all minds, a pious feeling of dependence and gratitude. We wish, finally, that the last object to the sight of him who leaves his native shore, and the first to gladden his who revisits it, may be something which shall remind him of the liberty and the glory of his country.[11]

Here Webster takes a rhetorical inventory of the sites in which patriotic national identity will be transmitted, as a result of the mnemotechnique of this monument: children will learn their nationality from their mothers, and later remember it as primal; workers will understand their collective importance as the instruments of national production; the religious will affirm America's millennial claims; and, finally, the formal memory of the monument itself will become a touchstone, a reflection, a refraction, and also evidence of the nation's ever-imminent greatness. In both a rhetorical and a political sense, then, the Bunker Hill monument eclipses the battle it commemorates: for while the details of the battle might be forgotten, the monument is a social and material fact in the present tense, made to be permanently projected into the future. It condenses the event and the cultural investment in the event, and brilliantly overcomes the originary historical moment. Moreover, typologically harnessing the energies of millennial America to the days of national crisis that inevitably "come upon all nations," it discharges in advance the crisis of historicity that threatens the represented immutability of the nation itself.

In contrast, Hawthorne's Grandfather thinks that the version of American history he provides is valuable not because of its formal, memorial domination of the children's minds but because of his unique voice, as one among many sources of knowledge. "When he talked to them, it was the past speaking to the present—or rather to the future, for the children were of a generation which had not become actual. Their part in life, thus far, was only to be happy, and to draw knowledge from a thousand sources. As yet, it was not their time to do."[12] Grandfather's pedagogy assumes that the more fully the children understand that national life is not simply a "cold array of outward action"[13] but is also subjectively motivated, and contradictory and ambiguous in its circulation through heroes, statesmen, "the people," and persons, the more critical the children will be as adult "citizens" in their nonetheless loving relation to the nation. Moreover, in recasting America through the personal and the private, Grandfather redefines the nation as well. He disavows its abstract and symbolic self-legitimation and insists that it is rooted in persons, individually and collectively, as they live and have lived everyday life.

In light of these two axes on which narrators fantasized about how American history might be told—the submission of a grateful public to the memory marked by monuments, and the seduction of children by a familial narrative that constitutes national identity in the private lives and subjective feelings of adult citizens—an act of strange historiographical collaboration takes place in *The Scarlet Letter*. I have described at some length how public spectacle operates in Hawthorne's representation of Puritan culture. It equates the collective political enterprise with the state, and with the law that polices the people's relation to the state; public spectacle elicits affect from persons and makes them citizens by routing that affect through love of the law and the regulation of the collective "imagination" and individual conscience, the law's portable memory.

The intention of the law to make people love it and refer themelves to it is affirmed and exemplified in three scaffold scenes. But what happens is more than the law intended. For proximity to the law and to the scaffold so destabilizes some people that the affect it rouses feels like madness, and this madness ultimately refracts on the law itself, bringing into representation its own dependence on unreason. Thus in the first scaffold scene, Hester Prynne barely escapes losing her mind and control of her body's desire to laugh, to scream, and to fling itself into the crowd; in the second, Arthur Dimmesdale does lose control, parading his repressed and unconscious desires in a radical suspension of intention and eruption of laughter; in the third, not only does Dimmesdale display his split self by confessing his sins in both the third and the first persons but creates a contagion of indeterminacy, so that the people who hear him confess his sexual transgression vary wildly in their recollection of what they saw, experienced, and felt.

Yet in this chaos of oversignification and surplus affect, a quiet filiopietistic moment takes place, which explains how this history of juridical dementia might be read in a nationalist tract. In the chapter "The New England Holiday" (21), which takes place just prior to the scaffold's final theatrical event, Hester disciplines Pearl. She chastizes her daughter for wanting to know why her private knowledge of Dimmesdale is improper, inappropriate for talk and action in the marketplace where the public sphere of Puritan culture also convenes.

> "Be quiet, Pearl! Thou understandest not these things," said her mother. "Think not now of the minister, but look about thee, and see how cheery is every body's face to-day. The children have come from their schools, and the grown people from their workshops and their fields, on purpose to be happy. For, to-day, a new man is beginning to rule over them; and so—as has been the custom of mankind ever since a nation was first gathered—they make merry and rejoice; as if a good and golden year were at length to pass over the poor old world!" (229)

The narrator then confirms Hester, and links her history of national identity to his own modern moment in post-revolutionary America. He notes that the "jollity that brightened the faces of the people . . . [in] this festal season of the year" would continue "to be during the greater part of two centuries" (230).

This passage has no consequences in the story. It stands as a narrative spectacle, a performance and a description of political socialization, and thus as a generic statement has extremely complicated bearing on our understanding of the text's mechanics of national identity. First, and most evident, here we see Hester teaching Pearl about politics. She proposes a way of experiencing the bonds of collective political life: do not think of the minister, his strangeness, nor, implicitly, of your own estrangement from society and the law; think of how happy "the people" are, who act annually "as if" in the next political year the ruler will transform the world, "as if" into gold. It is significant that this subjunctive locution recalls Hester Prynne's first political moment, when she enters the scene of her public torture "as if by her own free-will" (52).

Always too imaginative for her own good, Pearl's wish to disclose in the political public sphere what she privately knows and experiences runs against the American grain, for national identity apparently involves substituting a "golden" glow for consciousness of a "poor" or at least a locally problematic reality. To put it more strongly, the social contract that makes Puritan and American society intelligible requires persons to relinquish personal memory for collective identity. Collective identity is equivalent to collective amnesia: patriotism is constituted by the desire to overcome political and historical memory; "happiness," which Americans are fundamentally defined as in righteous pursuit of, is the result of being able to separate everyday from national life, in a ritual frame. On the face of it, then, the mother and the daughter play out the conflict between Daniel Webster's monumental history and Grandfather's personalized nationalist ethic, and Grandfather loses. Hester's exhortation, and the narrator's gloss on it, twine the utopian promise of national identity, the desire of persons to believe it, their desire to participate as citizens in its rituals, and, finally, their willingness to forget its failures. Pearl, in contrast, has not yet learned to "forget" strategically that which will not enable her to be "happy." Until she does this, in the narrator's view, she will be insufficient both as a citizen and a woman.

Earlier I characterized this forgetful tendency in Puritan culture as specifically an effect of the centrality of juridical theory and practice—as differentiated from, say, theological or economic discourse—to the legitimation of the colony's rulers. The law's reliance on spectacle transforms the temporal frame in which people experience social life into a new synchronic space, a juridical present tense. The present tense of the law, like all synchronic moments, actually condenses a number of diverse temporalities: the legal spectacle itself, with its own theatrical duration; the Providential and utopian promises of the political apparatus, which suspend the implications of individual and collective actions to some future, conclusive moment; the virtually corporeal memory of the spectacle, which plays out its logics in a variety of affective traces, for example, a burning feeling on the breast that the scarlet A touches. This is why legal spectacle in the novel is accompanied by references, literal and figurative, to birth and rebirth, for these signal the state's need to sever the relation between persons and their memories. The threatening aspect of personal memory, which I have called counter-memory, is that it reveals both that the state is not inevitable and that it is also, at times, irrelevant to the needs, desires, practices, and identities of citizens. Thus in *The Scarlet Letter*, the Puritan mnemotechnique seeks to dedicate both rational and irrational affect to the future of the polis: the madness of the law is not evidence of its defects, but rather a necessary effect of the state's legitimation strategy—to construct a "people" whose minds, memories, and knowledge will be defined in relation to a juridical present tense. Acting like a good citizen, Hester does not evidence irony when she tells Pearl to gain pleasure and knowledge in identifying with the happy amnesia of her fellow and sister citizens. It is the Puritan and the American thing to do.

But in representing and so strangely affirming as the central, formal point of cultural coherence the paradoxically amnesiac mnemotechnique of national identity, Hester and the narrator also affirm the two-hundred-year history of its social and psychic insufficiency. "Nevertheless," writes the post-Custom-House Hawthorne, "vixenly as she [the American eagle] looks, many people are seeking, at this very moment, to shelter themselves" in the "bosom" of the infantilizing federal state (5). This statement marks the outermost moment of modernity in *The Scarlet Letter*: "at this very moment" the state's confidence game is taking in more suckers. This is as close as we get to the "real" in the novel: real time, real desire, real collective political activity, and real betrayal of the national-utopian promise.

I have argued that "The Custom-House" and *The Scarlet Letter* preserve the possibility that utopia and politics might again come together in America: because history is truly happening at "this very moment," and because people do wish—in ways that reflect socialization and also less concrete, but powerful, desires—to be, politically, happy. Hawthorne effects this preservation simply, by suspending conclusions about the future of the national public sphere: literally, at the end of *The Scarlet Letter*, the marketplace is empty, evacuated, there is neither intracultural contact nor conversation, in the way nations are supposed by Hester and by Habermas always to have worked.[14] The nation is a negative. The populace is divided by gender into "houses," political and domestic: Puritan men carry on unrepresented tasks of civic self-preservation and women imagine a future polis, based not on relations of power as we know them but on relations of spirit in a world where bodies are virginal and abstract, having no history. The political language of happiness that marked Hester's earlier nationalist pedagogy is translated here to the post-political discourse of "sacred love" which will, she promises, "make us happy" (263).

Until that time, according to the text, the citizen's body, which is mainly a patriarchal form, will take the beating for the affective distortions that come from desiring proximity to a mass, abstract power that effectively delegitimates personal memory, everyday life, and private experience. *The Scarlet Letter* is full of such bodies, whose physical intimacy with the concrete and symbolic machinery of law actually transforms them physically, into unintelligible symbolized subjects. And as we have seen, "The Custom-House" too houses citizens physically preserved by their identification with

American transhistoricism, while also entirely desiccated and dysfunctional.

By now it should be clear that Hawthorne not only calls into question the politics and ethics of the nation's dominant modes of intelligibility and coherence but also brings into crisis the utopian value of national identity itself. Is it true that the nation should be the fundamental reference point of collective political identity, fantasy, and practice? Or is it possible that its occupation of what Stuart Hall has called "the horizon of the taken-for-granted" is just a symptom of its Providential and post-Enlightenment heritage?[15] Citizens and students of mass political culture have tended to assume that the modern nation always retains the trace of its revolutionary promises, at least to represent some version of "the people": but the example of early national America suggests that the promises and the techniques devised to realize them have lives of their own, provoking strained and asymmetrical relations within the physical map.[16] The implications of this generalization for the United States in particular can be seen in the way its dominant political culture has deployed utopia—brought it, as it were, into practice.

I have suggested that during this period the constitutional relations between the federal state and the local states were undergoing a crisis of what constituted "native" privilege that eventuated in the Civil War. But it should go without saying, although of course it does not, that in America it was not only Southerners who resisted being absorbed by the nation's millennial typology. In *The Scarlet Letter* and elsewhere, Hawthorne suggests that America may not fulfill the movement of history toward justice and humanity: rather, the federal nation is one category among many vying for cultural power within the native land, while claiming to have always already won, in the Providential scheme. He shows this in a number of ways, from a number of angles. He approaches the possibility of inhabiting a post-national mentality both as a philosopher of the quotidian, examining the way the alienation of modern life influences personal affect and collective relations, and as a worker, trying to make it himself in the system.

Most trivially, but crucially, he tells in "The Custom-House" a history of small resistances and thefts of privilege and time perpetrated against the state.[17] For example, rather than doing the commercial work of the nation they were assigned to do, both Hawthorne and his "official ancestor," Surveyor Pue, waste time (33). After "[p]oking and burrowing into the heaped-up rubbish" of the Custom-House, they write history (29); they also do a fair amount of "pacing," "lounging," idle reading, and shooting the breeze (8, 27); in addition, we see that one of Hawthorne's colleagues there writes poetry on "Uncle Sam's letter-paper" (27). Describing "daily life" in the Custom-House as a terrible violation of his desire "to live throughout the whole range of his faculties and sensibilities" (40), as a productive citizen and a thinker, Hawthorne posits inspecting the garbage and writing poetry instead of memos as small protests against a mutually parasitic and self-evacuating national system.

In contrast, while Hawthorne's official national identity wastes him, and while he wastes time occupying his privileged position, everything he does is significant locally. Both returning to and leaving Salem are acts of extreme ambivalence, and also psychically impossible: as he says, he either "possesses or did possess" affection for Salem (8). He speaks of his "native energy" (38), and his "native reserve" (4); he calls Salem his native home (4, 44), his natal spot, always, ideally, a kind of "magic" "Paradise" (11, 38, 13). Of course, by the end of the essay he has left both Salem and America, living in the realm of the dead, neither here nor there (44). This "solution" to his stressful negotiation of these different nodes of identity is at best prophetic and utopian, but in terms of the political present tense has no positive value at all.[18]

However, twelve years later, in his Civil War essay "Chiefly About War Matters," Hawthorne retheorizes not the inchoate everyday life resistances to national appropriation, but rather the experiential way the American claim for total political and symbolic self-presence violates what he knows about how political affect works. This essay, written under the pseudonym, "A Peaceable Man," is an extremely sensitive adjudication of the different claims for federal, state, local, and private identity that circulate through the American system, identities that become enunciated in the political fractions, the daily tensions, and the very bodies of American men.

Hawthorne records in this text a trip to meet Abraham Lincoln, "the man of men."[19] He seeks Lincoln "with my own eyes" first because he is frustrated that his only experience of the "general heart-quake of the country" was abstract, in the national press. In other words, he partly experiences the Civil War as a crisis of feeling political affect in a mass society. I will return to this problem of feeling later. Second, he assumes the right to be intimate with Lincoln, and desires "the customary free intercourse of Americans with their chief magistrate."[20] The word "magistrate" links Lincoln with the Puritan rulers and recasts the United States as a small town, where power creates strong fields of intimacy, not vast abstract fields of generic obligation and love. Third, and most important for my purposes, in this essay he registers his own metamorphoses of political identity, without consolidating them. As a relay through which different identities flow, Hawthorne chronicles his trip to Washington, mapping the cities and states through which he travels, and reporting the landscapes that greet him there: in New York, the streets were muddy; in New Jersey, a thin covering of snow; Philadelphia was mild and balmy.[21] But the "vague disturbance" in the "air" he experiences on this trip is not simply weather—it is war, itself all muddy and rusted. He concludes, "The whole business, though connected with the destinies of a nation, takes inevitably a tinge of the ludicrous."[22]

The essay changes its tone about national destiny, though, when Hawthorne reaches the Capitol. Catching the painter Emmanuel Gottlieb Leutze painting the patriotic frieze on the Capitol ceiling, Hawthorne understands that at this moment of constitutional panic, the nation's utopian claims are extremely useful: "The work will be emphatically original and American. . . . it looked full of energy, hope, progress, irrepressible movement onward, all represented in a momentary pause of triumph; and it was most cheering to feel its good augury at this dismal time, when our country might seem to have arrived at such a deadly stand-still."[23] The "absolute comfort" Hawthorne experiences at this symbolic representation of an otherwise fractured nation is itself ruptured, however, when he sees the huge cracks in the Capitol walls, symbolizing, he fears, what will happen "on the day when we drop the Southern stars out of our flag."[24]

At issue is not whether Hawthorne is simply proslavery: his complex relation to abolition can be bracketed for the moment. But Hawthorne's sympathy for the Southern position also derives from his deep sense of local identity, a sense which has become politically untenable, from the nationalist point of view, because of the slave agitation.

> There never existed any other government against which treason was so easy, and could defend itself by such plausible arguments, as against that of the United States. The anomaly of two allegiances (of which that of the State comes nearest home to a man's feelings, and includes the altar and the hearth, while the General Government claims his devotion only to an airy mode of law, and has no symbol but a flag) is exceedingly mischievous in this point of view; for it has converted crowds of honest people into traitors, who seem to themselves not merely innocent, but patriotic, and who die for a bad cause with as quiet a conscience as if it were the best. In the vast extent of our country,—too vast by far to be taken into one small human heart,—we inevitably limit to our own State, or, at farthest, to our own section, that sentiment of physical love for the soil which renders an Englishman, for example, so intensely sensitive to the dignity and well-being of his little island, that one hostile foot, treading anywhere upon it, would make a bruise on each individual breast. If a man loves his own State, therefore, and is content to be ruined with her, let us shoot him, if we can, but allow him an honorable burial in the soil he fights for.[25]

We know, from Hawthorne's campaign biography of Franklin Pierce, that he is capable of feeling and expressing the most blatant nationalism: there, he lauds Pierce's support of the 1850 compromise, which saved the "Union," and preserved "that common country which Providence brought into one nation, through a continued miracle of almost two hundred years, from the first settlement of the

American wilderness until the revolution."[26] It is harder to believe that, only a few pages earlier in "Chiefly About War Matters," "the peaceable man" has himself called secession "treason," while arguing that the "Union" has "an indefeasible claim to a more enduring national existence."[27]

In this passage, however, Hawthorne judges neither the righteousness of the war nor the issues that have produced it. Nor does he presume the sanctity of the United States, despite its utopian, "American" frame. Instead, he explicates how the abstract, or as he puts it, the "airy" machinery of the National Symbolic has established itself so forcefully as the dominant patriotic index that the local, experiential attachments and affiliations of even the most loyal citizens are regarded by the federal state as species of treason and political blasphemy. In the symbolic structure of this passage, the law and the flag are posited against the state, the altar, the hearth, and the soil. This split does not exist in the Puritan polis of *The Scarlet Letter*, where "the clerical band, the judicial robe, the pillory, the gallows, the fireside, or the church" are intimately linked social in-

stitutions (199). These, the modern loyal citizen also experiences intimately, like the Englishman whose body registers footprints hostile to his nation. But the United States is too abstract for Hawthorne at this moment, especially because, however utopian it may ultimately be, it has in the present codified an intense, high-stakes polarity between national interests and local identities.

Yet *The Scarlet Letter*, like many of Hawthorne's experiments in national identity, imagines that the federal or "General State" might be experienced positively—if not in everyday life, perhaps in local life—and with an intimacy akin to the compulsive identification Hawthorne feels for Salem. He imagines this in "Chiefly About War Matters" too, as he looks at Fort Ellsworth, and envisions the time, after military service, when it will become a monument. He is not interested in its history of glory in battle; like Fort Ticonderoga, Fort Ellsworth's decayed ruins will be, he predicts, material for poetry, which will root itself like "weeds" in the landscape and "make our country dearer." For "the more historical associations we can link with our localities, the richer will be the daily life that feeds upon the past, and the more valuable the things that have been long established."[28] In sum, commemorative literature will do the work of making intimate the subjective experience of national identity. Hawthorne imagines, here at least, no political strategy for the Union to take that will give it a direct line to the heart.

Here we apprehend the enigma of Hawthorne's nationalist literary pedagogy. When he approaches America as a philosopher of citizenship, he adjudicates the deep and serious claims the nation has to the love and obligation of its citizens, and tries to imagine ways of making unimpeded intimacy with the mass political system possible. Literature fills the space between the abstract "simultaneity"[29] of national existence and the quotidian temporalities of material life, which include personal, political, and historical memories and collective practices: as if the National Symbolic were, through literary transmission, etched lovingly with the reader's own personal monogram, and placed by the author on the person's body, hands, and brain. In contrast, when Hawthorne approaches the nation as a worker and a citizen of daily life, his *ressentiment* at the nation's modes of domination provokes an iconoclastic cynicism. In this position, he stages himself as a subaltern subject, victimized by a fraudulent political space and symbolic order. He then identifies with a whole new fashion of detail: from scraps of fabric, paper garbage, and children's play, to political, religious, and erotic fantasy, which stand in for familial, local, sectional, and regional nodes of collective knowledge.

Insofar as "Hawthorne" can be seen shuttling between these two nationally inflected positions, the argument of many Hawthorne critics that he embodies the contradictions of liberal pluralist culture seems unassailable. Even the aspect of the "local" that means "not-national" can be seen to constitute America as the horizon with respect to which persons define themselves. Ironically, Gramsci's list of what counts as archaic, politically paralyzing knowledge—of "one's own village or province . . . in the parish and the 'intellectual activity' of the local priest or ageing patriarch whose wisdom is law, or in the little old woman who has inherited the lore of the witches or the minor intellectual soured by his own stupidity or inability to act" virtually reproduces a cast list of *The Scarlet Letter* and "The Custom-House."[30] Rather than providing conclusive evidence of Hawthorne's radical embrace of local identities, the textual prominence of precisely this material might mark him as what Fanon would call the kind of colonized "native intellectual" who, unable to liberate himself from the "seeds of decay" produced by dominating cultures, takes up the cause of the indigenous peoples while still identifying himself with the elite.[31]

Still, the practices and knowledges of everyday life and personal memory serve in this work as a mnemonic of another sort. The material that operates amply in excess to patriotic memory, obligation, and desire may, indeed, provoke a redefinition of political life outside of the psuedo-dialectic of national-local identities I have been elaborating here. Seen en masse, these diverse sites of identity, knowledge, and practice provide a kind of antidote to American monomania. They not only break the frame of national self-presence but also deny the politics and the ethics of its claim to be the frame of frames, where political and social life are concerned. This foundational break makes it possible to recast the inquiry into the relation between utopia and politics in this way: if the nation were no longer held to be the ideal type of political structure that secures justice for its citizens, what other forms of identity might be construed to relegitimate its incorporation of utopia-in-practice? "Private" and personal memories, thoughts, and acts, unauthored by the state—sometimes "political" and "historical," sometimes disengaged from political reference—might then be seen, positively, as a kind of "voting." But it would not suffice to say that the "personal" would be the "political," for, crucially, these materials would be defined outside of their now defensive postures with respect to the national-utopian promise that has long conscripted their allegiance and their fantasy: they would be unintelligible to us, now. Hawthorne thus expresses, in my view, a problem of modern, mass national identity yet to be solved, in practice or in theory. He provides a field of negatives, condensed in the word "local," that are not simply critical of the nation in the mode of dissensus, but restlessly predictive of other collective-utopian political forms and social movements.[32] The affective intensity of local and everyday life identities provides a "floating buffer zone"[33] within the nation, refuting both its totalizing claims and its "horizonality" as a referent for social thought, even against Hawthorne's own intimate identification with the privileges of nationality.

In sum, Hawthorne's national work, in its defamiliarizing drive, runs up against a set of limits within hegemonic political culture: notably, I have argued here, the ambiguity with which federal and local interests intersect with the utopian privilege of America, and the collectivizing promise of the National Symbolic. But his critical analysis of the technology of modern citizenship also runs into personal, perhaps more banal obstacles, at the social axes on which his self-privileging takes place; I refer to the racial and gendered sites of his entitlement, which superintend the emancipated ethnic identity Hawthorne lives, that of a white man in a culture that sanctions this conjunction of identities. In "Alice Doane's Appeal," I have suggested, these axes are remembered as silences in the text. Women and Native Americans appear as traces in the text's "Appeal" to national political consciousness: that is, as objects of representation devoid of political agency. But in "Chiefly About War Matters" he vocalizes their place in a literary-nationalist pedagogy. He argues that poetry, which is permanently conjoined with history, should be dedicated to training children not to "sacrifice good institutions to passionate impulses and impracticable theories."[34] The "good institution" to which he refers remains characteristically unnamed. It might be the "Union," or it might be slavery—but in the political unconscious of the United States, he suggests, these institutions are not so distinct. Primally, he associates slavery with America. He names "the historical circumstance, known to few" that links the national and the economic institution: both Pilgrims and slaves were "brought forth" to the nation from the "womb" of the Mayflower, two sets of "kindred" immigrants linked by a "monstrous birth." The implication here is not only, as Bercovitch has argued, to herald "the continuities of American history," paradoxical as they are within the nation's symbolizing dialectics.[35] This passage also implies that, fundamentally, slavery makes America intelligible: without it, as without the South, we are no longer a nation, historically, politically, or providentially sanctioned, *e pluribus unum*. Slaves, in short, are not persons, not potential citizens, but are part of the national landscape and of the deep memories that sanctify it as politically a "country."

If racial privilege becomes glaringly the one local identity in which Hawthorne feels nationally uncontested, the politics of gender and nationalism take on vastly different and more intimate issues. I have spoken at length about how American manhood becomes, in Hawthorne's national work, a site and an origin of a certain affective pathology. This gender sickness, as Myra Jehlen and Anne Norton have argued, stems from the mind-body fractures that abstract American political life necessitates.[36] The customs and the laws of early national America are passionately homosocial, as Carey McWilliams has so painstakingly shown: the price of even the most normative public political fraternity appears to have been a confused and distorted masculine relation to the male body, to sexual desire, and to the political privileging of that desire vis à vis women, both in and outside of the home.[37]

But for Hawthorne the dire national consequences of the philosophical contruction of homosocial political culture do not in any way result in a positive construction of female political agency. I have described his repudiation of Hester's political theory and his narrator's wish that she "ought to be, concealed" in the home (81). When constructing the psychopathology of the masculine political subject, he usually denies the separation of domestic from political space. But in self-contradiction, his texts nonetheless maintain the adequacy of such territorializing for women. Rooted to the home, Hester has leave to speak the language of political intimacy he authorizes, but only while waiving her desire to enact it in public.

Elsewhere he reiterates his resistance to female participation in the political public sphere. This is, crucially, an antifeminist stance in two senses of the term: the older sense, "anti-female," and the newer, which refers to the feminist movement. For instance, in the book *Biographical Stories for Children*, he tells of the abomination embodied by Queen Christina of Sweden, an exact contemporary of Hester Prynne. It seems that Queen Christina, with "a bold and masculine character," liked Latin and Greek literatures and fancied herself a politician. Unfortunately, because she violated the terms of feminine pedagogy, she died alone and unloved. The narrator concludes,

> Happy are the little girls of America, who are brought up quietly and tenderly, at the domestic hearth, and thus become gentle and delicate women! May none of them ever lose the loveliness of their sex, by receiving such an education as that of Queen Christina![38]

We can read this as a contrafeminist reference, implicating the women of Hawthorne's day who were commenting on and transforming American politics as well as demanding the privileges of citizenship as already enjoyed by men. Paula Baker has suggested that national political parties provided crucial local sites of cultural masculinity in the American nineteenth century:[39] while despairing at the trivializing practices of party politics, and seeing its effects as a menace to his own manhood, Hawthorne seems to experience the possible intrusion of women into this sphere as a threat to his most privileged national body.

But other women were *repudiating* the political public sphere for the same reasons Hawthorne reared his pen against it. While he, however, had the privilege of assuming power within the sphere he mistrusted, these women, who can be characterized as domestic sentimentalists, actively did not seek, and wholly opposed themselves to, female participation in the political public sphere.[40] Like Hawthorne, they saw this sphere as sick, masculine, and masculinizing: "stirring speeches," "exciting scenes," and "heated and angry discussion of political subjects" were unbecoming to woman.[41] *Godey's Lady's Book*, which was subtitled "The Book of the Nation," brimmed, during the 1840s and 1850s, with instruction and commentary on the ethics and politics of female citizenship in America. The essay "Woman in her Social Relations" typically insists:

> The great policy of woman in the present age is, we believe, the correction of those errors in sentiment and education into which a few *ambitious* spirits have betrayed her; proving, by her contempt of everything like agitation or uncalled-for excitement, that her only proper hall of legislation is Home, and that

> she who makes the politics of home her peculiar study, discharges more faithfully her duty, enhances her own happiness, and that of those about her, adds much to the dignity of her position, and encircles, with an amaranthine wreath of purity and brightness, the cherished name of *Woman*.[42]

These women take on the struggle over what properly constitutes "woman's rights," and insist, like Hawthorne, that the political public sphere is a vicious masculine space. Yet, Amy Schrager Lang has suggested, Hawthorne's rage at public women was not so much against feminist as against the "feminine" women: despite the sentimentalist repudiation of feminist political ambitions, Hawthorne's work suggests that the very fact and form of any woman's public presence was "politically" threatening.[43] However, it was wishful to think that "the politics of home" protected women from the violations of national culture.

Lydia Maria Child's 1857 story "Home and Politics" reiterates much of what Hawthorne says about the nation's desecration

of local affections and affiliation: it plays out the logic of national identity in a way that reveals the vulnerability of the "person," the man, and the woman to the nation's instrumentalization of patriotic love. I end with this story because its attempt to stage the limitations of national identity, in the effects of its abstracting and instrumentalizing culture, speaks from a popular, subaltern position, and is not ambiguated by the schizophrenia of Hawthorne's own identification with the nation. Moreover, since the tale uses the presidential election of James Knox Polk to foreground its repudiation of the national referent, it ironically brings us to the moment when Hawthorne profits from his national, ethnic, and political alliances: for Polk is the president who appoints Hawthorne to the Salem Custom-House, as a perquisite of patronage politics. It shows how the nation exploits the different techniques for interpellation into the love and discipline of the National Symbolic, on the one hand, and party politics on the other; it reiterates, but with scathing differences, Hester's commentary on the utopian promise affirmed by the popular celebration of election days. Indeed, the story of "Alice White," Child's heroine, might be read as an antidote to that of the diaphanous Alice Doane, along with the other "wraithlike Alices who expressed womanhood" to Hawthorne.[44]

Alice White opens the story as a plain but virtuous elementary school teacher. An ideal American who transcends her vulgar class origins to encompass both civic and spiritual virtue, Alice lives daily what Child calls a "pastoral" mentality: uninterested in the "epic" ephemera of the political public sphere, Alice installs the enduring values of proper proportion, health, and self-culture in the little children who are her students. One day, on holiday from the city, a man named George Franklin happens upon Alice, and marvels at her simple agrarian virtue: although Franklin has political ambitions, as any man with such an American name would, she brings him to a better self, and a world of intellectual and domestic pleasures. That is, until "an evil hour," when "a disturbing influence" crossed their household:

> It came in the form of political excitement; that pestilence which is forever racing through our land, seeking whom it may devour; destroying happy homes, turning aside our intellectual strength from the calm and healthy pursuits of literature or science, blinding consciences, embittering hearts, rasping the tempers of men, and blighting half the talent of our country with its feverish breath.[45]

We learn here that the way America attaches itself to the affect of its citizens is through the contagion or plague of party politics. Enthralled by the prospect of William Henry Harrison, who ran in 1844, Franklin "lived in a species of mental intoxication. He talked louder than formerly, and doubled his fists in the vehemence of gesticulation. He was restless for newspapers, and watched the arrival of mails, as he would once have watched over the life of his child," also named Alice.[46] His sublimation of domestic affections in the political public sphere results in two events: first, he receives a patronage position during the Harrison/Tyler administration; second, baby Alice dies, no doubt from paternal love starvation.

Political life absorbs and intensifies Franklin's appetites. He spends more money; he gives more dinners; because his personal has become national-political, he leaves the materials of his counter-memory behind and loses his mind in a way akin to the juridical delirium brought about by the law in *The Scarlet Letter*. But before he can go utterly mad in the exercise of his privilege, the election of 1848 takes place. Franklin backs Henry Clay, the great Whig author of the "American System," against Polk, the war hero. Child takes us to a parade that commemorates the election, and tests our competence in deciphering national signs and in understanding the meaning of national choices, much as Hawthorne did in his representations of the Custom-House eagle and the flag.

The Whig parade passes by "with richly-caparisoned horses, gay banners, flowery arches, and promises of protection to every thing"—everything except, as Alice points out with a sigh, "women and children."[47] In contrast to this show of class finery and beneficent sentimental generic patriarchalism, the Democrats brandish an "army of horses; temples of Liberty, with figures in women's dress to represent the goddess; raccoons hung, and guillotined, and swallowed by alligators; the lone star of Texas everywhere glimmering over their heads; the whole shadowy mass occasionally illuminated by the rush of fire-works, and a fitful glare of lurid torches . . . "[48]

The content of the Democratic spectacle, which wields the lure of popular signs, of military victory on the Texas frontier, and the spectre and spectacle of American imperialism, reminds Alice, as it did many conservatives, of wild revolutionary mobs in France—even though this is simply carnival, the psuedo-insanity of the politically enfranchised. She makes no comment on the different political lexicons the parties employ, nor offers a judgment as to which she prefers. For this contest between the patrician and the populist strains of national political affiliation is almost ludicrous to Alice, who interprets their differences as false choices, different routes to the same privilege. The different motifs mask their formal identity as competitors for semiotic and thus political control over the National Symbolic during the next presidential term. In short, the different ways in which America reaches out to Alice personally appear as so many forms of negation, measures of her exile from a utopian realm that in theory protects and affirms her values, talents, and desires. Her husband, in contrast, has never felt more intimate with the federal state. He stakes their entire estate on the election of Clay, and loses everything, as Clay does. Alice's response to this catastrophe—her only possible vote—is to return to the perpetual present tense of pastoral life, but by another route: she goes insane. "In a few days," writes Child, "hers was pronounced a case of melancholy insanity. She was placed in the hospital, where her husband strives to surround her with every thing to heal the wounded soul. But she does not know him."[49]

Child concludes that this couple "is only one of a thousand similar wrecks continually floating over the turbulent sea of American politics."[50] But can this marriage be saved? Can the personal and the political be brought into some sort of mutually authorizing relation, in the mass political culture that has become the arena of American citizenship? Let us recap the evidence. Before Alice learned to love George Franklin, national identity was irrelevant to her. Not simply because she had no vote, and thus had not been interpellated as a citizen: for Alice was otherwise occupied in a struggle for survival, as a member of an underclass, and for dignity, as a single professional woman. When we see her teach her children, she manifests no pedagogy of political socialization: rather, she teaches the timeless values of ethics and self-discipline, both of the mind and the body. She has, as far as we can tell, no sense that she is in exile from power. However, once married to patriarchal national culture, in the person of George Franklin, Alice learns that her life practices are themselves irrelevant to the larger, more spectacular scene of urban culture and national politics. She remains rooted in the local: and her husband cannot, for the life of him, think a way to live the local and the national, even though his participation in national politics might involve simply a change of job. Seduced by the surplus affect and excessive rhetoric of the national frame, Franklin sees the quotidian as degraded, workaday, an undistingushed and emasculated category of experience.

Thus if there is no such thing as everyday life in the abstract state of the nation, and if there is much more coherence at the level of symbolic nationalist discourse than in personal, local, sectional, and regional practices, then the local lives of wives, mothers, children, and unpropertied laborers, and also of statesmen and professionals, are irrelevant to America, except in exceptional, ritual, and usually symbolic moments, as in Daniel Webster's speech. The sign "of what does not (yet) speak," they represent in Hawthorne's and in Child's work what de Certeau calls "*the memory of [a] wordless remnant*," haunting but not visibly transforming the technologies of national identity.[51] Constructing an everyday logic of America, then, is an impossible task, from the point of view of mass national culture. For the utopian nation can only recognize that which has entered the National Symbolic, which itself contains only affective objects that can be wrested from their historical, practical, and experiential contexts.

Having recognized a split between what we might call utopian America and the historical United States, we can also imagine that the pragmatics of national culture are as vital to its machinery as are those symbolic discursive practices in the context of which utopian "America" stands as the master-text to the historical nation. In "Home and Politics" "The Custom-House," and *The Scarlet Letter*, different modes of effecting what we must now call "the hegemony of the national" within the United States work together powerfully to engage everyday life, but mainly as a negative field of force.

The national fantasy in whose utopian promise Americans and New Englanders have invested identities and bodies, for the sake of happiness, addresses persons in their set of particular identities, and reconstrues them in two ways. Through the National Symbolic, they receive the mantle and the privilege of collectively held affect, a fantasy of boundless identity. This requires each subject to shed her attachment to her other, local identities, and to enter a new synchronic political order, which has a mystical relation to everyday history. In contrast, through political parties, citizens are distributed along hierarchical lines in the political public sphere according to the value of their gender, class, ethnic, racial, and regional identities. The National Symbolic embraces everyone with a memory and a conscience; political parties disperse social energies and substitute the lure of political self-interest for the sense that philosophers of the quotidian have, that politics ought to respond to needs, and that needs are attached to bodies, which need to negotiate complex relations of power.[52]

But in the United States, power is erotically attached to America. This national frame is abstract, like a man, or a Statue of Liberty. Since that sentence is false—for a man and a statue are only abstract if you repress their conditions of production—the subject who wants to avoid the melancholy insanity of the self-abstraction that is citizenship, and to resist the lure of self-overcoming the material political context in which she lives, must develop tactics for refusing the interarticulation, now four hundred years old, between the United States and America, the nation and utopia. She must look, perhaps to her other identities, for new sources of political confederation. She must break her attachment to abstract political fulfillment. For just as there is everyday life in the United States, although there is not in "America," utopian social relations might be sought or effected without reference to the national frame, which has been sullied by its long exploitation of the dream of political happiness it has expressed.

Finally, a caveat. As Hester and Hawthorne would have predicted, every four years "the people" still vote to become happy once again that a new man will try to keep the national-utopian images aligned, so that they seem inevitable and indivisible. I have described how Hawthorne's work reveals the incredible hope behind every such act of political faith, including the willingness to forget, in advance, its betrayal in the national public sphere. Thus there is no guarantee that Americans would rejoice if the historical nation, the United States, were to take off its utopian A—perhaps at the end of Empire. Saddened and shocked at the end of the seemingly eternal coupling of the United States and Utopia, might we not act like little Pearl, on witnessing an unalphabetized Hester for the very first time, and "suddenly burst into a fit of passion, gesticulating violently, and throwing [our] small figure[s] into the most extravagant contortions . . . piercing shrieks . . . [and] childish and unreasonable wrath" ?

NOTES

INTRODUCTION

1. Nathaniel Hawthorne, *The Scarlet Letter*, Centenary Edition of the Works of Nathaniel Hawthorne (Columbus: Ohio State University Press, 1962), 1: 43. Further page references to *The Scarlet Letter* will appear in parentheses.

2. For a broad statement about how nationalism has come to link love and obligation to state-supported institutions and technologies (such as print capitalism), see Benedict Anderson, *Imagined Communities: Reflections on the Origin and Spread of Nationalism* (London: Verso, 1983), whose work has been central to this project. Another foundational text, articulated in a quite different moment, national context, and mode of political engagement is Frantz Fanon's *The Wretched of the Earth*, trans. Constance Farrington, introduction by Jean-Paul Sartre (New York: Grove Press, 1963). See notes to chapter 1 for a more elaborate bibliography of works on the construction and reproduction of nations.

3. Elaine Scarry writes eloquently about the sensational, corporeal attributes of generic political identity as a national, not specifically American, phenomenon. The United States is, then, one local instance of an extremely complicated modern mechanism of political interpellation, which deserves specific representation and analysis. "The extent to which in ordinary peacetime activity the nation-state resides unnoticed in the intricate recesses of personhood, penetrates the deepest layers of consciousness, and manifests itself in the body itself is hard to assess; for it seems at any given moment "hardly" there, yet seems at many moments, however hardly, *there* . . . in the learned postures, gestures, gait, the ease or reluctance with which it breaks into a smile; *there* in the regional accent . . . Whether the body's loyalty to these political realms is more accurately identified as residing in one fragile gesture or in a thousand, it is likely to be deeply and permanently there, more permanently there, less easily shed, than those disembodied forms of patriotism that exist in verbal habits or in thoughts about one's national identity" (Scarry, *The Body in Pain: the Making and Unmaking of the World* [New York: Oxford University Press, 1985], 108–109).

4. See the intricate argument of John Irwin, in *American Hieroglyphics: The Symbol of the Egyptian Hieroglyphics in the American Renaissance* (New Haven: Yale University Press, 1980), 276–84. See also Gordon Hutner, *Secrets and Sympathy: Forms of Discourse in Hawthorne's Novels* (Athens: University of Georgia Press, 1988), 17–28. Hélène Cixous speculates about a similar logic of embodiment in the generic state's address to the patriarchal body in "Castration or Decapitation?" *Signs* 7, no. 1 (Autumn 1981): 41–55. For further discussion of how and why Hawthorne represents the patriarchal state as is and also transposes it into a figural she-eagle, see chapter 4.

5. Victor Burgin, "Diderot, Barthes, *Vertigo*," in *Formations of Fantasy*, ed. Victor Burgin, James Donald, and Cora Kaplan (New York: Methuen, 1986), 98. Burgin's configuration of bodies, politics, and texts hinges on both Freudian and Nietzschean theories of how transindividual desire works; I focus on how it circulates through popular and official positions within the public sphere of representation. Nietzsche writes that modern nation-states create public theaters of penal violence to citizens, in order to construct spectacular forms or pseudo-intimate fetishes of collective memory. Somewhere between the image-memory of pain and the need for intelligible fantasy comes the mixture of love and obligation inspired by the juridico-utopian ideology of the modern nation. See Friedrich Nietzsche, *On the Genealogy of Morals*, trans. Walter Kaufmann and R. J. Hollingdale, ed. Walter Kaufmann (New York: Vintage, 1967), 57–96, and Anne Norton, *Reflections on Political Identity* (Baltimore: Johns Hopkins University Press, 1988).

6. Among major Hawthorne critics, this view of Hawthorne as champion of radical individualism has been most strongly and subtly articulated by Nina Baym, in a series of books and essays, culminating in *The Shape of Hawthorne's Career* (Ithaca, N.Y.: Cornell University Press, 1976) and *The Scarlet Letter: A Reading* (Boston: Twayne, 1986). From a far less political, more philosophical angle, the social state of the "person" in crisis in these texts has been powerfully enunciated by Sharon Cameron, *The Corporeal Self: Allegories of the Body in Melville and Hawthorne* (Baltimore: Johns Hopkins University Press, 1981), and Emily Miller Budick, *Fiction and Historical Consciousness: The American Romance Tradition* (New Haven: Yale University Press, 1989). See also Dennis Pahl, *Architects of the Abyss: the Indeterminate Fictions of Poe, Hawthorne, and Melville* (Columbia, Mo.: University of Missouri Press, 1989) and Allan Gardner Lloyd-Smith, *Eve Tempted: Writing and Sexuality in Hawthorne's Fiction* (Totowa, N.J.: Barnes & Noble, 1983).

7. A strong argument for Hawthorne's populist sympathies is offered by Donald E. Pease, *Visionary Compacts: American Renaissance Writings in Cultural Context* (Madison: University of Wisconsin Press, 1987). For

the strongest counterargument, and there are many, see Larzer Ziff, *Literary Democracy: The Declaration of Cultural Independence in America* (New York: Viking Press, 1981).

8. For the history of Hawthorne's canonicity, see Richard H. Brodhead, *The School of Hawthorne* (New York: Oxford University Press, 1986), and Jane Tompkins, *Sensational Designs: The Cultural Work of American Fiction, 1790–1860* (New York: Oxford University Press, 1985).

9. For a brilliantly argued opposing view on the priority of intention in Hawthorne's texts, see Michael J. Colacurcio, *The Province of Piety: Moral History in Hawthorne's Early Tales* (Cambridge: Harvard University Press, 1984).

10. Bercovitch has developed a powerful argument for Hawthorne's place as a vessel for the explicit ideologies and contradictions of liberal American political culture, in its utopian and ideological aspects; I am often in harmony with his local readings. To the extent that this book holds that America's symbolic lexicon aims to create an aura of transhistorical invulnerability for the nation, I concur with Bercovitch's observations—but as my version of *The Scarlet Letter* proposes, the official state imaginary accounts fully neither for its own nor its citizens' experiences, memories, opinions, or desires. Bercovitch emphasizes the way *The Scarlet Letter* "expresses a particular culture's mode of resolving crisis"; by contrast, I am interested in the way several cultures come into play, contact, and power within the narrative, not to be resolved in any political frame, national or otherwise (Bercovitch, "Hawthorne's A-Morality of Compromise," *Representations* 24 [Fall 1988]: 9). See also Bercovitch, *The American Jeremiad* (Madison: University of Wisconsin Press, 1978); *The Puritan Origins of the American Self* (New Haven: Yale University Press, 1975); "The Problem of Ideology in American Literary History," *Critical Inquiry* 12, no. 4 (Summer 1986): 631–53; "The A-Politics of Ambiguity in *The Scarlet Letter*," *New Literary History* 19, no. 3 (Spring 1988): 629–54. Myra Jehlen attaches the kind of work on the political public sphere I describe here to Enlightenment and imperialist heritages: see her fine *American Incarnation: The Individual, the Nation, and the Continent* (Cambridge: Harvard University Press, 1986).

11. See Jonathan Arac, "The Politics of *The Scarlet Letter*," in *Ideology and Classic American Literature*, ed. Sacvan Bercovitch and Myra Jehlen (Cambridge: Cambridge University Press, 1986), 247–66; Donald Pease, *Visionary Compacts*. For allied texts, see Richard Brodhead, "Hawthorne and the Fate of Politics," *Essays in Literature* 11, no. 1 (Spring 1984): 95–103; Zelda Bronstein, "The Parabolic Ploys of *The Scarlet Letter*," *American Quarterly* 39, no. 2 (Summer 1987): 193–210, and Robert Levine, *Conspiracy and Romance: Studies in Brockden Brown, Cooper,*

Hawthorne, and Melville (Cambridge: Cambridge University Press, 1989).

12. To name two kinds of cultural history influential in their ways of adjudicating cultural overdetermination but not addressed specifically to Hawthorne, in the first case, or America, in the latter: William Boelhower, *Through a Glass Darkly: Ethnic Semiosis in American Literature* (New York: Oxford University Press, 1987); and Fredric Jameson's classic essays on ideology and utopia, "Imaginary and Symbolic in Lacan (1977)," in *The Ideologies of Theory: Essays, 1971–1986* (2 vols; Minneapolis: University of Minnesota Press, 1988), 1: 75–115; "Of Islands and Trenches: Neutralization and the Production of Utopian Discourse (1977)," *The Ideologies of Theory*, 2: 75–101; and "Reification and Utopia in Mass Culture," *Social Text* 1, no. 1 (1979): 130–48.

13. See, for example, Homi K. Bhabha, ed., *Nation and Narration* (London: Routledge, 1990); Stuart Hall, "Gramsci's Relevance for the Study of Race and Ethnicity," *Journal of Communication Inquiry* 10, no. 2 (Summer 1986): 5–27; Ernesto Laclau, *Politics and Ideology in Marxist Theory: Capitalism, Fascism, Marxism* (London: NLB, 1977); Chantal Mouffe and Ernesto Laclau, *Hegemony and Socialist Strategy: Towards a Radical Democratic Politics*, trans. Winston Moore and Paul Cammack (London: Verso, 1985); Fredric Jameson, "Third-World Literature in the Era of Multinational Capital," *Social Text* 15 (Fall 1986): 65–88 and Aijaz Ahmad, "Jameson's Rhetoric of Otherness and the 'National Allegory'," *Social Text* 17 (Fall 1987): 3–25; Tom Nairn, *The Break-Up of Britain: Crisis and Neonationalism*, (London: Verso, 1981); Doris Sommer, *One Master for Another: Populism as Patriarchal Rhetoric in Dominican Novels* (Lanham, Md.: University Press of America, 1983); and Gayatri Chakravorty Spivak, "Subaltern Studies: Deconstructing Historiography," in *In Other Worlds: Essays in Cultural Politics* (New York: Methuen, 1987), 197–221.

14. Some major texts of feminist revisionary political theory are: Ruth H. Bloch, "The Gendered Meanings of Virtue in Revolutionary America," *Signs* 13, no. 1 (Autumn 1987): 37–58; Mary G. Dietz, "Citizenship with a Feminist Face: The Problem with Maternal Thinking," *Political Theory* 13, no. 1 (February 1985): 19–37; Jean Bethke Elshtain, *Public Man, Private Woman: Women in Social and Political Thought* (Princeton: Princeton University Press, 1981); Leslie Friedman Goldstein, *The Constitutional Rights of Women: Cases in Law and Social Change* (Madison: University of Wisconsin Press, 1988); Joan R. Gundersen, "Independence, Citizenship, and the American Revolution," *Signs* 13, no. 1 (Autumn 1987): 59–77; Anne Norton, *Reflections on Political Identity*; Carole Pateman, *The Sexual Contract* (Stanford: Stanford University Press, 1988); Hanna Fenichel Pitkin, *Fortune Is a Woman: Gender and Politics in the Thought of Niccolò Machiavelli* (Berkeley and Los Angeles: University of California

Press, 1984); Iris Marion Young, "Polity and Group Difference: A Critique of the Ideal of Universal Citizenship," *Ethics* 99 (January 1989): 250–74.

15. Nina Baym suggests that Hester Prynne's gender informs her radical individualism against the claims of the state, and that Hawthorne is a kind of feminist. See note 6 above. A useful summary of the range of feminist critical responses can be found in Louise DeSalvo, *Nathaniel Hawthorne* (Atlantic Highlands, N.J.: Humanities Press International, 1987), 1–38. Of recent work, I'd especially like to cite that of Amy Schrager Lang, who has excellently argued for Hester's difference and even exile from the liberal model of the sovereign "subject" or "citizen"; see *Prophetic Woman: Anne Hutchinson and the Problem of Dissent in the Literature of New England* (Berkeley and Los Angeles: University of California Press, 1987), 161–92.

16. Eve Kosofsky Sedgwick, "Privilege of Unknowing," *Genders* 1 (Spring 1988): 102–24.

17. David Van Leer, "Hester's Labyrinth: Transcendental Rhetoric in Puritan Boston," in *New Essays on* The Scarlet Letter, ed. Michael J. Colacurcio (Cambridge: Cambridge University Press, 1985): 58.

18. On the juridical conceptions and conventions of national citizenship, see: José A. Cabranes, *Citizenship and the American Empire* (New Haven: Yale University Press, 1979); Michael Kent Curtis, *No State Shall Abridge: The Fourteenth Amendment and the Bill of Rights* (Durham, N.C.: Duke University Press, 1986); James H. Kettner, *The Development of American Citizenship, 1608–1870* (Chapel Hill: University of North Carolina Press, 1978); Sanford Levinson, *Constitutional Faith* (Princeton: Princeton University Press, 1988); Benjamin B. Ringer, *"We the People" and Others* (New York: Tavistock Publications, 1983); John P. Roche, "The Early Development of United States Citizenship," intro. by Robert E. Cushman, (Ithaca, N.Y.: Cornell University Press, 1949; rpt. in *Cornell Studies in American History, Literature, and Folklore* 1–7 [1944–62]; and Peter H. Schuck and Rogers M. Smith, *Citizenship Without Consent: Illegal Aliens in the American Polity* (New Haven: Yale University Press, 1985).

19. Kettner, *The Development of American Citizenship*, 287–88.

20. *Trop v. Dulles*, 78 S.Ct. 590 (1958).

21. Ibid., 597.

22. *Trop v. Dulles* 78 S.Ct. 590, 598. Warren cites Chief Justice Clark's opinion, 239 F.2d 527, 530.

23. Justice Brennan's argument, *Trop v. Dulles*, 78 S.Ct. 590, 603. For related illuminating histories and discussions of American citizenship, see also *Perez v. Brownell* 356 U.S. 44 (1958) and *Afroyim v. Rusk* 387 U.S. 253 (1967).

24. There is dissension on the court concerning the logic of assigning citizenship primal status. Justice Frankfurter asks, "Is constitutional dialectic so empty of reason that it can be seriously urged that loss of citizenship is a fate worse than death?" *Trop v. Dulles* 78 S.Ct. 590, 611. But the majority of justices say that it is and that forced expatriation is a species of political address even more brutal than physical torture.

25. The authors of the Constitution intended merely to ban torture with the Eighth Amendment; *Trop v. Dulles* significantly redefines "cruel and unusual" punishment by situating it along a juridico-ethical axis. See Anthony F. Granucci, "'Nor Cruel and Unusual Punishments Inflicted': The Original Meaning," *California Law Review* 57, no. 4 (October 1969): 839–65.

26. Cushman, Introduction, to Roche, "The Early Development of United States Citizenship," 5.

27. Ringer, *"We the People" and Others*, 103.

28. A useful documentary history of the struggle to redemocratize citizenship is Philip S. Foner, *"We the Other People": Alternative Declarations of Independence by Labor Groups, Farmers, Woman's Rights Advocates, Socialists, and Blacks, 1829–1975* (Urbana: University of Illinois Press, 1976). Curtis reports that Victoria Woodhull petitioned Congress to extend Fourteenth Amendment rights and protections explicitly to women; the congressional record shows senators producing a barrage of vagueness in their defense of constitutional patriarchalism (Curtis, *No State Shall Abridge*, 168).

29. For the constitutional history of the tension between consensual and birthright models of national identity, see Schuck and Smith, *Citizenship without Consent*, 9–89.

30. Roche, "The Early Development of United States Citizenship," 23.

31. Kettner, *The Development of American Citizenship*, 311.

32. Curtis, *No State Shall Abridge*, 26; Kettner, *The Development of American Citizenship*, 220–25; Roche, "The Early Development of United States Citizenship," 11.

33. *Dred Scott v. Sandford*, 60 U.S. (19 How.) 393 (1857); Taney cited in Roche, "The Early Development of United States Citizenship," 19.

CHAPTER ONE

1. Karl Marx, *The Eighteenth Brumaire of Louis Bonaparte* (1852; rpt. New York: International Publishers, 1963), 21.

2. Ibid., 19, 18.

3. For Jacques Lacan, the Symbolic order or function is the register of language and the law in which the subject-in-process discovers his historicity—a "past" that is always being realized. "The unconscious is that part of the concrete discourse, in so far as it is transindividual, that is not at the disposal of the subject in re-establishing the continuity of his conscious discourse. . . . The unconscious is that chapter of my history that is marked by a blank or occupied by a falsehood: it is the censored chapter. But the truth can be rediscovered; usually it has already been written down elsewhere. Namely: in monuments . . . in archival documents . . . in semantic evolution . . . in traditions, too, and even in the legends which, in a heroicized form, bear my history . . . and, lastly, in the traces that are inevitably preserved by the distortions necessitated by the linking of the adulterated chapter to the chapters surrounding it, and whose meaning will be re-established by my exegesis" (Jacques Lacan, "The Function and Field of Speech and Language in Psychoanalysis," in *Ecrits: A Selection*, trans. Alan Sheridan [New York: W.W. Norton, 1977], 49–50). Lacan applies this list of symbolic traces to the individual subject: his body, his memories, his language. My aim is to show how the modern nation installs itself within the memory and the conscience of citizens—in part by explicitly interpellating the citizen within a symbolic nationalist context (in July Fourth celebrations, for example) and in part by providing a general technology of memory that establishes the subject's "destiny" to receive her/his national inheritance. For other readings of Lacan's potential bearing on a theory of the subject-in-history, see Juliet Mitchell, "Introduction I," and Jacqueline Rose, "Introduction II," in Jacques Lacan and the *école freudienne*, *Feminine Sexuality*, ed. Juliet Mitchell and Jacqueline Rose, trans. Jacqueline Rose (New York: W. W. Norton, 1982), 1–57; and John Brenkman, "The Other and the One: Psychoanalysis, Reading, the *Symposium*," *Yale French Studies* 55/56 (1977): 396–456.

4. The most compelling argument for the utopian formation of this national intimacy has been made by Benedict Anderson, *Imagined Communities: Reflections on the Origin and Spread of Nationalism* (London: Verso, 1983).

5. See, for example, John P. McWilliams, Jr., *Hawthorne, Melville, and the American Character: A Looking-Glass Business* (New York: Cambridge University Press, 1984).

6. The classic, and still powerful, expression of this "moment" is in F. O. Matthiessen, *American Renaissance: Art and Expression in the Age of Emerson and Whitman* (New York: Oxford University Press, 1941). In Matthiessen's tradition of seeing literature as a symbolic relay between national formation and collective/libidinal fantasy, the following texts have laid important new ground for understanding the ways literary culture has engaged the American national-political apparatus: Robert Clark, *History*

and Myth in American Fiction 1823–1852 (New York: St. Martin's Press, 1985); Philip Fisher, *Hard Facts: Setting and Form in the American Novel* (New York: Oxford University Press, 1985); Myra Jehlen, *American Incarnation: The Individual, The Nation, and The Continent* (Cambridge: Harvard University Press, 1986); David S. Reynolds, *Beneath the American Renaissance: The Subversive Imagination in the Age of Emerson and Melville* (New York: Knopf, 1988).

7. Frantz Fanon, "The Pitfalls of National Consciousness," in *The Wretched of the Earth*, trans. Constance Farrington; preface by Jean-Paul Sartre (New York: Grove Press, 1963), 200.

8. Fanon, "On National Culture," in *The Wretched of the Earth*, 210.

9. Ibid., 233.

10. For discussions of the relation between the emergence of the modern nation and the history of populisms, see Anderson, *Imagined Communities*; David Forgacs, "National-Popular: Genealogy of a Concept," in *Formations: Of Nation and People* (London: Routledge & Kegan Paul, 1984), 83–98; and Ernesto Laclau, *Politics and Ideology in Marxist Theory* (London: NLB, 1977), especially 143–98.

11. In general my work in this area coincides with and has benefited from that of Anne Norton, *Alternative Americas: A Reading of Antebellum Political Culture* (Chicago: University of Chicago Press, 1986); Elaine Scarry, *The Body in Pain: The Making and Unmaking of the World* (New York: Oxford University Press, 1985), especially 108–33; and Doris Sommer, *One Master for Another: Populism as Patriarchal Rhetoric in Dominican Novels* (Lanham, Md.: University Press of America, 1983).

12. For example, the historical novel inevitably involves an allegory of power, but it usually does not "solve" in *political* language or logic the national problems it usually addresses. The conservative, radical, or contestatory implications of the relay between "art" and "politics" this kind of novel sets out to create might go in any ideological direction. Replacing the terms of "politics" with the logic of "art" might rupture the veil of inevitability that often characterizes a dominant political order; on the other hand, the very displacement of value from the realm of the political to the literary-symbolic formation might also figure the intractability of established political situations, as if relations of power constitute a Real that cannot be addressed or transformed in its own terms. In *The Political Unconscious: Narrative as a Socially Symbolic Act* (Ithaca, N.Y.: Cornell University Press, 1981), Fredric Jameson makes a similar argument about romances: their difference from the "Real" they construct may or may not valorize the historical/political referent. There too the critical project is to locate and to investigate the ideological space that produces a text's oppositional images of *realpolitik* and its antipode, whatever these may be.

13. *World*, March 16, 1885; quoted in Mary J. Shapiro, *Gateway to Liberty: The Story of the Statue of Liberty and Ellis Island* (New York: Vintage Books, 1986), 49–50; also in James B. Bell and Richard I. Abrams, *In Search of Liberty: The Story of the Statue of Liberty and Ellis Island* (Garden City, New York: Doubleday and Company, 1984), 35–36; Christian Blanchet and Bertrand Dard, *Statue of Liberty: the First One Hundred Years*, trans. Bernard A. Weisberger (New York: American Heritage, 1985), 90; Oscar Handlin, *Statue of Liberty* (New York: Newsweek, 1971), 54; Pierre Provoyeur and June Hargrove, eds., *Liberty: the French-American Statue in Art and History* (New York: Perennial Library, 1986), 163; and Marvin Trachtenberg, *The Statue of Liberty* 2d ed. (New York: Penguin Books, 1986), 183–84.

14. Quoted in Shapiro, *Gateway to Liberty*, 51.

15. See, for example, Lee Iacocca, "What Liberty Means to Me," *Newsweek*, 7 July 1986, 18–19.

16. Blanchet and Dard, *Statue of Liberty*, 41; they quote from Charles Blanc, *Le Temps*, 27 March 1878.

17. Frantz Fanon, *Black Skin, White Masks*, trans. Charles Lam Markmann (New York: Grove Press, 1967), 109–13.

18. Fanon, "On National Culture," *The Wretched of the Earth*, 209.

19. Trachtenberg, *Statue of Liberty*, 79.

20. See Michael Taussig, *Shamanism, Colonialism, and the Wild Man: A Study in Terror and Healing* (Chicago: University of Chicago Press, 1987), 199–203, 369.

21. Anderson, *Imagined Communities*, 67–68.

22. Ibid., 30.

23. Julia Kristeva, "Women's Time," trans. Alice Jardine and Harry Blake, *Signs* 7, no. 1 (Autumn 1981): 14.

24. The text of Emma Lazarus's poem, "The New Colossus" (1883), is quoted in Shapiro, *Gateway to Liberty*, 8:

> Not like the brazen giant of Greek fame,
> With conquering limbs astride from land to land;
> Here at our sea-washed, sunset gates shall stand
> A mighty woman with a torch, whose flame
> Is the imprisoned lightning, and her name
> Mother of Exiles. From her beacon-hand
> Glows world-wide welcome; her mild eyes command
> The air-bridged harbor that twin cities frame.
> "Keep, ancient lands, your storied pomp!" cries she
> With silent lips. "Give me your tired, your poor,

Your huddled masses yearning to breathe free,
The wretched refuse of your teeming shore. . . ."

25. "The statue does not record the past, except for the allusion to the Declaration of Independence. It anticipates continuously a future that is always in the process of becoming . . . " (Marina Warner, *Monuments and Maidens: The Allegory of the Female Form* [New York: Atheneum, 1985], 14).

26. See Neil Hertz, "Medusa's Head: Male Hysteria under Political Pressure," *Representations* 4 (Fall 1983): 27–54. Annette Kolodny has established that the symbolic fusion of nation and woman in the American case took place long before the statue's conception: "The personification of the new nation as feminine was hardly original with Freneau and, in fact, followed the contemporary habit of picturing Liberty, Justice, and indeed all the republican virtues, as latter-day Greek goddesses. What Freneau consistently and insistently infused into that image, however, was its inextricable connection to the larger femininity of soil and landscape, so that, whatever the ostensible object of the poem, the image of the nation as woman became one and the same with the image of the landscape . . . " (Kolodny, *The Lay of the Land: Metaphor as Experience and History in American Life and Letters* [Chapel Hill: University of North Carolina Press, 1975], 30).

27. Teresa de Lauretis, *Alice Doesn't: Feminism, Semiotics, Cinema* (Bloomington: Indiana University Press, 1984), 134, 151.

28. The sense that the Statue's power resides in its emphasis on immobility and passivity is affirmed by studies both of the nineteenth-century context of female statuary and the twentieth-century uses of the Statue's image. Although it is true that statues as such must imply movement, the Statue of Liberty *genders* immobility by representing it as female *activity* and, by implication, representing the nation as operating a priori as well. See especially Provoyeur and Hargrove, *Liberty*.

29. As Hertz suggests, in the event that the female political icon represents destructive, rather than positive, activity, her negative force is figured precisely as *physical activity*, her disruption of order seen as a rupture of ideal female stasis (see Hertz, "Medusa's Head").

30. Quoted in Blanchet and Dard, *Statue of Liberty*, 151. See also Iacocca, "What Liberty Means," and Tom Wolfe, "The Copper Goddess," *Newsweek*, 14 July 1986, 34–35.

31. Trachtenberg, *Statue of Liberty*, 196.

32. See Kaja Silverman, "*Histoire d'O:* The Construction of a Female Subject," in *Pleasure and Danger: Exploring Female Sexuality*, Carole S. Vance, ed. (London: Routledge & Kegan Paul, 1984), 320–49.

33. Marina Warner suggests another angle from which we can read

the gender-based meaning of the Statue's iconic passivity. "We can all take up occupation of Liberty, male, female, aged, children, she waits to enfold us in her meaning. But a male symbol like Uncle Sam relates to us in a different way, and the distinction between the two figures who have become emblematic of the United States indicates a common difference between male and female figures conveying ulterior meaning. The female form tends to be perceived as generic and universal, with symbolic overtones; the male as individual, even when it is being used to express a generalized idea . . . Liberty, like many abstract concepts expressed in the feminine, is in deadly earnest and one-dimensional . . . [I]f John Bull appears angry, it is his anger he expresses; Liberty is not representing her own freedom. She herself is caught by the differences, between the ideal and the general, the fantasy figure and the collective prototype, which seem to hold through the semantics of feminine and masculine gender in rhetoric and imagery, with very few exceptions" (Warner, *Monuments and Maidens*, 12–13).

34. See de Lauretis, *Alice Doesn't*, 103–57.

35. Julia Kristeva, "Women's Time," 13.

36. Eric Hobsbawm, "Mass-Producing Traditions: Europe, 1870–1914," in Eric Hobsbawm and Terence Ranger, *The Invention of Tradition* (Cambridge: Cambridge University Press, 1983), 279–80.

37. America was not established according to some notion of "cultural identity to justify [its] claims" but universal human rights. "Admittedly a sense of national identity developed after the achievement of independence but by then nationalism had a rather different and less distinctive function" (John Breuilly, *Nationalism and the State* [Manchester: Manchester University Press, 1982], 7). See also John F. Berens, *Providence and Patriotism in Early America, 1640–1815* (Charlottesville, Va.: University Press of Virginia, 1978); Lawrence J. Friedman, *Inventors of the Promised Land* (New York: Alfred A. Knopf, 1975); Linda Kerber, *Federalists in Dissent: Imagery and Ideology in Jeffersonian America* (Ithaca, N.Y.: Cornell University Press, 1970); Donald E. Pease, *Visionary Compacts: American Renaissance Writings in Cultural Context* (Madison: University of Wisconsin Press, 1987); Kenneth Silverman, *A Cultural History of the American Revolution* (New York: Columbia University Press, 1987); and Major L. Wilson, *Space, Time, and Freedom: The Quest for Nationality and the Irrepressible Conflict, 1815–1861* (Westport, Conn.: Greenwood Press, 1974). My reading of the conditions under which the American National Symbolic was produced, especially in the conjunction of American utopianism and the movement toward cultural nationalism, derives largely from this set of texts, in addition to Anderson, *Imagined Communities*. See also David S. Reynolds, *Beneath the American Renaissance*.

38. Silverman, *Cultural History of the American Revolution*, 492.

39. I derive this list directly from Norton, *Alternative Americas.*

40. Friedman, *Inventors of the Promised Land*, 139, 142.

41. Forgacs, "National-Popular," 92.

42. Sacvan Bercovitch, *The American Jeremiad* (Madison: University of Wisconsin Press, 1978); *The Puritan Origins of the American Self* (New Haven: Yale University Press, 1975); and "The Problem of Ideology in American Literary History," *Critical Inquiry* 12, no. 4 (Summer 1986), 631–53. An exemplary instance: "Of all symbols of identity, only *America* has united nationality and universality, civic and spiritual selfhood, secular and redemptive history, the country's past and paradise to be, in a single synthetic ideal. . . . The revelation of America serves to blight, and ultimately to preclude, the possibility of fundamental change" (*American Jeremiad*, 178–79).

43. Louis Marin, *Utopics: Spatial Play*, trans. Robert A. Vollrath (New Jersey: Humanities Press, 1984), 7. See also Karl Mannheim, *Ideology and Utopia*, trans. Louis Wirth and Edward Shils (New York: Harcourt, Brace, 1936); and Paul Ricoeur, *Lectures on Ideology and Utopia*, ed. George H. Taylor (New York: Columbia University Press, 1986).

44. For example, Bercovitch argues: "Hence the enormous conservative, restraining power in the alliance between utopia and ideology. It allows the dominant culture not merely to enforce rules of conduct, but to circumscribe the bounds of perception, thought, and desire. . . . [I]f the culture, that is, combines the conditions of modernization in the United States with the principles of a liberal democracy, then the need to preclude alternatives a priori, before they can become radical fact, assumes special urgency. We might say that the American ideology was made to fill that need" ("The Problem of Ideology in American Literary History," 644–45).

45. Nathaniel Hawthorne, *The House of the Seven Gables*, Centenary Edition of the Work of Nathaniel Hawthorne (Columbus: Ohio State University Press, 1965), 2: 1.

46. Nathaniel Hawthorne, *The Scarlet Letter*, Centenary Edition of the Works of Nathaniel Hawthorne, vol. I (Columbus: Ohio State University Press, 1962), 1: 36.

47. Nathaniel Hawthorne, *The Blithedale Romance*, Centenary Edition of the Works of Nathaniel Hawthorne (Columbus: Ohio State University Press, 1964), 3: 2.

48. For an argument that Hawthorne fully rejects liberal nationalism, see Michael J. Colacurcio, *The Province of Piety: Moral History in Hawthorne's Early Tales* (Cambridge: Harvard University Press, 1984). For critiques of Colacurcio's convictions about the degree of Hawthorne's deconstructive antiliberalism, see Bercovitch, "The A-Politics of Ambiguity in *The Scarlet Letter*," *New Literary History* 19, no. 3 (Spring 1988): 629–

54, and "Hawthorne's A-Morality of Compromise," *Representations* 24 (Fall 1988): 1–27; Lawrence I. Buell, *New England Literary Culture: From Revolution Through Renaissance* (Cambridge: Cambridge University Press, 1986); and George Dekker, *The American Historical Romance* (Cambridge: Cambridge University Press, 1987).

49. For the Enlightenment origins of this paradox, see Suzanne Gearhart, *The Open Boundary of History and Fiction: A Critical Approach to the French Enlightenment* (Princeton: Princeton University Press, 1984), 95–128. See also William Boelhower, *Through a Glass Darkly: Ethnic Semiosis in American Literature* (New York: Oxford University Press, 1987).

50. See Michel Foucault, "Of Other Spaces," *Diacritics* 16, no. 1 (Spring 1986): 22–27.

51. Friedrich Nietzsche, *On the Genealogy of Morals*, trans. Walter Kaufmann and R. J. Hollingdale, (New York: Vintage Books, 1967), 61.

52. See Fisher, *Hard Facts*.

53. See Nina Baym, *The Shape of Hawthorne's Career* (Ithaca, N.Y.: Cornell University Press, 1976), 23–24, and Colacurcio, *The Province of Piety*, 41–53. "The Hollow of the Three Hills" (1837) was eventually collected in *Twice-Told Tales* Centenary Edition of the Works of Nathaniel Hawthorne (Columbus: Ohio State University Press, 1974), 9: 199–204. "An Old Woman's Tale" was collected in *The Snow-Image* in 1851 and is reprinted in *"The Snow-Image" and Uncollected Tales*, Centenary Edition (Columbus: Ohio State University Press, 1974), 11: 240–50. "Alice Doane's Appeal" was never officially collected: it appears in *"The Snow-Image" and Uncollected Tales*, 266–80. All references to these tales will be contained in the text.

54. Two critically antithetical Hawthorne critics, Baym (in *The Shape of Hawthorne's Career*, 23–31) and Colacurcio (in *The Province of Piety*, 41–46), agree that these early tales are vague in their historical address and weak in their intellectual penetration, and as such do not provide the significant commentary on national culture characteristic of Hawthorne's later work.

55. In "Mrs. Hutchinson" (1830), *The Scarlet Letter* (1850), and *The Blithedale Romance* (1853), the public prominence of a theorizing woman, one who uses the same materials and addresses the same questions as the historicizing Hawthornean narrator, is always scandalous and always provokes some kind of textual discipline. This discipline appears both in representations of the woman's ethical, juridical, and physical chastisement (physical disfiguration, moral humiliation, and death in all cases) within the "story" or plot, and in the narrator's own metacommentary on the proprieties of gender. The most positive Hawthornean statement about the val-

ue of women's "public" knowledge can be found in *The House of the Seven Gables*: "It is often instructive to take the woman's, the private and domestic view, of a public man; nor can anything be more curious than the vast discrepancy between portraits intended for engraving, and the pencil-sketches that pass from hand to hand, behind the original's back" (122). But even this description regulates the proper operation of the woman-generated sign: it is most valuable when read as a supplement to public knowledge about public men; it is decorously circulated in a feminine underground, in an ephemeral aesthetic of faint lines and details.

56. Colacurcio has developed an argument about "Alice Doane's Appeal" that focuses on the drama of historical authorship engaged in by the narrator against Charles W. Upham, Edmund Spenser, Robert Calef, Cotton Mather and other historians of witchcraft. I defer to his treatment of the politics of authorship; my interest focuses instead on the politics and the technology of citizenship (*The Province of Piety*, 78–93).

57. Jameson, *The Political Unconscious*, 34.

58. "Celebrations of *Pope Day*, marked by parades and bonfires, are held in Salem until as late as 1817. . . . The traditional bonfire, a part of the *Pope Day* festivities, lingers as one of Salem's institutions; a favorite spot for the blaze is on top of *Gallows Hill*, usually on the eve of July 4th. In the original Salem *Pope Day*, little effigies of the Pope were carried then set on fire" (Frances Diane Robotti, *Chronicles of Old Salem: A History in Miniature* [Salem, Mass.: Newcomb and Gauss Co., 1948], 37).

59. See Hayden White, *Metahistory: the Historical Imagination in Nineteenth-Century Europe* (Baltimore: Johns Hopkins University Press, 1973), 29–31 and 135–162, and David Levin, *History as Romantic Art* (New York: Harcourt, Brace, and World, 1959), 3–23. See also Lawrence Buell, *New England Literary Culture*, especially "Reinventing Puritanism: The New England Historical Imagination," 191–280.

60. Taussig does not generalize the notion of "virginal historiography," but identifies it as a mode of cultural management in evidence among the Putumayo Indians: an icon of a female virgin (the Virgin of Caloto) "serves as a mnemonic of focal points in social history, points charged with the messianic time of persecution and salvation of the moral community. The mnemonic function replenishes the present with mythic themes and oppositions set into semiotic play in the theater of divine justice and redemption" (*Shamanism, Colonialism, and the Wild Man*, 197). Likewise, for Alice Doane—a character whose crisis is constituted by the awesome possibility that she has acted according to her own agency—symbolic and collective power resides in the passive *historicity* of the dialectical image, here the hymen.

61. Taussig, *Shamanism, Colonialism, and the Wild Man*, 198.

62. See Colacurcio, *The Province of Piety*, 283–313.

63. The question of why Hawthorne chooses two young women as his audience has been answered variously: Colacurcio sees them as the archetypal nineteenth-century audience of girls "nurtured on a soft but steady diet of gift books and other ladies' magazines"(79); traditional speculation identifies them as Hawthorne's wife, Sophia, and his sister, Rose. Hawthorne's repeated conflation of the female subject and the emergent subject of national history suggests to me that the emphasis here is on the erotic bases of collective political identity (but not to the exclusion of these other plausible possibilities).

64. It is suggestive, if nothing else, to note that Daniel Webster's speech commemorating the monument at Bunker Hill uses the same language of sentiment to describe the proper affect of "American" citizens. "Human beings are composed, not of reason only, but of imagination also, and sentiment; and that is neither wasted nor misapplied which is appropriated to the purpose of giving right direction to sentiments, and opening proper springs of feeling in the heart. Let it not be supposed that our object is to perpetuate national hostility, or even to cherish a mere military spirit. It is higher, purer, nobler. We consecrate our work to the spirit of national independence, and we wish that the light of peace may rest upon it for ever. We rear a memorial of our conviction of that unmeasured benefit which has been conferred on our own land, and of the happy influences which have been produced, by the same events, on the general interests of mankind" ("The Bunker Hill Monument," in *Great Speeches and Orations of Daniel Webster*, ed. and with an introduction by Edwin P. Whipple [Boston: Little, Brown, 1879], 125–26).

65. Mannheim, *Ideology and Utopia*, 94.

66. Jameson, "Reification and Utopia in Mass Culture," *Social Text* 1, no. 1 (1979): 144.

67. See for example, Baym, *The Shape of Hawthorne's Career*, 26.

68. See James Duncan Phillips, *Salem in the Eighteenth Century* (Boston and New York: Houghton Mifflin, 1937). "Halfway up the hill toward the town they passed the remains of the old palisade built in King Philip's War, twenty-five years before, to keep the Indians off the peninsula of Salem" (19). See also Robotti, *Chronicles of Old Salem*, 27–28.

69. Hawthorne has explicitly chosen elsewhere to represent King Philip's War: see "Main-Street," "The Gray Champion," and "The Indian Bible" chapter of *Grandfather's Chair*. However, even in these texts Hawthorne marginalizes the event. It is, says "Grandfather," "the bloodiest war that the Indians had ever waged against the white men"; but Hawthorne's main interest in all three texts is to talk about the white men who participated in the war, not about the war or Philip himself. Nathaniel Haw-

thorne, *The Whole History of Grandfather's Chair*, in *True Stories from History and Biography*, Centenary Edition of the Works of Nathaniel Hawthorne (Columbus: Ohio State University Press, 1972), 6: 50. For the most thorough critical analysis of Hawthorne's elision of the "other" Native Americans, see Kristin Herzog, *Women, Ethnics, and Exotics: Images of Power in Mid-Nineteenth-Century American Fiction* (Knoxville: University of Tennessee Press, 1983).

70. McWilliams, *Hawthorne, Melville, and the American Character*, suggests that Gallows Hill is here posed as the negative mirror of Bunker Hill (42, 89). In addition—as if to rescue it for idealist history—local studies of Salem often foreground the centrality of Gallows Hill in celebrations of national identity. The *Visitor's Guide to Salem*, for example, reports that on Gallows Hill "bonfires have been lighted on the eve of 'the Fourth of July' and on the occasion of other celebrations. The hill is covered with 'wood-wax' which is usually in full flower about July 4, when the effect of the flaring fire on the golden flowers and masses of people collected in groups about the hills is picturesque in the extreme" (*Visitor's Guide to Salem* [Salem, Mass.: Essex Institute, 1895]), 130. See also Sidney Perley, "Where the Salem 'Witches' Were Hanged," in *Essex Institute Historical Collections* 57, no. 1, (January 1921): 1–18.

71. Pease, *Visionary Compacts*, 52–56.

CHAPTER TWO

1. For the accepted genealogy of the novel, see Charles Ryskamp, "The New England Sources of *The Scarlet Letter*," *American Literature* 31 (November 1959): 257–72.

2. Critical theory is engaged in an ongoing struggle to define what constitutes "ideology"—broadly, whether it is best defined as a set of codified values or an imaginary field that mediates subjects' relations to the Real. The binary pair "utopia" and "ideology" is thus hobbled as a frame for analyses of cultural politics. For further elaboration of the debate over what ideology is and how it works, see John B. Thompson, *Studies in the Theory of Ideology* (Berkeley: University of California Press, 1984).

3. James Holstun, *A Rational Millennium: Puritan Utopias of Seventeenth-Century England and America* (New York: Oxford University Press, 1987), 246–47.

4. John Winthrop, "A Modell of Christian Charity," *Winthrop Papers, 1623–1630* (Boston: Massachusetts Historical Society, 1931), 2: 293.

5. I take the concept "genealogy" from Michel Foucault, in arguing that *The Scarlet Letter* provides two different kinds of analysis of the Pu-

ritan and American materials. Genealogy designates a history liberated from origins, genetic progression, and a movement toward unity; and "the traits it attempts to identify are not the exclusive generic characteristics of an individual, a sentiment, or an idea, which permit us to qualify them as 'Greek' or 'English': rather, it seeks the subtle, singular, and subindividual marks that might possibly intersect in them to form a network that is difficult to unravel" (145). "Genealogy, as an analysis of descent, is thus situated within the articulation of the body and history. Its task is to expose a body totally imprinted by history and process of history's destruction of the body," including the individual and collective "stigmata of past experience . . . desires, failings, and errors" (148). "Nietzsche, Genealogy, History," in *Language, Counter-Memory, Practice*, ed. Donald F. Bouchard, trans. Donald F. Bouchard and Sherry Simon (Ithaca, N.Y.: Cornell University Press, 1977).

6. Nathaniel Ward, *The Simple Cobler of Aggawamm in America*, ed. P. M. Zall (Lincoln: University of Nebraska Press, 1969), 25.

7. Ethyn Williams Kirby, *William Prynne: A Study in Puritanism* (Cambridge: Harvard University Press, 1931), 42. To place this practice in the Puritan historical context, see Edwin Powers, *Crime and Punishment in Early Massachusetts, 1620–1692: A Documentary History* (Boston: Beacon Press, 1966), 195–211; for its place in a more general history of punishment, see Edward Peters, *Torture* (New York: Basil Backwell, 1985).

8. The maternalization of the patriarchs was a common trope. Ministers "often called themselves breasts of God, and milk imagery was interchangeably dispensed among several theological roles: the minister, the Word, and God's promises. Thomas Shepard explains the parable of the ten virgins in allegorical terms by defining ministers as "those that sell" God's promises, or breasts. See David Leverenz, *The Language of Puritan Feeling: An Exploration in Literature, Psychology, and Social History* (New Brunswick, N.J.: Rutgers University Press, 1980), 142–3. John Cotton's *Spiritual Milk for American Babes*, "a volume used as a text-book by six generations of Massachusetts progeny . . . administered to the babes what was regarded as milk 'for their Souls Nourishment, drawn out of the Breasts of both Testaments'." (Charles Francis Adams, *Three Episodes of Massachusetts History: The Settlement of Boston Bay, the Antinomian Controversy, a Study of Church and Town Government* [New York: Russell and Russell, 1965], 2: 778–79).

9. Michael J. Colacurcio, "Footsteps of Ann Hutchinson: The Context of *The Scarlet Letter*," *ELH* 39, no. 3 (September 1972): 459–94; " 'The Woman's Own Choice': Sex, Metaphor, and the Puritan 'Sources' of *The Scarlet Letter*," in Colacurcio, ed. *New Essays on* The Scarlet Letter (New York: Cambridge University Press, 1985), 101–135. Colacurcio's essay "The Woman's Own Choice" uses many of the same archival materials

as the present study does: I take his focus on the Puritan and moral problem of female sexuality and spiritual privacy in *The Scarlet Letter* as given, and as an allied interpretation. Nonetheless, my work diverges in its choice to foreground juridical over theological rhetoric and history in the novel, and to see female sexuality as a stand-in (a metonym) for a more "political" interest in staging the juridical semiotics of American collective identity. A strong and strongly feminist reading of the Puritan theo-sexual material in *The Scarlet Letter* has been constructed by Margaret Olofson Thickstun, *Fictions of the Feminine: Puritan Doctrine and the Representation of Women* (Ithaca, N.Y.: Cornell University Press, 1988), 132–56.

10. Most notably, Nina Baym. See her *The Shape of Hawthorne's Career* (Ithaca, N.Y.: Cornell University Press, 1976) and "The Significance of Plot in Hawthorne's Romances," in *Ruined Eden of the Present: Hawthorne, Melville, and Poe: Critical Essays in Honor of Darrel Abel*, ed. G. R. Thompson and Virgil L. Lokke (West Lafayette, Ind.: Purdue University Press, 1981), 49–70.

11. John Winthrop, "Arbitrary Government," *Winthrop Papers, 1638–1644*, (Boston: Massachusetts Historical Society, 1944), 4: 480.

12. A valuable history of the state of Puritan adultery law has been provided by Hugh J. Dawson, "Hester Prynne, William Hathorne, and the Bay Colony Adultery Laws of 1641–42," *ESQ* 32, no. 3 (1986): 225–31.

13. Winthrop, "Arbitrary Government," 482.

14. Powers, *Crime and Punishment in Early Massachusetts: A Documentary History*, 62. Taken from *Massachusetts Colony Records* 4, pt. 1, 60–61 (1651). Powers writes in a footnote that "Attempts to regulate dress occurred as early as 1634—MCR vol. 1, 126 (1634); 183 (1636); 274–275 (1639) . . . " (575).

15. See Ward, *Simple Cobler*, 24–32, on the fashion excesses of the female aristocracy. "I truly confesse it is beyond the ken of my understanding to conceive, how those women . . . disfigure themselves with such exotick garbes, as . . . transclouts them into gantbar-geese, ill-shapen-shotten-shell-fish, Egyptian Hyeroglyphicks, or at the best into French flurts of the pastery . . . " (26).

16. Frederick Newberry, *Hawthorne's Divided Loyalties: England and America in His Works* (Cranbury, N.J.: Associated University Presses, 1987), 178–79.

17. The most crisis-oriented interpretation of legal history during this period can be found in Robert Emmet Wall, Jr., *Massachusetts Bay: The Crucial Decade, 1640–1650* (New Haven: Yale University Press, 1972). Other valuable sources include: George Athan Billias, ed., *Law and Authority in Early Massachusetts* (Barre, Mass.: Barre Publishers, 1965); Daniel R. Coquillette, ed., *Law in Colonial Massachusetts, 1630–1800*,

Publications of the Colonial Society of Massachusetts v. 62 (Boston: The Colonial Society of Massachusetts, 1984); Stephen Foster, *Their Solitary Way: The Puritan Social Ethic in the First Century of Settlement in New England* (New Haven: Yale University Press, 1971); George Lee Haskins, *Law and Authority in Early Massachusetts: A Study in Tradition and Design* (New York: The Macmillan Company, 1960); David Thomas Konig, *Law and Society in Puritan Massachusetts, Essex County, 1629–1692* (Chapel Hill: University of North Carolina Press, 1979); Perry Miller, *Orthodoxy in Massachusetts, 1630–1650* (Cambridge: Harvard University Press, 1933); Edmund S. Morgan, *The Puritan Dilemma: The Story of John Winthrop*, ed. Oscar Handlin (Boston: Little, Brown, 1958); Edwin Powers, *Crime and Punishment in Early Massachusetts, 1620–1692.*

18. John Winthrop, *The History of New England from 1630–1649*, ed. James Savage (Boston: Little, Brown, 1853), 2: 140, 228, 257. Winthrop, though disgusted by the narrow "politic principles" that seemed to motivate Bellingham's perversely democratic allegiances, tried to find ways to respect his fellow magistrate. Speaking of Bellingham and Richard Saltonstall, his ally, Winthrop writes that "it might be conceived in charity, that they walked according to their judgments and conscience, and where they went aside, it was merely for want of light, or their eyes were held through some temptation for a time, that they could not make use of the light they had" (257). Such an extenuating argument has significant resonances for the representation of Dimmesdale, addressed below.

19. Colacurcio, "Footsteps of Anne Hutchinson."

20. Bellingham first governed the Massachusetts Bay Colony in 1641. He returned to the governorship in 1654 and served again from 1665 to 1672. See Charles Ryskamp,"The New England Sources of *The Scarlet Letter*," which situates the novel between the years 1642 and 1649, and places John Winthrop at the actual helm.

21. For a biased, but accurate and brief, biography of Bellingham, see James Savage, *A Genealogical Dictionary of the First Settlers of New England* (Boston: Little, Brown, 1860), 161–62.

22. For an excellent discussion of the narrator's language of "sympathy," see David Van Leer, "Hester's Labyrinth: Transcendental Rhetoric in Puritan Boston," in Colacurcio, *New Essays on* The Scarlet Letter, 57–100.

23. See Haskins, *Law and Authority in Early Massachusetts.*

24. The classic, encyclopedic exposition of this struggle over the "sympathy" of nature is Otto Friedrich von Gierke, *Natural Law and the Theory of Society, 1500–1800*, trans. and introduction by Ernest Barker (1934; rpt. Boston: Beacon Press, 1957); for a more condensed analysis of the natural-law issue in seventeenth-century political philosophy, see J. P. Sommerville, *Politics and Ideology in England, 1603–1640* (London:

Longman, 1986); the American Puritan reception of this problem is still best elaborated in the chapters "The Uses of Reason" and "Nature" in Perry Miller, *The New England Mind: The Seventeenth Century* (New York: Macmillan, 1939), 181–235; for the literary elaboration of its American fortune, see Myra Jehlen, *American Incarnation: the Individual, the Nation, and the Continent* (Cambridge: Harvard University Press, 1986).

25. All of the histories mentioned in note 4 discuss the negative voice issue in varying degrees. Winthrop's *Journal* and the *Winthrop Papers*, vol. 4, also contain valuable close-to-the-source discussion of the conflict.

26. T. H. Breen, *The Character of a Good Ruler: A Study of Puritan Political Ideas in New England, 1630–1730* (New Haven: Yale University Press, 1970), 73ff. Chapter 2, "A Family Quarrel, 1630–1660," configures the same historical crises in Puritan juridical discipline alluded to by the narrator (35–86).

27. Winthrop, *The History of New England from 1630 to 1649*, 2: 141.

28. *Winthrop Papers*, 4: 383.

29. Wall, *Massachusetts Bay: The Crucial Decade*, 11–12.

30. Winthrop, *The History of New England from 1630 to 1649*, 2: 183.

31. Typically, Winthrop and Bellingham argued different sides of this issue: "This stiffness of his and singularity in opinion was very unpleasing" to Winthrop (*The History of New England from 1630 to 1649*, 2: 139).

32. Edward Johnson apotheosizes in verse the Governor's juridical preeminence: "Richardus now arise must thou, Christ seed hath thee to plead,/ His peoples cause, with equall Laws, in wildernesse them lead; Though slow of speech, thy counsell reach, shall each occation well,/Sure thy sterne looke it cannot brook those wickedly rebell./With labours might, thy pen indite doth Lawes for peoples learning:/That judge with skill, and not with will, unarbitrate discerning; *Bellingham* thou, on valiant now, stop not in discontent,/For Christ with crown, will thee renown, then spend for him, be spent;/As thou hast done thy race still run till death, no death shall stay,/Christ's work of might, till Scripture light, bring Resurection day" (*Wonder-Working Providence of Sions Saviour in New-England* in *Wonder-Working Providence of Sions Saviour in New-England (1654) and Good News from New-England (1648)*, ed. Edward J. Gallagher [Delmar, N.Y.: Scholars' Facsimiles and Reprints, 1974], 67–68).

33. Christopher Hill, *The Century of Revolution, 1603–1714* (New York: W. W. Norton, 1961), 67–68.

34. Kirby, *William Prynne*, 170–71. William M. Lamont's *Godly Rule: Politics and Religion, 1630–60* (London: Macmillan, 1969) also

places Prynne ideologically and politically in the Puritan fight to empower the common law.

35. For the personal and political fortunes of Coke's life and work, see Sir William Holdsworth, *A History of English Law* (London: Methuen, 1924), especially 5: 427–56.

36. Ibid., 5: 238–54, 434–38, 485–88.

37. For a discussion of the political lives of both Noye and Finch, see W. J. Jones, *Politics and the Bench: The Judges and the Origins of the English Civil War* (London: Allen and Unwin, 1971), 92–95, 139–41.

38. See Powers, *Crime and Punishment in Early Massachusetts*, 1–14, 30–99, for the history of legal codification in Massachusetts Bay.

39. John Cotton, "Abstract of the Lawes of New England as Proposed by John Cotton," in *Hutchinson Papers* (1865; rpt. New York: Burt Franklin, 1967), 1: 181–205.

40. Nathaniel Ward, *Body of Liberties (1641)*, in Powers, *Crime and Punishment in Early Massachusetts*, 533–48.

41. In 1646, Dr. Robert Child, along with six other residents of the Massachusetts Bay Colony, petitioned the General Court to extend the citizenship rights of England to all inhabitants of the New England colony. "Notwithstanding, we cannot, according to our judgements, discerne a setled forme of government according to the lawes of England, which may seem strange to our countrymen, yea to the whole world, especially considering we are all English. Neither do we so understand and perceyve our owne lawes or libertyes, or any body of lawes here so established, as that thereby there may be a sure and comfortable enjoyment of our lives, libertyes, and estates, acording to our due and naturall rights, as freeborne subjects of the English nation." Child et al. attribute the juridical insecurity of the citizens to "an overgreedy spirit of arbitrary power" and, among other things, "a negative or destructive vote unduly placed, and not well regulated." ("A Remonstrance and Petition of Robert Child, and Others," in *Hutchinson Papers* [Albany, N.Y.: Publications of the Prince Society, 1865], 1: 216–217.) This remonstrance provoked a long answer by the General Court, which both asserts that its laws do fall into line with English law, and that the petitioners "must either harden theire hearts or confesse theire guilt, and be careful to reforme theire arbitrary obedience, as we are to keep off arbitrary government. We may say the same for the second, the Negative vote." Their response is extremely sarcastic and anti-populist, as might be predicted. ("A Declaration of the General Court at Boston 4 [9] 1646, concerning a Remonstrance and Petition exhibited at the Last Session of this Court by Doctor Child, Thomas Fowle, Samuel Maverick, Thomas Burton, John Smith, David Yale, and John Dand" ibid., 236–7.)

42. S. F. C. Milsom, *Historical Foundations of the Common Law* (London: Butterworths, 1969), 85.

43. For the strongest articulation of this position, see Winthrop on "Arbitrary Government," *Winthrop Papers,* vol. 4.

44. Winthrop, ibid., 476. In addition, Robert Emmet Wall, Jr., *Massachusetts Bay: The Crucial Decade*, notes that the "Declaration of the General Court" against Child's Remonstrance publicly obscures the colony's punishment for adultery, because of worry about discrepancies between the colony's law and that of England (176–77).

45. The patriarchal analogy between God, kings or legislators, and fathers has been deployed both on behalf of aristocratic, monarchical, absolutist hierarchies and more populist reconstructions of social authority. But the double reading of this analogy as a "theory" of legitimacy and a "description" of sexual hierarchy (what Gordon J. Schochet calls a "genetic" or "anthropological" explanation of legitimacy) has characterized arguments all along the political spectrum. Schochet cites Dudley Digges, for example: "In the early days of the world, Digges wrote . . . 'patriarchs lived so long and fathered so many children that they might people a Nation out of their own loynes, and be saluted *Pater Patriae* without a metaphor; the same being their subjects and their children'." (Gordon J. Schochet, *Patriarchalism in Political Thought: The Authoritarian Family and Political Speculation and Attitudes Especially in Seventeenth-Century England* [Oxford: Basil Blackwell, 1975], 104.)

46. Even Bellingham's election was contested: see Winthrop's *The History of New England from 1630 to 1649*, 2: 35, 52–55.

47. Ibid., 2: 52.

48. This would be Colacurcio's argument, "The Woman's Own Choice."

49. Michael Davitt Bell, *Hawthorne and the Historical Romance of New England: the Sacrifice of Relation* (Princeton: Princeton University Press, 1971), 136.

50. Winthrop, "A Modell of Christian Charity," *Winthrop Papers*, 2: 288.

51. Brian Tierney, *Religion, Law, and the Growth of Constitutional Thought, 1150–1650* (Cambridge: Cambridge University Press, 1982), 38.

52. Miller, *The New England Mind: The Seventeenth Century*, 190–191, 418. See also Charles Lloyd Cohen, *God's Caress: the Psychology of Puritan Religious Experience* (New York: Oxford University Press, 1986).

53. Each of the texts listed in note 16 employs Winthrop as Hawthorne does, both as the exemplary Puritan of his historical moment, and as

a major historian of his own time. See especially Cohen, *God's Caress*; Sacvan Bercovitch, *The Puritan Origins of the American Self* (New Haven: Yale University Press, 1975).

54. "Arbitrary Government" and "A Modell of Christian Charity" are in the *Winthrop Papers* (2: 282–95 and 4: 468–88). "On Liberty" is reproduced in Robert C. Winthrop, *Life and Letters of John Winthrop* (Boston: Ticknor and Fields, 1867), 339–42. All future references to these works will be cited by page number in the body of the text.

55. For the history of this idea, see Albert 0. Hirschman, *The Passions and the Interests: Political Arguments for Capitalism Before Its Triumph* (Princeton: Princeton University Press, 1977).

56. C. S. Lewis discusses the philological resonance of "conscience" and "synteresis" in *Studies in Words* (Cambridge: Cambridge University Press, 1967), 181–213; Cohen, *God's Caress*, depicts its Puritan incarnation, 120–121; as does Miller, *The New England Mind: The Seventeenth Century*, 193, 270.

57. Once again, Perry Miller established the convention of seeing splits or tensions within the Puritan state—*The New England Mind* project is an interrogation of the inconsistencies within this structure. Bell says that Hawthorne's view of the Puritans is the common one in the nineteenth century: "But the great theme of the historical romance of New England was not the conflict between Puritanism and external tyranny but the conflict within Puritanism itself between the forces of tyranny and the forces of liberty" (Michael Davitt Bell, *Hawthorne and the Historical Romance of New England* [Princeton: Princeton University Press, 1971], 159).

58. See Colacurcio, "The Woman's Own Choice."

59. Foster, *Their Solitary Way*, 41, 48.

60. Michel Foucault comments on the status of this method in its historical context: *Discipline and Punish: The Birth of the Prison*, trans. Alan Sheridan (New York: Vintage Books, 1979), 3–31.

61. St. Thomas Aquinas, *Summa Theologiae* (New York: McGraw-Hill, 1975), 37: 81.

Winthrop excerpts Aquinas' response to an objection he attributes to Augustine, "who holds that *while men judge about temporal laws when they are making them, yet once they are passed and established it is not lawful to question them, but instead to apply them*" (81). Aquinas' response to this question distinguishes between natural and divine law. In contrast to Winthrop in "On Liberty" and "A Modell of Christian Charity," Aquinas does not here foreground the concept of depraved nature. Rather, positive law ideally contains natural right, but cannot legislate it, because it is natural. "Consequently judgement must be passed according to written laws, otherwise it would fall short of natural right or of positive right" (81). Hence: if a legal code contains something contrary to natural right, "it is unjust and has no binding force." Furthermore, if a law is too harsh, the juror has the right to judge according to equity, "*severity contrary to our welfare*" being the intention of no lawmaker. In sum, a certain kind of antinomianism is permissible according to the light of nature.

62. Baym, *The Shape of Hawthorne's Career*, 133.

63. Bercovitch, *The Puritan Origins of the American Self*, 114.

64. Miller, *The New England Mind: The Seventeenth Century*, especially chapter 5.

65. For a reading of Puritan discourse in accord with this reading of Puritan symbolic practice in *The Scarlet Letter*, see Ann Kibbey, *The Interpretation of Material Shapes in Puritanism* (Cambridge: Cambridge Unversity Press, 1986).

66. Lewis, *Studies in* Words, 12–17.

67. Bell, *Hawthorne and the Historical Romance of New England*, 136. See also Larry J. Reynolds, "*The Scarlet Letter* and Revolutions Abroad," *American Literature* 57, no. 1 (March 1985): 61.

CHAPTER THREE

1. See, for example, Larzer Ziff, *Literary Democracy: The Declaration of Cultural Independence in America* (New York: Viking, 1981), 124–25.

2. Michel Foucault, "Nietzsche, Genealogy, History," in Donald F. Bouchard, ed., *Language, Counter-Memory, Practice* (Ithaca, N.Y.: Cornell University Press, 1977), 148. The discussion of the body directly following also derives from this work.

3. B. Katherine Brown's summary of historians' disagreement over who exactly had the franchise in Puritan Massachusetts suggests that Hawthorne's "public" is constituted not by the voting members of the town but by the more varied group emerging from the colony's religious and mercantile community. The ambiguity about this group's members would have been especially acute during the 1640s, when the relative independence of the colony from English rule led to a struggle within the community over how to delimit the public franchise in the New England context. See B. Katherine Brown, "The Controversy Over the Franchise in Puritan Massachusetts, 1954 to 1974," in *Puritan New England: Essays on Religion, Society, and Culture*, ed. Alden T. Vaughan and Francis J. Bremer (New York: St. Martin's Press, 1977), 128–54. See also Timothy H. Breen, "Who Governs: The Town Franchise in Seventeenth-Century Massachusetts," *The William and Mary Quarterly* 3d. ser., 27, no. 3 (July 1970): 460–74. Breen notes that the *Body of Liberties*, for the first time, gave all Puritan and non-

Puritan male inhabitants of the colony the "libertie to come to any publique Court, Councel, or Towne meeting, and either by speech or writeing to move any lawfull, seasonable, and materiall question, or to present any necessary motion, complaint, petition, Bill, or information"—so long, that is, as he did not "behave himselfe offensively" (463). The privilege of voting is denied to all of "the people," as such, but this is the first moment when the right to intervene in the political public sphere is particularly distributed according to gender position.

4. See David Van Leer, who convincingly situates the narrator's values in the context of transcendentalist sympathies. But Van Leer's reading needs to be complicated by the fact that the discourse of the heart and of love that so characterizes the transcendentalist theory of the subject is immanent in Puritan rhetoric of the soul and of the sociality of "bodies" in the political sphere (David Van Leer, "Hester's Labyrinth: Transcendental Rhetoric in Puritan Boston," in Michael J. Colacurcio, ed., *New Essays on* The Scarlet Letter [New York: Cambridge University Press, 1985]: 57–100). For another crucial angle on the narrator, which reads him as a representative cultural psychology, with respect to questions of narrative and gender authority, see David Leverenz, "Mrs. Hawthorne's Headache: Reading *The Scarlet Letter*," *Nineteenth Century Fiction* 37, no. 4 (March 1983): 552–75.

5. David Reynolds comments that the love of such juridical excess characterized the popular "sensational novel" whose codes dominated the public reception of the text (but, says Reynolds, Hawthorne used them to generate "moral ambiguity" rather than the "crass diversion" of the popular genre) (David S. Reynolds, *Beneath the American Renaissance: The Subversive Imagination in the Age of Emerson and Melville* [New York: Alfred A. Knopf, 1988], 264).

6. See also Michael J. Colacurcio, "'The Woman's Own Choice': Sex, Metaphor, and the Puritan 'Sources' of *The Scarlet Letter*," in Colacurcio, ed. *New Essays on* The Scarlet Letter, 101–35.

7. Michael J. Colacurcio, "Footsteps of Ann Hutchinson," *ELH* 39, no. 3 (September 1972): 459–94; Amy Schrager Lang, *Prophetic Woman: Anne Hutchinson and the Problem of Dissent in the Literature of New England* (Berkeley: University of California Press, 1987): 161–92.

8. Hibbins's death by unjust persecution for having a perverse personality is remembered twice in the novel: 49, 116. Thomas Hutchinson, whose history of the colony was familiar to Hawthorne, notes that Hibbins, like Hutchinson, was named "witch" by the law for being too sharp-tongued and self-possessed a woman. It is worth reproducing Hutchinson's text in full, to show evidence of (a) the collaboration between Puritan law and the supernatural that Hawthorne also shows operating in the popular

juridical mind of the Bay Colony and (b) the literal politics of embodiment in patriarchal political culture.

> The most remarkable occurrence in the colony, in the year 1655, was the trial and condemnation of Mrs. Ann Hibbins for witchcraft. Her husband, [William Hibbins], who died in the year 1654, was an agent for the colony in England, several years one of the assistants, and a merchant of note in the town of Boston; but losses in the latter part of his life had reduced his estate, and increased the natural crabbedness of his wife's temper, which made her turbulent and quarrelsome, and brought her under church censures, and at length rendered her so odious to her neighbors as to cause some of them to accuse her of witchcraft. The jury brought her in guilty, but the magistrates refused to accept the verdict; so the cause came to the general court, where the popular clamour prevailed against her, and the miserable old woman was condemned and executed. Search was made upon her body for tetts, and in her chests and boxes, for puppets, images, &c. but there is no record of any thing of that sort being found. Mr. Beach, a minister in Jamaica, in a letter to Doctor Increase Mather in the year 1684, says,
>
>> You may remember what I have sometimes told you your famous Mr. Norton once said at his own table before Mr. Wilson the pastor, elder Penn, and myself, and wife &c. who had the honour to be his guests. That one of your magistrates wives, as I remember, was hanged for a witch, only for having more wit than her neighbors. It was his very expression, she having, as he explained it, unhappily guessed that two of her prosecutors, whom she saw talking in the street, were talking of her; which, proving true, cost her her life, notwithstanding all he could do to the contrary, as he himself told us.
>
> It fared with her as it did with Joan of Arc in France. Some counted her a saint and some a witch, and some observed solemn marks of Providence set upon those who were very forward to condemn her, and to brand others upon the like ground with the like reproach.

See Thomas Hutchinson, *The History of the Colony and Province of Massachusetts-Bay*, ed. Lawrence Shaw Mayo (Cambridge: Harvard University Press, 1936), 1: 160–61. See also Alfred S. Reid, *"The Yellow Ruff" and* The Scarlet Letter (Gainesville: University of Florida Press, 1955); David Ketterer, "'Circle of Acquaintance': Mistress Hibbins and the Hermetic Design of *The Scarlet Letter*," *English Studies in Canada* 9, no. 3 (September 1983): 294–311.

9. Edward Peters notes that while seventeenth-century political theory and popular discourse described torture as legitimate tool of the state, post-Enlightenment thought "focused often on torture as violating their most essential tenets, that of the natural dignity of humans and that of the individual natural right of humans to decide upon the means of preservation of their dignity" (87). It is at this time, he suggests, that literature itself deployed torture as an instrument of literary interest. This historical and typically idealist transformation of the material thing to the idea of the thing might well explain the manifestations of ambivalence toward the legal apparatus expressed in *The Scarlet Letter.* While "our common nature" might well be violated by the physical violations of the scaffold and the pillory, in the narrator's view, the mnemotechnical value of the scaffold's theatricalization of human suffering is central to the novel's implicit claim of its own superiority to the historical law. See Edward Peters, *Torture* (New York: Basil Blackwell, 1985).

10. See Jacques Lacan and the *école freudienne*, *Feminine Sexuality*, ed. Juliet Mitchell and Jacqueline Rose, trans. Jacqueline Rose (New York: W. W. Norton, 1982).

11. It is important to emphasize that the scaffold scene is not the first time Hester is brought into the law's symbolic order: her memories on the scaffold reveal her multiple interpellations into the family and marriage. On the scaffold, with the installation of the New Law, these prior relations of submission to duty appear as mirages to her. Thus the New Law, and her symbolic position within it, are her only "realities": and here she is especially crucial to the legitimation of the local embodiment of the symbolic order.

12. That they do not "love" their own authority properly is apparent not only in the men's subliminal battles but also in their betrayal of the very laws they represent in the community. Jacques Donzelot notes that preceding the institution of separate and distinct social services within the community, the physician and the priest were counted on to "police" the family; however, the methods and goals of the physician were considered to conflict directly with those of the priest, because the physician could cure the very ailments that otherwise controlled certain kinds of legal and moral transgressions (specifically venereal disease, the presence of which at least theoretically limited sexual prodigality). Thus these two figures were the representative of the law in the family's "private" realm and yet within that hierarchical position, battled for jurisdiction. In this light Dimmesdale and Chillingworth, whose positions in regard to the law seem roughly contiguous, are punished not only because they are agents of the law in each other's and Hester's interior world, but also because their competition potentially destabilizes public structures of patriarchal authority. As with Bellingham, the public figure has no private life, no privates; every act re-

dounds on the law. See Jacques Donzelot, *The Policing of Families*, trans. Robert Hurley and with an introduction by Gilles Deleuze (New York: Pantheon Books, 1979).

13. Chillingworth's supernatural legalism somehow leaks into the popular imagination as well: the physician's associations with Sir Thomas Overbury's murder ("under [yet] some other name"—has he transformed his identity with respect to passion and the law, in yet another life?), with "savage" culture, and with "miraculous cures" create "vulgar" ideas (127) about the source of his authority. On the Overbury affair's mixture of political, scientific, and amorous scandal, see Reid, *"The Yellow Ruff" and* The Scarlet Letter.

14. The narrator explicitly says that Chillingworth's "concord of paternal and reverential love for the young pastor" was considered the only possible substitute for any heterosexual/married love Dimmesdale might have fostered (125).

15. "Homosocial," rather than "homoerotic" or "homosexual," describes the state of alliance among men that derives its great interest and attractiveness for men by remaining a *symbolic*, as opposed to sexual, affiliation—an identification at the level of the phallus, without the pressure of acting through the penis. I elaborate here on the work of Eve Kosofsky Sedgwick, *Between Men: English Literature and Male Homosocial Desire* (New York: Columbia University Press, 1985).

16. My analysis of the propping of masochism, sadism, and sexual pleasure within Dimmesdale is informed by Jean Laplanche, *Life and Death in Psychoanalysis*, trans. and with an introduction by Jeffrey Mehlman (Baltimore: Johns Hopkins University Press, 1976), 85–102. Freud (only half-jokingly) argues that the autoerotic economy of pleasure-violence is inscribed not only within the family and the individual subject but in the realm of political desire as well. See Sigmund Freud, "A Child Is Being Beaten" and "Fetishism," in *Sexuality and the Psychology of Love*, ed. Philip Rieff (New York: Collier Books, 1963), 107–32, 214–19.

17. As a result of his particularly Puritan split from the language Dimmesdale speaks, a split created by his own and the communities' fetishization of himself as minister—a body and a body of discourse—he silences himself and turns on his physical body, fetishizing it as the public does, but playing out his various disassociations on it violently. The slippage between a Marxian and a psychoanalytic notion of fetishism is played out within and between Dimmesdale's "two persons": his ministerial body and discourse is commodified (it gives him "value" in the world) and simultaneously he places a negative value on that which he must consider his private language and private body, though no less ministerial for all that.

18. As Colacurcio reminds us, one reason Dimmesdale invites Wilson

to ascend the scaffold is that that image repeats the historic relation of Winthrop, Cotton, and Wilson in the persecution of Ann Hutchinson. See Michael J. Colacurcio, "Footsteps of Ann Hutchinson."

19. Such a configuration of the fractured subjectivity, the ravaged body, and the sinful state, was theorized by Nathaniel Ward.

> That State is wise, that will improve all paines and patience rather to compose, then tolerate differences in Religion. There is no divine Truth, but hath much Coelestiall fire in it from the Spirit of Truth, nor no irreligious untruth, without its proportion of Antifire from the spirit of Error to contradict it: the zeale of the one, the virulency of the other, must necessarily kindle Combustions. Fiery diseases seated in the spirit, imbroile the whole frame of the body: others more externall and coole, are lesse dangerous. They which divide in Religion, divide in God . . . there is no reconciliation, without atonement; that is, without uniting in him, who is One, and in his Truth, which is also one. (Nathaniel Ward, *The Simple Cobler of Aggawamm in America,* ed. P. M. Zall [Lincoln: University of Nebraska Press, 1969], 9)

20. In Larry J. Reynolds' view, this transformation in the novel refers to Hawthorne's general sympathy with resistance and general repudiation of revolution. His fine essay, "*The Scarlet Letter* and Revolutions Abroad," reinforces my argument that the shift in the narrator's sympathies is a conservative political one. But since his reading concentrates more on "Hawthorne's" sympathies than on the effect of those sympathies on the project of articulating the various positions that compose national identity, his discussions of characters' motives fall short of explaining how the revolutionary aura of individual subjects (which they mostly derive from foreign revolutions) redounds on the problem of collective and national identity in America. See Reynolds, "*The Scarlet Letter* and Revolutions Abroad"; see also Jonathan Arac, "The Politics of *The Scarlet Letter,*" in Sacvan Bercovitch and Myra Jehlen, eds., *Ideology and Classic American Literature* (Cambridge: Cambridge University Press, 1986), 247–66.

21. In his discussion of the sexual politics of *The Scarlet Letter*, George Dekker similarly notes how Hawthorne expresses "political" rage at female theorizing through an analysis of its gender-castrating effects on Hester. But to Dekker this shows that "nineteenth-century feminism reincarnates the schismatic and 'enthusiastic' impulses of seventeenth-century Puritanism" (248), whereas I argue here that the novel's ambiguation of Hester's gender is less interested in women as a historical group and more engaged in the theorization of "woman" within her own Symbolic Order, thus setting up a logic of equivalence between Hester's counter-law and the excesses of the patriarchal law whose crisis is the historical event of *The Scarlet Letter.* See George Dekker, *The American Historical Romance*

(New York: Cambridge University Press, 1987), 244–54. See also David Van Leer, "Hester's Labyrinth: Transcendental Rhetoric in Puritan Boston," for an argument similar to Dekker's.

22. Fredric Jameson, "Of Islands and Trenches: Neutralization and the Production of Utopian Discourse," *The Ideologies of Theory: Essays, 1971–1986* (Minneapolis: The University of Minnesota Press, 1988), 2: 101.

23. See Jacques Lacan's elaboration of the phrase "woman is a symptom." His reminder that "images and symbols *for* the woman cannot be isolated from images and symbols *of* the woman" suggests the impossibility of thinking outside of the discursive field developed historically on behalf of protecting the Father. The Hawthornean narrator's representation of the Female Symbolic expresses a fantasy and a reading of what "woman" would want, if she could pose herself as a historical subject of language. As it is, negated in the realm of history, she must play Isis to her own Osiris by embracing the utopian mode. As a result, the narrator has the pleasure of writing both her terrifying theory and his consoling analysis of its perversity. See Jacques Lacan and the *école freudienne*, *Feminine Sexuality*, ed. Juliet Mitchell and Jacqueline Rose (New York: W. W. Norton, 1982), 171ff., 90. See also Neil Hertz, "Medusa's Head: Male Hysteria under Political Pressure," *Representations* 4 (Fall 1983): 27–54; Fredric

Jameson, "Imaginary and Symbolic in Lacan," *The Ideologies of Theory: Essays, 1971–1986* (Minneapolis: University of Minnesota Press, 1988), 1: 115.

24. Eliot's "praying towns" were actually founded in 1651 (Hutchinson and other early historians place them in 1650, but modern historians disagree), but I presume that the narrator's description of Dimmesdale's visit to Eliot "among his Indian converts" (182) means to refer to the convened space of the utopian settlements Eliot dedicated to "civilizing" and "Christianizing" Native Americans. On Hawthorne's other national-utopian use of Eliot, see Lauren Berlant, "Fantasies of Utopia in *The Blithedale Romance*," *American Literary History* 1, no. 1 (Spring 1989): 30–62.

25. In truth, the minister did not act "alone": he and Hester mutually "consecrat[ed]" "[w]hat we did" (195). But "alone" rings out in this narrative as the isolating consequence of the law's violation. Note the pattern of repetition: "Standing alone in the world,—alone, as to any dependence on society, . . . alone, and hopeless of retrieving her position . . . she cast away the fragments of a broken chain" (164); "'O Hester!' cried Arthur Dimmesdale. . . . 'There is not the strength or courage left me to venture into the wide, strange, difficult world, alone!' . . . He repeated the word. 'Alone, Hester!'" (198). From conscience's point of view one's shameful activity is always alone.

26. For an opposing point of view of the narrator's relation to judgement, see Daniel Cottom, "Hawthorne versus Hester: The Ghostly Dialectic of Romance in *The Scarlet Letter*," *Texas Studies in Literature and Language* 24, no. 1 (Spring 1982): 47–67. Cottom argues that the narrator's equivocations about the ethical status of his characters signify his desire to be outside of a juridicial apparatus—his "primary allegiance is to imagination rather than assertion" (47).

27. This double shift in political subjectivity—through the feminine, for the patriarchal—has also been described in terms of liberal subjectivity and specifically American sentimentality. See Mary Kelley, *Private Woman, Public Stage: Literary Domesticity in Nineteenth-Century America* (New York: Oxford University Press, 1984).

28. Nancy Armstrong, *Desire and Domestic Fiction: A Political History of the Novel* (New York: Oxford University Press, 1987).

29. By "inevitability" I mean simply that utopia and the law are two generic social formations of desire that are inevitable in the same way that desire is ongoing.

30. "Cultural work" is Jane Tompkins' term for what early American novels did for the formation of cultural identity. See Jane P. Tompkins, *Sensational Designs: The Cultural Work of American Fiction, 1790–1860* (New York: Oxford University Press, 1985).

31. See Sacvan Bercovitch, "Hawthorne's A-Morality of Compromise," *Representations* 24 (Fall 1988): 1–27, on Endicott's meaning as the harbinger of the new New Law.

32. See Benedict Anderson, *Imagined Communities: Reflections on the Origin and Spread of Nationalism* (London: Verso, 1983), 67–68.

CHAPTER FOUR

1. An allied argument for the complex contemporaneity and cultural politics of the novel is made by Zelda Bronstein, "The Parabolic Ploys of *The Scarlet Letter*," *American Quarterly* 39, no. 2 (Summer 1987): 193–210.

2. See Sacvan Bercovitch, "Hawthorne's A-Morality of Compromise," *Representations* 24 (Fall 1988): 1–27. Bercovitch reads this crisis of national fragmentation as Hawthorne's prophetic response to the impending War Between the States. Here and in the following chapter I suggest different and broader ways to configure the scope of the national conflagration.

3. Criticism of "The Custom-House" has generally insisted that despite its ironic tone and deliberate hyperbole, Hawthorne demonstrates in it a longing for romantic self-expression, truth, and authenticity. The most

challenging forms of this argument can be found in Kent Bales, "Hawthorne's Prefaces and Romantic Perspectivism," *ESQ* 23, no. 2 (2nd Quarter 1977): 69–88; Nina Baym, "The Romantic Malgré Lui: Hawthorne in 'The Custom-House'," *ESQ* 19, no. 1 (1973): 14–25; Christine Brooke-Rose, "A for But: 'The Custom House' in Hawthorne's *The Scarlet Letter*," *Word and Image* 3, no. 2 (April-June 1987): 143–55; Edgar A. Dryden, *Nathaniel Hawthorne and the Poetics of Enchantment* (Ithaca, N.Y.: Cornell University Press, 1977), 132–42; Dan McCall, "The Design of Hawthorne's 'Custom-House,'" *Nineteenth-Century Fiction* 21, no. 4 (March 1967): 349–58; David Stouck, "The Surveyor of 'The Custom-House': A Narrator for *The Scarlet Letter*," *The Centennial Review* 15 (1971): 309–29; Marshall Van Deusen, "Narrative Tone in 'The Custom-House' and *The Scarlet Letter*," *Nineteenth-Century Fiction*, 21 no. 1 (1967): 61–71. For a critique of traditional psychological readings of "The Custom-House," see John Franzosa, "'The Custom-House,' *The Scarlet Letter*, and Hawthorne's Separation from Salem," *ESQ* 24, no. 2 (1978): 57–71. Despite Franzosa's opposition to these readings, he still relies on the categories of self and other that found the previous interpretive errors. Another strain in the criticism goes not to the Romantic Hawthorne, but rather the Political: Steven Nissenbaum "The Firing of Nathaniel Hawthorne," *Essex Institute Historical Collections*, 114, no. 2 (April 1978): 57–86; David S. Reynolds, *Beneath the American Renaissance: The Subversive Imagination in the Age of Emerson and Melville* (New York: Alfred A. Knopf, 1988), 118–20.

4. In addition, we see that the military and the civil branches of government have an ambiguous involvement, perhaps like that of the Puritan church and state, in the novel proper: while "in theory" the branches are separate, in practice, we later learn, the civil branch is saturated with impediments that originate in military experience. Most prominently, the "civil branch" of the federal government is full of incompetent old soldiers. Hawthorne appropriates their discourse to describe his own troubled relation to his official acts. The military heritage of the United States is of ongoing concern to Hawthorne's understanding of state-patriarchal power. But in the American novels written between 1850 and 1853, the military appears more as a discourse and an ornament to power than it does as an element in plot.

5. In desperation Hawthorne-as-sibyl flings her "leaves forth upon the wind" (3) and hopes that readers who can decipher her riddles and prophecies will find them; without this audience, all a sibyl utters is nonsense, "the corpse of dead activity" which one reads with "saddened, weary, half-reluctant interest" (29). In Hawthorne's identification with this model of authorship, two kinds of authority constitute the status of writing:

the sibylline author possesses "truth" and the privileged reader appreciates the text, which is the only means by which its truth has significant value. Hawthorne never explicitly calls the leaf-flinging author a sibyl in "The Custom-House." This figure recurs frequently in his public and private writing, and in the story "Old News" is named outright: "They [newspaper editors] scatter their leaves to the wind, as the sibyl did, and posterity collects them, to be treasured up among the best materials of its wisdom. With hasty pens, they write for immortality." The sibyl's "news" is valuable in its very un-iconicity, its temporality: the nation's inability to treasure this at the moment of its utterance is a sign of its compulsive self-misprision. (Nathaniel Hawthorne, "Old News," in *The Snow-Image and Uncollected Tales*, Centenary Edition of the Tales of Nathaniel Hawthorne [Columbus: Ohio State University Press, 1974], 11: 132.)

Hawthorne's alliance of his text with such news is one of the many signs of the novel's alliance with the epic: for the sibyl who prophesies (the Cumaean sibyl) is also the one who leads Aeneas to the underworld on the way to his discovery of Greece. The world of the dead is, of course, where Hawthorne "lives" as he sings the Puritan tale. In any case, Hawthorne seems to imply that "The Custom-House" is among other things a kind of epic poem, a history, and a prophecy by a poet who has, in a way, survived the violence of nations. For a more general debate about whether the American novel of this period is or isn't the "middle-class epic," see Myra Jehlen, "New World Epics: The Novel and the Middle-Class in America," *Salmagundi* 36 (Winter 1977): 49–68, and a response by Carolyn Porter, *Seeing and Being: The Plight of the Participant Observer in Emerson, James, Adams, and Faulkner* (Middletown, Conn.: Wesleyan University Press, 1981), 9–18.

6. See, for example, the picture in Samuel Chamberlain, *A Stroll Through Historic Salem*, (New York: Hastings House, 1969), 33. This "error" of Hawthorne's has been noted but not exploited by Hugh J. Dawson, "*The Scarlet Letter*'s Angry Eagle and the Salem Custom-House," *Essex Institute Historical Collections* 122 (1986): 30–34, and Bercovitch, "Hawthorne's A-Morality of Compromise."

7. Nathaniel Hawthorne, "Old Ticonderoga," in *The Snow-Image and Uncollected Tales*, Centenary Edition of the Tales of Nathaniel Hawthorne (Columbus: Ohio State University Press, 1974), 11: 186–91. I will refer to this in the text by volume and page number.

8. I appropriate here Todorov's description of Christopher Columbus's form of imaginative/imperialist engagement with the American landscape. See Tsvetan Todorov, *The Conquest of America: The Question of the Other*, trans. Richard Howard (New York: Harper and Row, 1984), 27 and passim.

9. For a history of the production of an abstract "citizen" whose textuality hides his white, male body, see Michael Warner, *The Letters of the Republic* (Cambridge: Harvard University Press, 1990).

10. Nina Baym, *The Shape of Hawthorne's Career* (Ithaca, N.Y.: Cornell University Press, 1976), 146.

11. Since, in my view, "The Custom-House" stages "Hawthorne" as an exemplary case in the modern (1850) production of national identity, the historical "facts" about Hawthorne's desire to remain a Custom-House patriarch have no a priori significance here. But the currently fashionable reading of the biographical information ratifies my reading of the fictive representation of American political formations in his work. See the discussion in note 12, on Nissenbaum, "The Firing of Nathaniel Hawthorne."

12. Stephen Nissenbaum makes an impassioned argument for Hawthorne's complicity in the patronage system he parodies in "The Custom-House." Nissenbaum overemphasizes what he calls Hawthorne's "literary sleight-of-hand" in his neglect to tell the story of how he procured the Custom-House Surveyorship. He argues that Hawthorne recounts his presence in the political public sphere as a simply magical, fairy-tale affair. But while Nissenbaum's information about Hawthorne's political self-promotion shows how invested the author was in becoming an "official," the essay does not take into account the way Hawthorne actually seeks, in

this preface, to account for his compulsion to head the local house of state, as the "President's" surrogate (12). For instance, he attributes his return to Salem to an expectation embedded in his paternal tradition that he will become a "patriarch," in the traditional sense. In addition, the city is simply in his bones: "It is not love, but instinct" (11). He also says he sincerely wanted to become "a man of affairs" and not just a social theorist or "dreamer" (26). The multiplicity of "motives" here is evidence that "The Custom-House" should be read not as autobiography (misguided or otherwise) but as an experiment in explicating the logic of national fantasy: of the desire he has to take up residence within the nation's "bosom" (5), to make himself vulnerable to the exiling force of the nation's "besom" (8). Such a project includes autobiographical narratives, but the compulsion to be national is also linked to transpersonal phenomena, phenomena that might and have implicated any subject in the national project. See Stephen Nissenbaum, "The Firing of Nathaniel Hawthorne," 57–86. Similar comments might be made contra Donald E. Pease, *Visionary Compacts* (Madison: University of Wisconsin Press, 1987), 49–80; Reynolds, *Beneath the American Renaissance*, 118–20.

13. These three texts on the centrality of motherhood to *The Scarlet Letter* stage Hawthorne's relation to his mother, (and less importantly to his sister, Elizabeth, and his wife, Sophia) as a strong motive behind the narrative of *The Scarlet Letter*. While not all making the same argument,

these texts all psychologize "Hawthorne's" excess or overidentification with women in the novel to depatriarchalize our reading of it, certainly a worthy intent. I see two general problems here. One is the usual assertion that biographical material is closer to intention and intention closer to "meaning" than other material might be. Even Baym, who foregrounds the speculative nature of her reading, tends to assert the authenticity of biographically attributed motive over whatever strategic or transpersonal cultural material might also contribute to the narrative. I simply disagree with that critical procedure. Two, such an emphasis on the mother tends to obscure how specifically fatherhood emerges in this text, and not as a symbolic category. While I think reproduction is foregrounded in *The Scarlet Letter*, it seems clear to me that paternity itself signifies at least as strongly as maternity, and that along with an intense interest in the female body Hawthorne plays out a desire to reconfigure the masculine. See Nina Baym, "Nathaniel Hawthorne and His Mother: A Biographical Speculation," *American Literature* 54, no. 1 (March 1982): 1–27. Joanne Feit Diehl, "Re-reading *The Letter*: Hawthorne, the Fetish, and the (Family) Romance," *New Literary History* 19, no. 3 (Spring 1988): 655–73: Gloria C. Erlich, *Family Themes and Hawthorne's Fiction: The Tenacious Web* (New Brunswick, N.J.: Rutgers University Press, 1984).

14. Fredric Jameson, "Post-Modernism: or, The Cultural Logic of Late Capitalism," *New Left Review* 146 (July-August 1984): 53–92.

15. Nina Baym, *The Scarlet Letter* (Boston: Twayne, 1986), 101–107; also Jonathan Arac, "The Politics of *The Scarlet Letter*," in Sacvan Bercovitch and Myra Jehlen, eds. *Ideology and Classic American Literature* (Cambridge: Cambridge University Press, 1986), 247–266.

16. I paraphrase the formulations of Freud, in "The Uncanny," *The Standard Edition of the Complete Psychological Works of Sigmund Freud*, trans. James Strachey, in collaboration with Anna Freud, assisted by Alix Strachey and Alan Tyson (London: The Hogarth Press, 1955), 17: 217–52. For an opposed view, see Dryden, *The Poetics of Enchantment*, 145–58. Dryden takes the thematic of home in "The Custom-House" as a sign of Hawthorne's mixed feelings toward exile and his desire for the origin.

17. Linking all these bodies is the *immortality* of national or collective marks of identity: the marks of political participation the body takes on are transpersonal and ultimately diachronic, like numbers on a tourist map of national monuments that lead you to explanations about some historical moment whose materiality you, the tourist, are now experiencing.

18. For a more pro-populist reading of Hawthorne's work, see Pease, *Visionary Compacts*, 81–107.

19. The decapitated Surveyor, like Deidrich Knickerbocker and Surveyor Pue, embodies yet a third patriarchal "tradition" in "The Custom-

House," in addition to the tradition of American political patriarchs and of Hawthorne's own familial fathers. These ancestral men are hinge figures, subjects who do not author anything, but who cast themselves explicitly as cultural translators, bridging local tales and national audiences. In addition, each tells a similar tale of clashing between the interests of bodies and the law: staging the inevitability that the law will mark the body—at once killing it, making it mortal, and giving it a permanency beyond itself.

20. Nathaniel Hawthorne, "A Rill from the Town-Pump," *Twice-Told Tales*, The Centenary Edition of the Works of Nathaniel Hawthorne (Columbus: Ohio State University Press, 1974), 9: 141–48. Further references will be signified in the text by volume and page number.

21. John Winthrop, the ur-governor of Massachusetts Bay, is here joined by John Endicott (the colony's first governor and well-known military hero) and Francis Higginson (one of the first ministers ordained in the colony [in 1629], a founding theorist of Puritan juridical hegemony, one of the colony's earliest historians). According to their nineteenth-century reception, the band of men represents the Puritan state's three disciplinary arms: legal, military, and religious.

CHAPTER FIVE

1. Agnes Heller, *Everyday Life*, trans. G. L. Campbell (1970; rpt. London: Routledge and Kegan Paul, 1984), 239 and passim; Antonio Gramsci, "Notes for an Introduction and an Approach to the Study of Philosophy and the History of Culture," in *An Antonio Gramsci Reader*, ed. David Forgacs (New York: Schocken Books, 1988), 326; Michel de Certeau, "On the Oppositional Practices of Everyday Life," *Social Text* 1, no. 3 (1980): 3–43, and, in a longer and different translation, *The Practice of Everyday Life*, trans. Steven Randall (Berkeley: University of California Press, 1984); Henri Lefebvre, "Toward a Leftist Cultural Politics: Remarks Occasioned by the Centenary of Marx's Death," trans. David Reifman, in *Marxism and the Interpretation of Culture*, ed. and with an introduction by Cary Nelson and Lawrence Grossberg (Urbana: University of Illinois Press, 1988), 77–88; Henri Lefebvre, *Everyday Life in the Modern World*, trans. Sacha Rabinovitch (Evanston: Harper and Row, 1971). See also Fredric Jameson, "The Realist Floor-Plan," in *On Signs*, edited by Marshall Blonsky (Baltimore: Johns Hopkins University Press, 1985), 374; Andrew Ross, "The Everyday Life of Lou Andreas-Salomé: Making Video History," in Richard Feldstein and Judith Roof, eds. *Feminism and Psychoanalysis* (Ithaca: Cornell University Press, 1989), 157–58.

Lefebvre distinguishes between "daily life" and "everyday life": the former a more mythic, pre-rationalized space, the latter a space of time regulated by a variety of markets, politics, and other modern formations. Given *The Scarlet Letter*'s projection of the former from the position of the latter, I use these two terms interchangeably, and mean them to signify an interplay of the freedom and constraint Lefebvre's work keeps separate.

2. Gramsci, "Notes for an Introduction and an Approach to the Study of Philosophy and the History of Culture," 326.

3. de Certeau, *The Practice of Everyday Life*, 138–39.

4. For a careful and comprehensive narrative of the struggle to equate the nation with the federal state, see Robert H. Wiebe, *The Opening of American Society: From the Adoption of the Constitution to the Eve of Disunion* (New York: Alfred A. Knopf, 1984). Much work is now being done on the local political uses of "national" forms: as in David G. Hackett, "The Social Origins of Nationalism: Albany, New York, 1754–1835," *Journal of Social History* 21, no. 4 (Summer 1988): 659–81; Paula Baker, "The Culture of Politics in the Late Nineteenth Century: Community and Political Behavior in Rural New York," *Journal of Social History* (Winter 1984): 167–93. From a more theoretical, political angle, William Boelhower's *Through a Glass Darkly: Ethnic Semiosis in American Literature* (New York: Oxford University Press, 1987) provides an extremely interesting argument for the fundamental "Americanness" of the national-local struggle.

5. "War of position" is Antonio Gramsci's term, which describes how forms of antagonism transpire within Western structures of political consent. See Forgacs, ed., *An Antonio Gramsci Reader*, 225–30; 440–41; and passim. Ernesto Laclau and Chantal Mouffe elaborate and deploy this concept to stage how relations between ideology and practical politics transpire, in *Hegemony and Socialist Strategy*, trans. Winston Moore and Paul Cammack (London: Verso, 1985), 136–38 and passim.

6. Sacvan Bercovitch, "Hawthorne's A-Morality of Compromise," *Representations* 24 (Fall 1988): 9.

7. For a more psycho-ethical reading of Hawthorne's uses of silence and mystery, see Gordon Hutner, *Secrets and Sympathy: Forms of Disclosure in Hawthorne's Novels* (Athens, Ga.: University of Georgia Press, 1988).

8. Nathaniel Hawthorne, Preface, *The Whole History of Grandfather's Chair*, in *True Stories from History and Biography*, Centenary Edition of the Works of Nathaniel Hawthorne, (Columbus: 1972), 6: 5.

9. For more sophisticated versions of this kind of material history, see the extremely useful "Everyday Life in America" series: David Freeman Hawke, *Everyday Life in Early America* (New York: Harper and Row, 1988); Jack Larkin, *The Reshaping of Everyday Life, 1790–1840* (New York: Harper and Row, 1988); Daniel E. Sutherland, *The Expansion of Everyday Life, 1860–1876* (New York: Harper and Row, 1989). See also Robert Lacour-Gayet, *Everyday Life in the United States before the Civil*

War, 1830–1860, trans. Mary Ilford (New York: Frederick Ungar, 1969); Louis O. Saum, *The Popular Mood of Pre-Civil War America* (Westport, Conn.: Greenwood Press, 1980).

10. Daniel Webster, "The Bunker Hill Monument," in *Great Speeches and Orations of Daniel Webster*, ed. and with an introduction by Edwin P. Whipple (Boston: Little, Brown, 1879), 135.

11. Ibid., 126.

12. Hawthorne, *The Whole History of Grandfather's Chair*, 51.

13. Ibid., 5.

14. Here is Habermas's original definition: "A portion of the public sphere comes into being in every conversation in which private individuals assemble to form a public body. They then behave neither like business or professional people transacting private affairs, nor like members of a constitutional order subject to the legal constraints of a state bureaucracy. Citizens behave as a public body when they confer in an unrestricted fashion—that is, with the guarantee of freedom of assembly and association and the freedom to express and publish their opinions—about matters of general interest" (Jürgen Habermas, "The Public Sphere: An Encyclopedia Article," trans. Sara Lennox and Frank Lennox, *New German Critique* 1, no. 3 [Fall 1974]: 49).

15. Stuart Hall, "The Toad in the Garden: Thatcherism among the Theorists," in *Marxism and the Interpretation of Culture*, ed. and with an introduction by Cary Nelson and Lawrence Grossberg (Urbana: University of Illinois Press, 1988), 44.

16. Fredric Jameson's construction of the politics of the "ideologeme" has much relevance, then, for construing the history of national identity. See his *The Political Unconscious* (Ithaca, N.Y.: Cornell University Press, 1981), 87–88, 115–19.

17. I appropriate the contestatory category of petty theft, *la perruque*, with its aura of counter-politics, from de Certeau, "On the Oppositional Practices of Everyday Life," 3.

18. The language of "native paradise" I use here to describe Hawthorne's Salem also characterizes the language I used, in "The Nationalist Preface," to decribe America: but the apparent rhetorical homology between these two political sites reveals, ultimately, a struggle, within the United States, over which site has priority, and over how they mutually derive meaning and authority. For a different reading of Hawthorne's argument (mainly about *The House of the Seven Gables*), which concludes that Salem is America *in nuce*, see Brook Thomas, *Cross-Examinations of Law and Literature: Cooper, Hawthorne, Stowe, and Melville* (Cambridge: Cambridge University Press, 1987), 45–90.

19. Nathaniel Hawthorne, "Chiefly About War Matters," *The Com-*

plete Works of Nathaniel Hawthorne, ed. George Parsons Lathrop (Boston: Houghton Mifflin, 1883), 12: 308.

20. Ibid.

21. Though put forth in the most casual of tones, Hawthorne's interest in the American map is of national significance. Critics Nina Baym and Michael J. Colacurcio both use his discussion of mapping, in the sketch "Sir William Phips," to argue over whether Hawthorne sees literature as different from and superior to history (Baym) or as simply a better means to its production (Colacurcio). See Baym, *The Shape of Hawthorne's Career* (Ithaca, N.Y.: Cornell University Press, 1976), 35; Colacurcio, *The Province of Piety* (Cambridge: Harvard University Press, 1984), 55. But the cartographical politics of America have been brilliantly discussed in terms more germane to this discussion of national citizenship in Boelhower's *Through a Glass Darkly* and Jehlen's *American Incarnation* (Cambridge: Harvard University Press, 1986).

22. Hawthorne, "Chiefly About War Matters," 304.

23. Ibid., 306.

24. Ibid., 307. It is interesting to note that, right after this meeting, Leutze paints Hawthorne's portrait, as if he were already one among many national icons. This is Sophia's view, in any case. See Nathaniel Hawthorne, *The Letters, 1857–1864*, Centenary Edition of the Works of Nathaniel Hawthorne (Columbus, OH: Ohio State University Press, 1987), 18: 444.

25. Ibid., 314–15.

26. Nathaniel Hawthorne, *The Life of Franklin Pierce*, foreword by Richard C. Robey (New York: Garrett Press, 1970), 111.

27. Hawthorne, "Chiefly About War Matters," 307.

28. Ibid., 317.

29. Benedict Anderson, *Imagined Communities: Reflections on the Origin and Spread of Nationalism* (London: Verso, 1983), 67–68.

30. Gramsci, "Notes for an Introduction and an Approach to the Study of Philosophy and the History of Culture," 325.

31. Frantz Fanon, "On National Culture," in *The Wretched of the Earth*, trans. Constance Farrington, preface by Jean-Paul Sartre (New York: Grove Press, 1963), 220–21.

32. My suggestion that Hawthorne configures a pragmatic-utopian politics of "local" affect and identities provides a twist on Jonathan Arac's excellent analysis of the politics of Hawthornean indeterminacy. Arac sees American symbolic indeterminacy as "violated" by the pragmatics of political action; in this chapter I mean to supplement this by arguing that the indeterminate sign can be politically "specific" in the way it marks the lim-

its or even the exhaustion of a certain national form of political thinking. See "The Politics of *The Scarlet Letter*," in *Ideology and Classic American Literature*, ed. Sacvan Bercovitch and Myra Jehlen (Cambridge: Cambridge University Press, 1986), 247–66.

33. I refer to Gayatri Chakravorty Spivak's model of how subaltern consciousness works in colonial and postcolonial political systems. See "Can the Subaltern Speak?" in *Marxism and the Interpretation of Culture*, ed. and with an introduction by Cary Nelson and Lawrence Grossberg (Urbana: University of Illinois Press, 1988), 285.

34. Hawthorne, "Chiefly About War Matters," 317.

35. Bercovitch, "Hawthorne's A-Morality of Compromise," 22–23. See also James Bense, "Nathaniel Hawthorne's Intention in 'Chiefly About War Matters,'" *American Literature* 61, no. 2 (May 1989): 214. For an argument that retains the friction between the skeptical and the prophetic tendencies of Hawthorne's national vision, see Richard Brodhead, "Hawthorne and the Fate of Politics," *Essays in Literature* 11, no. 1 (Spring 1984): 95–103.

36. Myra Jehlen, *American Incarnation*; Anne Norton, *Reflections on Political Identity* (Baltimore: Johns Hopkins University Press, 1988). See also T. Walter Herbert, "Nathaniel Hawthorne, Una Hawthorne, and *The Scarlet Letter*: Interactive Selfhoods and the Cultural Construction of Gender," *PMLA* 103, no. 3 (May 1988): 285–97.

37. Wilson Carey McWilliams, *The Idea of Fraternity in America* (Berkeley: University of California Press, 1973). See also E. Anthony Rotundo, "Body and Soul: Changing Ideals of American Middle-Class Manhood, 1770–1920," *Journal of Social History* 16 (Summer 1983): 23–38.

38. Nathaniel Hawthorne, "Queen Christina," *Biographical Stories for Children*, in *True Stories from History and Biography*, Centenary Edition of the Works of Nathaniel Hawthorne (Columbus: Ohio State University Press, 1972), 6: 283.

39. Paula Baker, "The Domestication of Politics: Women and American Political Society, 1780–1920," *American Historical Review* 89, no. 3 (June 1984): 620–47. See also Lee Virginia Chambers-Schiller, *Liberty, A Better Husband: Single Women in America: The Generations of 1780–1840* (New Haven: Yale University Press, 1984).

40. There is a huge bibliography on this subject. Classically, Ann Douglas, *The Feminization of American Culture* (New York: Avon Books, 1977); Jane Tompkins, *Sensational Designs* (New York: Oxford University Press, 1985); Barbara Welter, *Dimity Convictions: The American Woman in the Nineteenth Century* (Athens: Ohio University Press, 1976). Most recently, Sara M. Evans, *Born for Liberty: A History of Women in America* (New York: The Free Press, 1989).

41. Kate Berry, "How Can an American Woman Serve Her Country?" *Godey's Lady's Book* 43 (December 1851): 365, 362. See also Haddie Lane, "Woman's Rights," *Godey's Lady's Book* 40 (1850): 269–73.

42. Henry E. Woodbury, "Woman in her Social Relations," *Godey's Lady's Book* 45 (1852): 337.

43. Amy Schrager Lang, *Prophetic Woman: Anne Hutchinson and the Problem of Dissent in the Literature of New England* (Berkeley: University of California Press, 1987), 1–14.

44. Darrel Abel, *The Moral Picturesque: Studies in Hawthorne's Fiction* (West Lafayette: Purdue University Press, 1988), 171.

45. Lydia Maria Child, "Home and Politics," in *Autumnal Leaves: Tales and Sketches in Prose and Rhyme* (New York: C.S. Francis, 1857), 109.

46. Ibid., 110–11.

47. Ibid., 114–15.

48. Ibid., 115.

49. Ibid., 117.

50. Ibid., 118.

51. de Certeau, "On the Oppositional Practices of Everyday Life," 22.

52. Social theory, post-Habermas, has begun to address the relation between various local political and social affiliations and the nationally framed bourgeois public sphere. An especially rigorous instance of political analysis of the local (framed as the complex site where "need" is experienced) and the national is in Nancy Fraser, *Unruly Practices: Power, Discourse, and Gender in Contemporary Social Theory* (Minneapolis: University of Minnesota Press, 1989), 144–87. Applied to the United States, Fraser's rather Eurocentric model of the state would need revision, but her work still vitally provides another politically viable language for the kind of (post-nationally-concentrated) cultural identity politics I am imagining here.

INDEX

"A" (Hester's), 69–71, 105, 133, 136–37, 142, 161–63, 165, 184, 188, 200; as monument, 66
Alice Doane, 35, 37, 39, 40, 45, 172
Alice Doane, character, 38, 41–44, 49, 213; see also *Alice Doane's Appeal*
Alice Doane's Appeal, 21, 35–55, 57–58, 167, 171–72, 178, 187, 209, 231 n. 53, 232 n. 56; memory in, 50–51; monument, 43
America: defined, 4, 16; origin of, 163
American eagle, 170, 186, 214; as woman, 5, 69, 169, 177, 188, 201, 214, 220 n. 4
American Renaissance, 29
Amnesia, 39, 54, 75, 132, 152, 158, 166, 179, 194; in *Alice Doane's Appeal,* 50; definition of, 57; and Dimmesdale, 138; national, 134, 172, 204
Anderson, Benedict, 25–26, 28, 219 n. 2, 225 n. 4, 226 n. 10, 227 nn. 21, 22, 229 n. 37, 249 n. 32, 257 n. 29
Aquinas, Saint Thomas, 92, 253 n. 15
Arac, Jonathan, 9, 221 n. 11, 247 n. 20, 257 n. 32
"Arbitrary Government," 83, 88, 92–93, 236 nn. 11, 13, 240 nn. 43, 44, 241 nn. 54, 61. *See also* Winthrop, John
Armstrong, Nancy, 147–48
Augustine, Saint, 88, 241 n. 61

Bacon, Sir Francis, 80
Baker, Paula, 211, 255 n. 4, 258 n. 39
Bartholdi, Frederic, 23

Baym, Nina, 220 n. 6, 223 n. 15, 231 nn. 53–54, 233 n. 67, 236 n. 10, 248 n. 21, 250 n. 3, 252 n. 13, 253 n. 15, 257 n. 21
Bell, Michael Davitt, 241 n. 57, 242n. 67
Bellingham, Richard, 61, 72–89, 100, 109, 118, 134, 153–54, 194, 237 nn. 18, 20, 21, 238 nn. 31–32, 240 nn. 46–47, 245 n. 12
Benjamin, Walter, 24
Bercovitch, Sacvan, 9, 17, 32, 93, 194, 209, 221 n. 10, 230 nn. 42, 44, 48, 241 n. 53, 249 nn. 31, 2, 251 n. 6, 255 n. 6, 258 n. 35
Biographical Stories for Children, 210–11, 258 n. 38
Birth of A Nation, 16
The Blithedale Romance, 231 n. 55
Body, 7, 13, 16, 34, 45, 61–63, 68–69, 90, 94, 97, 99, 149–50, 157–59, 161; of Chillingworth, 153, 157; of citizen, 34, 56, 161, 163, 201; in *The Custom-House,* 165, 175–76, 186; of Dimmesdale, 121–22, 124, 126, 152–53, 157, 246 n. 17; female, 27–28, 52, 55, 148; of Hawthorne, 157–59, 185; of Hester Prynne, 10–14, 137, 141; iconic, 23–24; as landscape, 45, 52; and law, 101, 149, 254 n. 19; male, 115–16, 119–22, 153, 176, 210; politic, 24, 88; of John Winthrop, 89
Body of Liberties, 81–82, 242 n. 3. *See also* Ward, Nathaniel
Boelhower, William, 222 n. 12, 231 n. 49, 255 n. 4, 257 n. 21
Breen, Timothy, 78, 238 n. 26, 242 n. 3
Breuilly, John, 229 n. 37
Brodhead, Richard H., 221 n. 8, 258 n. 35
Bronstein, Zelda, 249 n. 1
Brown, B. Katherine, 242 n. 3
Budick, Emily, Miller, 220 n. 6
Buell, Lawrence I., 231 n. 48
Burgin, Victor, 220 n. 5

Cabranes, José A., 223 n. 18
Calef, Robert, 232 n. 56
Cameron, Sharon, 220 n. 6
Chamberlain, Samuel, 251 n. 6
Chief Justice Clark, 223 n. 22
"Chiefly About War Matters," 203–6, 209, 256 n. 19
Child, Dr. Robert, 82, 239 n. 41, 240 n. 44
Child, Lydia Maria, 8, 212–16, 259 nn. 45–50. See also *Home and Politics*
Chillingworth, Roger, character, 61, 84, 100, 106–7, 117–21, 124, 129, 145, 154, 157, 246 nn. 13–14; body, 153, 157; and law, 98, 245 n. 12
Citizen body: defined, 161, 163, 201; Hawthorne as, 3–4, 164–65, 205; of Hester Prynne, 106; versus native, 193–94, 203; as tourist, 34, 46, 53, 57, 144, 168, 174, 214; as woman, 94, 155–57, 163, 200
Citizenship, 4, 9, 11–13, 163, 165, 199, 201; ascriptive, 14; birthright, 14–15; construction, 14–15, 24, 29, 152; consensual, 14; Hawthorne and, 13, 16, 192; nature of, 15–20; in Puritan legal history,

103; rebirth of, 26. *See also* United States Constitution
Civil War, 15, 202–4, 206
Cixous, Hélène, 220 n. 4
Clay, Henry, 214–15. See also *Home and Politics*
Cohen, Charles Lloyd, 241 nn. 53, 56
Coke, Sir Edward, 80, 239 n. 35
Colacurcio, Michael, 67, 84, 109, 221 n. 9, 230 n. 48, 231 nn. 53–54, 232 n. 56, 233 nn. 62–63, 235 n. 9, 237 n. 19, 240 n. 48, 241 n. 58, 243 nn. 6–7, 246 n. 18, 257 n. 21
Collective identity, 24–25, 54, 62, 66, 68–69, 89, 95, 97, 163; definition of, 199; in "The Market-Place," 58; Puritan, 61, 132; in *The Scarlet Letter,* 60, 87, 151
Conscience, 64, 91–95, 114, 126, 133, 141, 146, 161, 205, 216; of Dimmesdale, 127; Dimmesdale as, 124; as moral link between law and citizen, 98
Consciousness, 63; proto-national, 152
Cotton, John, 79, 81–82, 235 n. 8, 239 n. 39, 247 n. 18
Counter-memory, 6, 60, 62–63, 95, 99–100, 102, 112, 116–17, 119–21, 132–33, 135, 142–43, 149–50, 162–63, 166, 171, 179, 180–81, 184, 187; categorized, 162; definition, 200; definition in *The Scarlet Letter,* 62
The Custom House, 2–4, 7, 10, 63, 106, 155, 163–71, 174–79, 181–83, 185–89, 192, 201–4, 207, 216, 249n. 3, 251 n. 5, 252 nn. 11–12, 253 nn. 16, 19; body in, 165, 175–76, 186; and national fantasy, 178

de Certeau, Michel, 192–93, 216, 254 n. 1, 255 n. 3, 256 n. 17, 259 n. 51
Dekker, George, 231 n. 48, 247 n. 21
de Lauretis, Teresa, 27–28, 228 n. 27, 229 n. 34
DeSalvo, Louise, 223 n. 15
Dimmesdale, Arthur, character, 61, 72, 74, 84–86, 94, 100, 106–7, 109, 111–12, 114, 116–19, 121, 123, 125–35, 141, 143–48, 151–52, 154, 157, 159, 171, 175–76, 198, 237 n. 18, 246 nn. 14, 16–18, 248 nn. 24–25; and amnesia, 133; body, 121–22, 124, 126, 152–53, 157, 246 n. 17; conscience, 127; as conscience, 124; innocence, 146; and law, 98, 122, 132–34, 245 n. 12; and madness, 123–24, 129
Doane, Leonard, character, 41-44, 49, 54. See also *Alice Doane's Appeal*
Donzelot, Jacques, 245 n. 12
Dred Scott, 11, 15
Dryden, Edgar A., 250 n. 3, 253 n. 16

Eliot, John, 144, 248 n. 24
Endicott, John, 187, 254 n. 21
Everyday life, 166, 179–85, 191–93, 197, 199, 201–3, 207–8, 215, 254 n. 1

Fanon, Frantz, 21, 24, 208, 219 n. 2
Flag, American, 168–69, 214
Foner, Philip S., 224 n. 28

Forgacs, David, 31, 226 n. 10, 230 n. 41
Foster, Stephen, 237 n. 17
Foucault, Michel, 6, 62, 99, 234 n. 5, 241 n. 60, 242 n. 2. *See also* Counter-memory
Fourteenth Amendment, 13–14, 16. *See also* United States Constitution
Franklin, Benjamin, 174
Franzosa, John, 250 n. 3
Fraser, Nancy, 259 n. 52
Freud, Sigmund, 246 n. 16, 253 n. 16
Friedman, Lawrence, 30–31

Gender, 67; and Hester Prynne, 247 n. 21; and iconicity, 27; and identity, 31, 211–12, and law, 101–10, 143, 105; in Marx, 20; and representation, 175–77
General Miller, character, 171, 174–75
Godey's Lady's Book, 211, 259 nn. 41–42
Gramsci, Antonio, 192–93, 207, 255 nn. 2, 5, 257 n. 30
The Gray Champion, 233 n. 69

Habermas, Jürgen, 201, 256 n. 14
Hall, Stuart, 202, 222 n. 13, 256 n. 15
Happiness, politics of, 197–201, 217
Harrison, William Henry, 213
Haskins, George Lee, 237 nn. 17
Hathorne, William, 81
Hawke, David Freeman, 255 n. 9
Hawthorne, Elizabeth, 252 n. 13
Hawthorne, Nathaniel, 231 n. 53; as author, 5–6, 8, 33, 38, 99, 183–85, 250 n. 5; body, 157–59, 185; and citizenship, 12–13, 16, 192; as citizen, 2–4, 164–65, 205; and cultural nationalism, 55; as father, 178–79, 182, 212; and monuments, 54, 182; as narrator, 38, 101–2, 104, 110, 134–40, 148; and national identity, 2–3, 5, 16–17, 34, 45, 49, 157, 163–89, 193–94, 202–12, 216; neutral territory, 183; as official, 2, 203; and utopia, 33
Heller, Agnes, 192, 254 n. 1
Herbert, T. Walter, 228 n. 36
Hertz, Neil, 228 nn. 26, 29, 248 n. 23
Herzog, Kristin, 234 n. 69
Hibbens, Ann, 85, 109, 243 n. 8
Higginson, Francis, 187, 254 n. 21
Hill, Christopher, 80
Hobsbawm, Eric, 29
The Hollow of the Three Hills, 35–37, 231 n. 53
Holstun, James, 61, 234 n. 3
Home and Politics, 8, 212–16, 259 nn. 45–50. *See also* Child, Lydia Maria
The House of the Seven Gables, 157, 232 n. 55, 256 n. 18
Hutchinson, Ann, 74, 104, 108
Hutchinson, Thomas, 243 n. 8
Hutner, Gordon, 220 n. 4, 255 n. 7
Hymen, in *Alice Doane's Appeal,* 40, 43–44, 48, 56, 232n. 61

Iacocca, Lee, 227 n. 15, 228 n. 30
Icon, 22, 168, 169
Iconicity: and gender, 22, 26–27, 149, 153, 169, 188, 214; as national, 25, 169–70, 217

Ideology, 17, 234 n. 2
Irving, Washington, 1, 185
Irwin, John, 220 n. 4

Jameson, Fredric, 38, 139, 181, 222 n. 12, 226 n. 12, 248 nn. 22–23, 256 n. 16
Jefferson, Thomas, 174
Jehlen, Myra, 9, 210, 221 n. 10, 226 n. 6, 238 n. 24, 251 n. 5, 257 n. 21
Johnson, Edward, 238 n. 32

Kelley, Mary, 249 n. 7
Kettner, James H., 223 n. 18, 224 nn. 31–32
Kibbey, Ann, 242 n. 65
Kolodny, Annette, 228 n. 26
Kristeva, Julia, 26, 28

Lacan, Jaques, 225 n. 3, 248 n. 23
Laclau, Ernesto, 226 n. 10, 255 n. 5
Landscape, 33, 35, 46, 48, 50–53, 64, 133, 143–45, 148, 166–67, 172–73, 187, 195, 206, 210; as body, 45, 52; and politics, 52; as symbolic, 34, 47, 55. *See also* Space
Lang, Amy Schrager, 109, 212, 223 n. 15, 243 n. 7, 259 n. 43
Laplanche, Jean, 246 n. 16
Law, 42, 44, 46, 59–61, 63–64, 66–75, 79, 80–89, 92–95, 100–101, 103–5, 111, 113, 118, 121, 130, 133–35, 146, 151, 153, 156–57, 175, 197–98, 245 n. 12; and body, 101, 149, 254 n. 19; and Chillingworth, 98, 245 n. 12; civil and common, 88–89; and Dimmesdale, 58, 122, 132–34, 245 n. 12; female, 107–8, 135–45, 154, 247 n. 21; and gender, 101–10, 143, 105; and Hester, 112–13, 134, 245 n. 11; homosocial, 210; literary, 155; of love, 89–90, 94; love of, 43, 198; and madness, 100, 103, 124, 130, 143–45, 149, 198, 214–15; natural, 76, 103, 143; patriarchal, 135, 138, 143; of resemblance, 41; and sexuality, 85–86; and spectacle, 198–200; sumptuary, 70–73; and utopia, 59–60, 62, 95, 101–2, 149–50, 152, 158, 249 n. 29. *See also* Winthrop, John
Lazarus, Emma, 26, 227 n. 24
Lefebvre, Henri, 192, 254 n. 1
The Letters, 1857-1864, 257 nn. 24–25
Leverenz, David, 235 n. 8, 243 n. 4
Levin, David, 40
Levine, Robert, 221 n. 11
Levinson, Sanford, 223 n. 18
Lewis, C. S., 241 n. 56
The Life of Franklin Pierce, 205–6
Lincoln, Abraham, 204
Literary nationalism, 21, 29–30, 165, 181–82, 184–85, 187–88, 205, 207, 210
Love, 42–43, 46–47, 89–90, 94, 136–37, 144, 159, 162; of law, 43, 198; and Hester Prynne, 154–56; law of, 89–90, 94

McWilliams, John P., Jr., 21, 234 n. 70
McWilliams, Wilson Carey, 210
Madness and law, 103, 124, 130, 143, 144–45, 149, 198, 214–15; collective, 129; and Dimmesdale, 123–24, 129; and Hester, 102, 114–17, 198

Magna Carta, 80, 82
Main-Street, 233 n. 69
Mannheim, Karl, 32, 53
Marin, Louis, 32, 230 n. 43
Marx, Karl, 19–20, 31
Mather, Cotton, 50, 232 n. 56
Matthiessen, F. O., 225 n. 6
Memory, 51, 63–64, 93–95, 97–98, 130, 132, 157–58, 196, 208, 210, 216; in *Alice Doane's Appeal,* 50-51; female, 35–37, 156–57, 162; Hester's, 111–12; loss, 132; national, 164, 175; as official, 98, 112, 116, 171, 187; popular, 185. *See also* Amnesia; Counter-memory; Mnemotechnique
Miller, Perry, 93, 237 n. 17, 238 n. 24, 241 n. 56–57
Mitchell, Juliet, 225 n. 3
Mnemotechnique, 8, 34–35, 37, 39, 40, 45, 51, 54, 63, 66, 69, 78, 95, 98, 133, 163, 165, 174, 178, 183; literary, of national identity, 180; Puritan, 133, 200
"A Model of Christian Charity," 88–89, 91, 240 n. 50, 241 nn. 54, 61. *See also* Winthrop, John
Monument, 58, 153, 172, 195–97, 206; the "A" as, 66; in *Alice Doane's Appeal,* 43; and Hawthorne, 54, 182; Hester Prynne as, 120
Mrs. Hutchinson, 231 n. 55

Narrator: of *The Scarlet Letter,* 101–1, 104, 110, 134–40, 148, 200; in body, 157–58; as lawyer, 146–47
National character, 21, 171; consciousness, 168; culture, 21, 30; memory, 164, 175; symbol, 22–23
National fantasy, 5, 7, 11, 16–17, 21–22, 26, 102, 216; and *The Custom-House,* 178; defined, 5; and identity, 8, 17; and utopia, 162, 189; woman and national, 31, 110, 135
National identity, 2–3, 7, 11–13, 17, 20, 24, 102, 119; and amnesia, 200; and body, 253 n. 17; construction of, 21, 25; in crisis, 8, 21, 29–30, 54, 216; and *The Custom-House,* 178–84; and gender, 31, 211–12; and Hawthorne, 2–3, 5, 16–17, 34, 45, 49, 157, 168–89, 193–94, 202–12, 216; problems with, 12; in *The Scarlet Letter,* 199, and woman, 106
Nationality, 14; and federal and state relations, 202; versus local identity, 5, 16, 164, 170, 202–3, 205, 207–8; and utopia, 32
National Symbolic, 5, 8, 20–22, 24, 26–31, 33–35, 102, 110, 155, 158–59, 168, 180–84, 188, 216; origin of, 155
Newberry, Frederick, 236 n. 16
The New Colossus, 26–27, 227 n. 24. *See also* Lazarus, Emma; Statue of Liberty
Nietzsche, Friedrich, 34, 220 n. 5
Nissenbaum, Stephen, 178, 250 n. 3, 252 nn. 11–12
Norton, Anne, 30-31, 210, 220 n. 5, 222 n. 14, 226 n. 11, 230 n. 39, 258 n. 36
Noye, William, 80, 239 n. 37

Old News, 251 n. 5
Old Ticonderoga, A Picture of the Past, 171–73
An Old Woman's Tale, 35–36, 194, 231 n. 53
"On Liberty," 88, 91–93. *See also* Winthrop, John

Pateman, Carol, 222 n. 14
Patriarchy, 5, 8, 14, 42, 45, 61, 63, 84, 133–39, 152–54, 162, 176–79, 209, 211
Pearl, character, 59, 67, 72, 76, 78, 82–84, 86–87, 95, 112–14, 128, 134–35, 139, 141–42, 145, 198–200, 217
Pease, Donald, 9, 54, 220 n. 7, 229 n. 37, 252 n. 12, 253 n. 18
Peters, Edward, 235 n. 7, 245 n. 9
Phillips, James Duncan, 233 n. 69
Polk, James Knox, 212, 214
Porter, Carolyn, 251 n. 5
Powers, Edwin, 70, 239 nn. 38, 40, 235 n. 7, 236 n. 14, 237 n. 17
Prynne, Hester, character, 59, 61, 64–78, 82–83, 85–87, 93, 100, 103–16, 118–19, 121–26, 130, 133–48, 151–59, 162, 167, 173, 175–77, 183–84, 191–92, 194, 198–201, 210, 212, 217, 248 n. 25; body, 110-14, 137, 141; as citizen, 106; and law, 112–13, 134, 245 n. 11; and love, 154–56; and madness, 102, 114–17, 198; as monument, 120; as National Symbolic, 110; and new law, 98, 245 n. 11; as phallus, 117; as woman, 140; as gendered negation, 140–41
Pyrnne, William, 66, 80, 162
Public sphere, 5, 12, 22, 28, 58–59, 63, 117, 133–34, 136, 148, 155–56, 162, 176, 183, 199, 211–12, 216
Puritan: collective identity, 61, 132; culture, 58, 59, 61, 74, 93, 127, 132, 134–35, 163–64, 200; law, 60, 74, 79–82, 89–90, 162, 188, 200; history of law, 79–82; mnemotechnique, 133, 200; semiotics, 93–95, 129-31, 133, 149, 151, 161

Queen Christina, character, 210-11, 258 n. 38. See also *Biographical Stories for Children*
Queen Elizabeth, 80

Reagan, Ronald, 23
Reid, Alfred S., 224 n. 8, 246 n. 13
Reverend Wilson, character, 72, 84–85, 104, 112, 125, 128, 246 n. 18
Revolutionary War, 54–55, 131–32, 154, 158, 163–65, 173–74
Reynolds, David S., 226 n. 6, 229 n. 37, 243 n. 5, 250 n. 3
Reynolds, Larry J., 247 n. 20
Ricoeur, Paul, 32
A Rill from the Town-Pump, 185–88
Ringer, Benjamin, 13, 223 n. 18
Rose, Jacqueline, 225 n. 3
Ryskamp, Charles, 234 n. 1, 237 n. 20

The Scarlet Letter, 4, 6–8, 10–11, 16, 58–90, 93–95, 97–159, 161–68, 175–78, 180, 183–

The Scarlet Letter (*continued*) 184, 188, 191–95, 197–202, 206–7, 214, 216, 219 n. 1, 230 n. 46, 231 n. 55
Scarry, Elaine, 219 n. 3, 226 n. 11
Schochet, Gordon J., 240 n. 45
Schuck, Peter, 14, 223 n. 18, 224 n. 29
Scott, Walter, 195
Sedgwick, Eve Kosofsky, 10, 246 n. 15
Seven Tales of My Native Land, 16, 35, 37, 45, 53, 156, 193
Sexuality, 35, 45, 52, 63–64, 67, 118; and adultery, 116; female, 148; homosocial, 120; and law, 86; and law in *The Scarlet Letter,* 85–86; marital, 116; of witchcraft, in *Alice Doane's Appeal,* 44
Shapiro, Mary J., 227 n. 24
Shepard, Thomas, 253 n. 8
Silverman, Kaja, 228 n. 32
Silverman, Kenneth, 29, 229 n. 37
"Sir William Phips," 257 n. 21
Smith, Rogers, 14, 223 n. 18, 224 n. 29
The Snow-Image and Uncollected Tales, 231 n. 53, 251 nn. 5, 7
Sommer, Doris, 226 n. 11
Space, 166, 181, 183; as gendered sites, 37, 209; as racial sites, 209; and time, 25–27, 29, 118, 136–37, 141, 143–44, 150, 152, 158, 163, 174, 192, 195, 200
Spivak, Gayatri Chakravorty, 208, 258 n. 33
Statue of Liberty, 22–28, 33, 44, 51, 195, 217, 227 nn. 13–16, 19, 24, 228 nn. 25, 28–30, 33. *See also* Icon; Iconicity
Subjectivity, 16, 20, 34–35, 64, 89, 104, 106, 115, 143, 154, 168; Dimmesdale's, 127; juridical, 101; national, 171; political, 19; in *The Scarlet Letter,* 62
Surveyor Pue, character, 183–84, 203, 253n.19. See also *The Custom-House*

Taussig, Michael, 40, 42, 232 n. 60
Thickstun, Margaret Olofson, 236 n. 9
Thomas, Brook, 256 n. 18
Thompson, John B., 234 n. 2
Todorov, Tsvetan, 251 n. 8
Tompkins, Jane, 221 n. 8, 249 n. 30, 258 n. 40
Trachtenberg, Marvin, 27, 228 n. 31
Trop v. Dulles, 12–13, 224 nn. 24–25
True Stories from History and Biography, 234 n. 69, 255 n. 8, 258 n. 38
Twice-Told Tales, 231 n. 53, 254 n. 20

United States Constitution, 169, 175; history of citizenship, 11–16, 78
United States Supreme Court, 12
Upham, Charles Wentworth, 39, 232 n. 56
Utopia, 7, 17, 25–26, 32-34, 60, 61, 63, 74, 87, 102, 113, 132, 139–40, 143–45, 148, 154–55, 159, 166, 192, 204, 216, 234 n. 2; and America, 28, 30–32, 53, 59, 162–63, 202, 206, 209, 216–17; and fantasy, 162, 189; homosocial, 120;

and law, 59-60, 62, 95, 101–2, 149-50, 152, 158; and law and desire, 249 n. 29; and nationality, 32; and politics, 201; and sexuality, 28, 153–55

Van Leer, David, 10, 237 n. 22, 243 n. 4, 248 n. 21
A Visitor's Guide to Salem, 54, 234 n. 70

Wall, Robert Emmet, Jr., 236 n. 17, 238 n. 29, 240 n. 44
Ward, Nathaniel, 65, 72, 82, 236 n. 15, 247 n. 19. See also *Body of Liberties*
Warner, Marina, 228 n. 33
Warner, Michael, 252 n. 9
Warren, Earl, 12–13, 223 n. 22
Webster, Daniel, 195–96, 199, 216, 233 n. 64
White, Hayden, 40
The Whole History of Grandfather's Chair, 8, 195–99, 233 n. 69
Winthrop, John, 61, 70, 73–75, 78–79, 81–85, 87, 89–94, 97, 106, 112, 128–29, 132–34, 144, 187, 230 n. 25, 237 nn. 18, 20, 238 n. 31, 240 nn. 43–44, 46–47, 53, 241 n. 61, 247 n. 18, 254 n. 21; body, 89. *See also* Law
Witchcraft, 37–39; and sexuality, 44. See also *Alice Doane's Appeal;* Hibbens, Ann
Wolfe, Tom, 228 n. 30
Woman: as citizen, 156; as icon, 27, 38, 44, 69, 110, 134, 137, 154–55, 157, 177; and law, 107–8; and national identity, 106; as object of National Fantasy, 28, 31, 110, 135; as outlaw in *The Scarlet Letter,* 85; as submissive, 120; as subversive, 36, 107–9, 113–15, 117, 120, 134, 135, 138, 140–42, 147, 210–11; as theorist, 86–87, 135–40, 156. *See also* American eagle; Body; Citizen body; Law; Prynne, Hester; Sexuality
"Woman in Her Social Relations," 211
Woodhill, Victoria, 224 n. 28

Ziff, Larzer, 221 n. 7, 242 n. 1